CHILDREN'S MUSEUMS

An American Guidebook

SECOND EDITION

Joann Norris

McFarland & Company, Inc., Publishers
Jefferson, North Carolina, and London

ALSO OF INTEREST

*The Historic Railroad: A Guide to Museums, Depots
and Excursions in the United States*
(by John R. Norris and Joann Norris; McFarland, 1996)

LIBRARY OF CONGRESS CATALOGUING-IN-PUBLICATION DATA

Norris, Joann, 1947–
Children's museums : an American guidebook /
Joann Norris. — 2nd ed.
p.   cm.
Includes index.

ISBN 978-0-7864-4000-9
softcover : 50# alkaline paper ∞

1. Children's museums—United States—Guidebooks.
I. Title.
AM11.N67   2009   069.083 — dc22   2008047785

British Library cataloguing data are available

Cover images ©2009 Shutterstock

Manufactured in the United States of America

*McFarland & Company, Inc., Publishers
Box 611, Jefferson, North Carolina 28640
www.mcfarlandpub.com*

Children's Museums
Second Edition

To my six grandchildren and two great-grands,
who love to see, do, touch, explore and imagine.
Thank you for sharing many of those times with me.
Grandpa would have been unbelievably proud of you all.

Acknowledgments

A special thanks to all of the curators who provided information
for this book, not just about their own museums but about other
museums of which they had knowledge (and thought I might not).
Thanks for your professionalism and helpfulness,
not only to me, but to your peers.

Contents

Preface

The Children's Museum of Indianapolis is still the largest children's museum in the United States, with 24,000 square feet of floor space and an average yearly attendance of more than 1,000,000 people. Although there are now several large museum that come close to rivaling these numbers, most children's museums' statistics come nowhere close to these figures. This does not mean that a visit to one of the smaller museums would not be beneficial, both for fun and educational purposes. My husband and I took our children to the Indianapolis museum in the early 1980s. Several years later, we took our grandchildren to a small museum in Sebring, Florida. It's hard to say which day (or which group of children) was the most enjoyable (probably the grandchildren!). Then, in 1998, my son and daughter-in-law took their twin toddlers, along with their cousins and their young daughters, to the Children's Museum of Indianapolis (makes a grandmother proud). Each visit was great enough to convince all parties concerned that they wanted to continue this family tradition.

The Indianapolis museum is a member of several associations, but smaller museums tend not to spend their tightly budgeted monies on association memberships. Because they are not affiliated with any associations it may be difficult for the nation's public to find out about them. (See the Appendix for information about associations.) I knew that it would take a lot of time and research to seek out these smaller museums. The museums listed in this book are children's museums, large and small, for which I was able to obtain information; my hope is that parents will use the information to plan quality family time with their children, whether it be a single morning excursion or part of a larger vacation experience. Included in most listings is information about other sites of interest fairly near the museum.

Research methods for this edition were considerably different from the research methods used for the 1998 edition. Much of the research for that book was done in public libraries, through the U.S. mail, and by phone or fax or both. While the research for this edition also required lots of written correspondence with various museums and agencies that are connected in some way to museums, most of the research was done through hours of work on the internet. This points out how technology was changed in the last 10 years. The big technological pride of most small museums in 1997–98 was having a fax machine — what a difference today! Today, even many of the smaller museums have their own websites. It should be noted that just because one is unable to locate a museum's website does not mean that that museum is not in existence. Since most small museums are run by volunteers, and not all volunteers have access to or an interest in computers, having a website is not yet considered "mandatory." I believe it will soon be as common, however, as having a fax and a phone.

Introduction

All museums listed in this book claim to have participatory, interactive, hands-on exhibits and or displays of specific interest to children, or to have formally organized education programs especially for children. This does not mean that only children would enjoy these activities, or that only children's activities are available at that museum. Many large museums that do not specifically advertise themselves as a "children's museum" are offering a children's exhibit hall or even a separate building specifically for children.

In the mission statements provided by most of the museums listed in this book, the intent of the museum staff and other personnel is to provide a safe and free place where children can see, touch, do, explore, create, imagine, and interact with their environment, thereby learning more than might be possible in a more structured environment. According to Howard Gardner, professor of education and co-director of Project Zero at Harvard University, this kind of learning can greatly influence their work as they get older. He says:

> I think the museum for young people is one of the most hopeful institutions in the world today. The youth museum gives more people a chance to develop their intelligences and to find out what they can do both for themselves and for their community — how they can develop abilities which can not only be productive for them, but which can be productive for others.... [They] can really help kids go beyond the unschooled mind, to engender genuine understanding, while at the same time preserving the best of the five-year-old mind. If kids have a chance to go to children's museums or discovery museums to learn about their own minds, the kinds of things they can do and what it means to discover stuff, they really have the best chance to do creative work when they're older.

The oldest children's museums in the United States opened in Boston and Brooklyn around the turn of the century. Growth was slow, but today, children's museums are a growing venture in the United States, and, indeed, the world. Although there were only a dozen or so well-known museums in the 1970s, a large number of museums opened in the 1980s. Since then, children's museums have opened all over the country, in urban and rural settings, in small and large buildings, with a huge number of exhibits and with a small number of exhibits. Visits to these museums can last from one hour to several hours, but in all cases, children and their adult companions are encouraged to explore, interact and experiment with art, nature, science and technology. Many of the larger museums also offer interactive activities on-line at their websites.

It is difficult to really get an accurate record of how many children's museums are in existence. From the beginning of the research part of this book until publication, some museums have closed and others have opened — largely because of a lack of funding. Most children's museums, hoping to attract families and school groups, require only small entrance fees, and some have no fees at all. It seems logical, then, that funding has to come from outside sources and is essential in keeping the museum running. (Membership in the ASTC or the AYM can help provide information about such funding. See the Appendix for further information.)

It is strongly suggested that you call or fax the museum shortly before your visit for current information, especially about hours, admissions costs, and parking costs. Many of the larger museums also have websites or e-mail addresses which are included in their listing and from which you can obtain current information. Many museums cater especially to school groups and will close to the public when a school group is in attendance, so you would not be able to visit at that time. Many museums also require reservations because they are run by volunteers who work only when there is a reservation scheduled.

Admissions fees listed are for individuals and were valid in 2008. Nearly all museums do offer special group rates, and teachers can use the information in these listings to contact the museums for group rates.

Museum Information

(*by State*)

ALABAMA

Children's Hands-On Museum
Tuscaloosa

Participatory education is the goal of the Children's Hands-On Museum. Two to twelve year olds and their caregivers are the targeted audience. High quality, entertaining and interactive exhibits and programs emphasize the community, the physical environment, science, history, and the arts.

Staff and volunteers are on the premises to answer questions on the exhibits which include "Choctaw Indian Village," "First National Bank of Tuscaloosa," "Maxwell General Store," "Barber's Shop," "Grandmother's Attic," "Planetarium," "Captain Tim Parker," "Images," "Beavers' Bend," "The Evening Times," "DCH Health System," "The Japan House," "Once Upon a Farm" and more.

Info in brief: Hands-on, participatory museum for children and their caregivers.

Location: 2213 University Boulevard in downtown Tuscaloosa.

Hours: Tuesday–Friday, 9 A.M. to 5 P.M.; Saturday, 10 A.M. to 4 P.M. Closed all major holidays.

Admissions: Under 1, free; all others, $5. Children must be accompanied by adults.

Nearby sites of interest: Paul W. Bryant Museum, the Alabama Museum of Natural History, the University of Alabama Arboretum, The Mercedes-Benz U.S. International Visitors Center.

For further information write to Children's Hands-on Museum, 2213 University Boulevard, Tuscaloosa, Alabama 35401, or call (205) 349-4235 or fax (205) 349-4276. *www.chomonline.org*

Discovery 2000
Birmingham

Discovery 2000 is a small hands-on discovery learning children's museum with creative, fun experiments like dressing as a fireman or observing baby animals. Other exhibits include an IMAX Dome Theater and "Adventures in Science."

Location: Old Loveman's department store on 19th Street and Third Ave. N.

Nearby sites of interest: Downtown Tours, DeSoto Caverns, Heart of Dixie Railroad Museum, Ruffner Mountain Nature Center, Sixteenth Street Baptist Church, Southern Museum of Flight, Alabama Jazz Hall of Fame, Alabama Sports Hall of Fame, Alabama Theatre, and more.

Admissions: Member ASTC.

For further information write Discovery 2000, 1320 22nd St. South, Birmingham, Alabama 35203, or call (205) 714-8414.

EarlyWorks Children's History Museum
Huntsville

One of three museums in the south's largest hands-on history museum complex (Alabama Constitution Village, the Historic Huntsville Depot and EarlyWorks Children' History Museum). EarlyWorks Museum was designed for children to touch, climb, pull, and explore. Visitors can communicate with a Talking Tree, play a tune on giant-sized instruments, experience building in the Kidstruction Zone, explore a 46-ft. keelboat, shop in an old General Store, and try on 1800's clothing in the Federal House. Pre-schoolers will enjoy Biscuit's Backyard designed especially for them, with a garden, grocery store, water table and even karaoke.

Info in brief: Three-complex family museum with hands-on, participatory exhibits.

Location: Huntsville.

Hours: Tuesday–Saturday, 9 A.M.-4 P.M.; Closed Thanksgiving, December 24 and 25, and January 1st.

Admissions: Single Museum: toddlers, $4; youth and seniors, $8; adult, $10. Two museums: toddlers, $4; youth and seniors, $13; adult, $15. All 3 museums: toddlers, $4; youth and seniors, $17; adults, $20.

Uniqueness: The south's largest hands-on history museum; Complex of 3 museums.

Nearby sites of interest: Many historic sites nearby.

For further information write to Early Works, 404 Madison Street, Huntsville, AL 35801, or call (256) 564-8100 or fax (256) 564-8151. *www.earlyworks.com*

The Exploreum Museum of Science
Mobile

The Gulf Coast Exploreum Science Center was the brain child of the Junior League of Mobile. Further funds and enthusiasm were provided by other mobile organizations, including the Mobile, A.S. Mitchell Foundation which donated the Bragg-Mitchell Mansion and surrounding 12-acres to be used as the museum. Because the Mansion had been listed on the National Register of Historic Places in 1972, the Board of Trustees decided not to use the mansion for the museum, but instead, raised $1.3 million to build a 10,000 sq. ft. contemporary building on the property. The museum opened in 1983 with the goal to "increase science literacy among the people of south Alabama and the Gulf Coast region, residents and visitors."

Very quickly, the museum had outgrown its space, and the Exploreum staff began making plans to move to another National Historic Landmark, the Matt Sloan Fire Station (and surrounding area), offering an "expanded, state-of-the-art science center and IMAX theater." This new Exploreum officially opened in 1998, offering more than 100 interactive exhibits, the IMAX theater and numerous educational programs.

Permanent exhibit areas include the "Hands on Hall," "Wharf of Wonder" (the newest addition), "Minds on Hall" (virtual exhibits), "The CIBA Lab," "Virtual Journeys Digital Theater," and more.

Info in Brief: Hands-on, participatory children's "Science Museum."

Location: 65 Government Street in the heart of historic downtown Mobile, between Royal and Water streets.

Hours: Monday–Saturday, 9 A.M. to 6 P.M.; Sunday, 11 A.M. to 6 P.M. Closed Mardi Gras Fat Tuesday, and Easter.

Admissions: Exhibits: under 2, free; child (2–12), $17; youth (13–18) and seniors (60+), $18; adult (19–59), $20. IMAX: under 2, free; child, $6; youth, and seniors, $6.50; adult, $7.75. Exhibit and IMAX Combo: under 2, free; child, $22; youth and seniors, $23; adult, $25. Memberships available. Member of ASTC.

For further information write to The Exploreum Science Center, 65 Government St., Mobile, Alabama 36607, phone: (251) 208-6873 or (877) 625-4FUN. *www.explorium.com*

McWane Science Center
Birmingham

The McWane Center is a 150,000 sq. ft. state-of-the-art family museum located in downtown Birmingham. A combination of two former museums, *Discovery Place* and *Red Mountain Museum*, McWane's museum site includes an aquarium, retail store, restaurant and an IMAX Dome Theater. Exhibits offer visitors the experiences of interacting with the building blocks of science in the Science Quest area, going on a simulated space mission in the Challenger Learning Center, and exploring the World of Water, where special habitat tanks present windows to the aquatic world and the processes that take place there. Very young visitors will enjoy "Just Mice Size," (the world from a mouse's point of view), where they can investigate, explore, build and experiment. McWane Science Center also serves as a depository of natural artifacts for collection, storage, and interpretive display.

Info in brief: An interactive family/children's museum.

Location: 2nd Avenue, North and 19th Street in downtown Birmingham in the historic and refurbished Loveman's department store building. McWane Science Center is the cornerstone of Birmingham's downtown revitalization.

Hours: September–May: Monday–Friday, 9 A.M.–5 P.M.; Saturday, 10 A.M.–6 P.M.; Sunday, noon to 6 P.M. June–August: Monday–Saturday, 10 A.M.–6 P.M.; Sunday, noon–6 P.M. Special Spring Break hours: Monday–Friday, 9 A.M. to 6 P.M. Closed Thanksgiving, Christmas Eve and Christmas Day, New Year's Day, and Easter.

Admissions: Exhibit Hall: under 2, free; seniors (65+) and kids (2–12), $8; all others, $11. Combo ticket (Exhibit Halls and IMAX) under 2, free; seniors and kids, $12; all others, $16. IMAX Educational Film: under 2, free; seniors and kids, $7.50; all others, $8.50. IMAX Feature Length Movies: under 2, free; seniors and kids, $9; all others, $10. Sundays—$5 IMAX Dome Theater tickets.

Nearby sites of interest: Downtown Tours, DeSoto Caverns, Heart of Dixie Railroad Museum, Ruffner Mountain Nature Center, Sixteenth Street Baptist Church, Southern Museum of Flight, Alabama Jazz Hall of Fame, Alabama Sports Hall of Fame, Alabama Theatre, and more.

For further information write to McWane Science Center, 200 19th St., N., Birmingham, AL 35203 or call (877) 4McWane or (205) 714-8300 or fax (205) 714-8400. E-mail: *info@mcwane.org*

Sci-Quest: The North Alabama Science Center, Inc.
Huntsville

Sci-Quest is a hands-on science center with more than 125 permanent, interactive exhibits designed to engage, educate and entertain in seven different subject areas. The center (museum) offers permanent and traveling exhibits, educational programs for children, and a *3-D Immersive Theater*. The Immersive Theater is an interactive, 3-D experience with touch-screen computer monitors that enable each visitor to experience his/her own customized adventure. New to the museum is the Roaming Dome.

Hours: (Labor Day thru Memorial Day) Tuesday–Friday, 9 A.M.–4 P.M.; Saturday, 10 A.M.–6 P.M.; Sunday, 1 P.M.–5 P.M., Closed Mondays. (Check on line for summer hours.) Member ASTC.

Admissions: General admission (includes unlimited access to Sci-Quest's permanent exhibits): children, $8; seniors, $8.50; adults, $9. Immersion Theater add-on admission, $4; Roaming Dome Admission, $2. Parking is free and "plentiful."

For further information write to Sci-Quest, the North Alabama Science Center, Inc., 102-D Wynn Drive, Huntsville, AL 35805 or call (256) 837-0606 or fax (256) 837-4536. E-mail: *info@sci-quest.org*

ALASKA

The Imaginarium:
Science Discovery Center
Anchorage

The Imaginarium, opened in 1987, is a "Science Discovery Center for All Ages," with "hands-on, minds-on" exhibits including a marine touch tank, live reptiles, bubbles and a planetarium. Special programs include daily demonstrations, birthday parties and other events. The Imaginarium also offers a state-wide outreach program, which takes "the wonder of science" to remote schools and communities throughout Alaska.

Info in brief: A hands-on science museum and planetarium for children and their caregivers.

Location: Downtown Anchorage, Suite G in the Glacier Brewhouse building.

Hours: Monday–Saturday, 10 A.M. to 6 P.M.; Sunday, noon to 5 P.M. Closed all major holidays.

Admissions: Under 2, free; children (2–12), $5; adults, $5.50. Memberships available. Member ASTC.

For further information write to The Imaginarium, 737 West Fifth Avenue, Suite G, Anchorage, Alaska 99501, or call (907) 276-3179. *www.anchoragemuseum.org*

ARIZONA

Arizona Museum for Youth
Mesa

The Arizona Museum for Youth is a public/private partnership between the City of Mesa and the Arizona Museum for Youth Friends, Inc. The goal of the museum, since its inception in 1978, has been to introduce "children to the visual excitement and cultural enrichment provided by fine arts." Holding its first exhibit experience in 1981, the museum is now one of only two museums in the United States with a fine arts focus. In its current facility — a 17,000 sq. ft. former grocery store — the museum now offers a unique program of workshops, classes and special events along with its exhibitions.

The display of the exhibits themselves is a unique concept. Three times each year, the entire museum is transformed (or re-transformed) into a water park, a ranch, a foreign country, a zoo, a Broadway theatre, or even a grocery store. All existing exhibits are interspersed with participatory activities which reinforce and enhance the visual experience always offered. Local merchants and community members often donate articles for these displays which encourage hands-on, creative play.

Info in brief: Unique hands-on fine arts museum for children, offering visual and tactile experiences.

Hours: (Fall and spring exhibits) Tuesday–Friday and Sunday, 1 P.M. to 5 P.M.; Saturday, 10 A.M. to 5 P.M.; (summer exhibits) Tuesday–Friday, 9 A.M. to 5 P.M.; Saturday, 10 A.M. to 5 P.M.; Sunday, 1 P.M. to 5 P.M.

Admissions: Under 2, free; others, $2.

Unique exhibitions: Three museum-wide participatory exhibits offered each year, each based on a theme with an emphasis on the fine arts.

Nearby sites of interest: Mesa Arts Center, Arizona Museum for Youth, Mesa Historical Museum, Arizona Museum of Natural History and other tourist attractions in Phoenix and Mesa.

For further information write to the Arizona Museum for Youth, 35 N. Robson St., Mesa, Arizona 85201, or call (602) 644-2467.

Arizona Museum of Natural History
Mesa

This natural history museum of the Southwest offers exhibits ranging from dinosaurs to ancient Indian civilizations to the settlement of the West. The *Adventure Center* offers several permanent hands-on, interactive exhibits for children of all ages, as well as changing exhibits, a history courtyard where visitors pan for gold, a native peoples' gallery with a replica village and pottery, an indoor waterfall, and a fully accessible gift shop. The newest exhibition, *Hohokam! Ancient Monuments of the Salt River Valley*, offers archeological materials such as ancient temples and vast networks of enormous irrigation canals that lie beneath the streets of Mesa.

Info in brief: The valley's only natural history museum that also includes hands-on activities for children.

Location: One block north of Main Street in downtown Mesa.

Hours: Tuesday–Friday, 10 A.M.–5 P.M.; Saturday, 11 A.M.–5 P.M.; Sunday, 1 P.M.–5 P.M. Closed Mondays and holidays.

Admissions: Ages 2 & under, free; children (3–12), $4; students (13+ with ID), $6; seniors (65+), $7; adults, $8.

Nearby sites of interest: Mesa Arts Center, Arizona Museum for Youth, Mesa Historical Museum, and other tourist attractions in Mesa and Phoenix.

For further information write to the Arizona Museum of Natural History, 53 N. Macdonald, Mesa, AZ 85201 or call (480) 644-2230. *www.azmnh.org*

Arizona Science Center
Phoenix

The Arizona Science Center is a hands-on science museum for children. Exhibits include activities on energy, physics, the human body, bubbles, weather and more. Live science demonstrations are offered regularly, along with special programs and workshops. An ice cream shop is also on site.

Info in brief: A hands-on children's museum.

Hours: Monday–Saturday, 9 A.M. to 5 P.M.; Sunday, noon to 5 P.M.

Admissions: Contact museum for current admissions charges.

For further information write to the Arizona Science Center, 147 E. Adams St., Phoenix, Arizona 85004-2394, or call (602) 256-9388.

Children's Museum of Phoenix
Museo de los Niños

Phoenix

The Children's Museum of Phoenix is located in the 70,000 sq. ft. historic Monroe School building in the heart of downtown Phoenix. All exhibits are hands-on and interactive, engaging the "minds, muscles and imaginations of 0–10 year olds." This is one of the first "Common Sense Green" museums in the country. Visitors will be able to "make a meal" in the Texture Café; test climbing skills in the 3-story climber, snuggle up and read in the reading loft, and more.

Location: Historic Monroe School building in downtown Phoenix, at the corner of 7th St. and Van Buren.

Hours: Tuesday–Sunday, 9 A.M. to 4 P.M.; closed Mondays except for special holidays.

Admission: Members, free; nonmembers, $9; children under the age of 1, free.

Nearby sites of interest: U.S. Airways Center, The Arizona Science Center, Chase Field and the Civic Center.

For further information write to the Children's Museum of Phoenix, P.O. Box 2439, Phoenix, AZ 85002 or call (602) 253-0501 or fax (602) 307-9833. *www.childrensmuseumofphoenix.org* E-mail: *info@chilmusephx.org*

Hall of Flame Museum of Firefighting

Phoenix

Children can explore all aspects of the 1952 fire engine on display at the Hall of Flame Museum of Firefighting. Over 100 other pieces of vintage firefighting apparatus and equipment are also on display with several fire engines on view from various countries around the world. Besides the 1952 fire engine, several hands-on fire safety exhibits are also available for children to experience.

Info in brief: Special interest collections museum with several hands-on exhibits for children.

Hours: Monday–Saturday, 9 A.M. to 5 P.M.; Sunday, noon to 4 P.M.

Admissions: Small admissions charge.

Unique exhibits: Exhibits dedicated to firefighting apparatus, equipment and history.

Nearby sites of interest (in Phoenix): Arizona Science Center, Arizona Doll and Toy Museum, Arizona Hall of Fame Museum, Deer Valley Rock Art Center, Desert Botanical Garden, The Heard Museum, Heritage Square, The Medical Museum, Museo Chicano, Phoenix Art Museum, Phoenix Museum of History, Phoenix Police Museum, The Phoenix Zoo, Pioneer Arizona Living History Museum, Plotkin Judaica Museum of Greater Phoenix, Pueblo Grande Museum, Shemer Art Center and Museum, Telephone Pioneer Museum, and other Phoenix tourist attractions.

For further information write to Hall of Flame Museum of Firefighting, 6101 E. Van Buren, Phoenix, Arizona 85008-3410, or call (602) ASK-FIRE (275-3473). *www.hallofflame.org*

Halle Heart Center at
the American Heart Association

Tempe

This small museum gives children and adult visitors an interesting hands-on way of learning about cardiovascular disease (the number one cause of death in the United States) and its prevention. Contact the museum before visiting.

Info in brief: Special interest education center/museum for people of all ages, but with definite hands-on activities for children and their caregivers.

Hours: Walk-ins welcome Monday–Friday; 1 P.M. to 4 P.M., by appointment only.

Admissions: Free.

Unique exhibits: All exhibits dedicated to teaching about cardiovascular disease and its prevention.

Nearby sites of interest (in Tempe): Arizona Historical Society, Arizona State University Art Museum (and other sites on campus), Salt River Project History Center, Tactile Museum for the Blind and Visually Impaired (mobile), Tempe Art Center and Sculpture Garden, Tempe Historical Museum, Niels Petersen House Museum, and the Island of Big Surf water park.

For further information write to Halle Heart Center at the American Heart Association, 2929 S. 48th St., Tempe, Arizona 85282-3145, or call (602) 414-5353.

Pioneer Arizona Living History Museum
Phoenix

Pioneer Arizona was actually in the planning for about 13 years before officially opening its doors in 1969. Current plans call for further additions and improvements to the facilities. The nonprofit museum's collection of original and reconstructed buildings currently displays various architecture and lifestyles from throughout Arizona, and encourages learning through the participatory living history concept.

Exhibits include the Saloon, Restaurant, Gift Shop, Opera House, Farm Machine Display, Carpenter Shop, Victorian House, Print Shop, Dress Shop, Exhibit of Weapons, Tinware and Locks, Blacksmith, Farm House, Miners Cabin, Arista (ore grinder), Bandstand, Church, Teacherage, School House, Cemetery, Stage Stop (Ruins), Ranch Complex and Spring House and Root Cellar, Barn and Corral, Flying V Cabin, Ashurst Cabin, Presidio and Spanish Colonial Horses, Northern Complex, Last Chance Saloon, Southern House, Sheriff's Office, Bank, Wagonmaker Shop (Ruins), and Rock Wall.

Info in brief: An educational, living history museum of interest to the entire family.

Location: 30 min. north of downtown Phoenix on Interstate 17.

Hours: Winter (October 1–May 31): Wednesday thru Sunday, 9 A.M.–5 P.M. Summer (June 1–September 30), Wednesday thru Sunday, 8 A.M.–2 P.M.

Admissions: Under 5, free; students (6–18), $5; seniors (60+), $6; adults, $7.

Unique exhibits: The Opera House where Lily Langtry sang.

For further information write to Pioneer Arizona, 3901 W. Pioneer Rd., Phoenix, Arizona 85027, or call (523) 465-1052 or fax (523) 465-0683. E-mail: *pioneerarizona@earthlink.net*

Silva House
Phoenix

One of the group of houses open in Heritage Square (original townsite of Phoenix), the Silva House is maintained by the Salt River Project, and all exhibits in the house focus on the history of water and electric power use in the Valley along with local turn-of-the-century lifestyles. Activities for children change according to the educational focus of the museum for that time. Be sure to contact the museum before visiting.

Since opening in 1980, the main focus of the Silva House has been community service to school and other groups, but exhibits and activities are also open to the public. The targeted groups are school age children and their caregivers.

Info in brief: One part of a living history museum (Heritage Square) which has some activities for children and their caregivers.

Location: Historic Heritage Square, the original townsite to Phoenix, listed on the National Register of Historic Places.

Hours: Monday–Saturday, 10 A.M. to 4 P.M.; Sunday, noon to 4 P.M.

Admissions: Free.

Unique exhibits: All exhibits are approved by the Salt River Project and emphasize water and electric power use in the Valley.

Nearby sites of interest (in Phoenix): See the Hall of Flame Museum of Firefighting entry.

For further information write to the Silva House, 628 E. Adams, Phoenix, Arizona 85004, or call (602) 236-5451 *www.silvahouse.com*

Tempe Historical Museum
Tempe

The wonderful world of Tempe's history is presented through hands-on activities, interactive displays, videos and changing exhibits, all capturing Tempe's unique flavor and experiences.

Info in brief: A history museum with several hands-on exhibits for children and their families.

Hours: Monday–Thursday and Saturday, 10 A.M. to 5 P.M.; Sunday, 1 P.M. to 5 P.M. Closed Fridays and major holidays.

Admissions: Free

For further information write to the Tempe Historical Museum, 809 E. Southern Ave., Tempe, Arizona 85282-5205, or call (480) 350-5100. *www.tempe.gov/museum*

Tucson Children's Museum
Tucson

Founded in early 1991, the mission of the Tucson Children's Museum is to provide a fun and creative environment with hands-on experience for all. Families with children ages 2 to 12 can spend a day at the museum exploring the 12 rooms filled with more than 125 hands-on activities. Theme areas include Rocks and Minerals, The Five Senses, the Cardio-Pulmonary System, Six Simple Machines, Electricity, Self Esteem, Predicting Time, Optics, Careers, Music, Railroads and more.

Several family events, workshops and activities are also sponsored by the museum throughout the year. Four full-time and ten part-time staff members run the museum and the special activities. The 16,000 sq. ft. building is owned by and leased from the City of Tucson.

Info in brief: Hands-on museum specifically for children and their caregivers.

Location: Historic Carnegie Library Building on Sixth Avenue.

Hours: Tuesday thru Saturday, 10 A.M.–5 P.M.; Sunday, noon–5 P.M. Closed Christmas and Thanksgiving. Open daily Memorial Day thru Mid-August. (The museum suggests visitors call for exact hours before visiting.)

Admissions: Under 2, free; children, $3; seniors, $5; adults, $7.

For further information write to the Tucson Children's Museum, 200 S. Sixth Ave., Tucson, Arizona 85701 , or call (520) 792-9985. *www.tucsonchildrensmuseum.org*

ARKANSAS

The Children's Museum of Arkansas
Little Rock

Located in the former Union Station in Little Rock, the Children's Museum of Arkansas offers interactive exhibits for children from pre-school to elementary ages. Permanent exhibits include a farmers market, construction area, and more.

Hours: Sunday–Friday, 10 A.M. to 5 P.M.; Saturday, 1 P.M. to 5 P.M.

Admissions: 1 & under, free; seniors (over 59), $3; child & adult, $4. Member ASTC.

Nearby sites of interest: Aerospace Education Center, Arkansas Arts Center (offering 5 unique museums or historic sites), the Historic Arkansas Museum, Little Rock Zoo, Museum of Discovery (art and history), State Capitol, Villa Marre, and the State Capitol.

For further information write The Children's Museum of Arkansas, Union Station, 1400 W. Markham, #200, Little Rock, Arkansas 72201, or call (501) 374-6655.

Mid-America Science Museum
Hot Springs

Known as MASM, Mid-America Science Museum is Arkansas' largest hands-on science center. MASM seeks to "stimulate a lifelong interest in science, spark curiosity, reshape attitudes and stir the imagination." Their goal is "informal science education that encourages learning in ways not ordinarily found in the workplace, classroom, or home." Over 100 hands-on exhibits, housed on three different levels, are available to help visitors explore the wonders of energy, matter, life and perception. Outreach programs are also offered for all ages.

MASM is also home to the world's most powerful Tesla Coil (officially listed in Guinness World Records in 2007, and is Arkansas' first Smithsonian Affiliate. Another claim to fame is the fact that three of "Sir Roland Emmett's Wondrous, Whimsical Creations" were used in the classic movie, *Chitty Chitty Bang Bang*. A Laser Show and Simulator Ride are also on site.

Info in brief: A hands-on family museum.

Location: On more than 21 acres of beautiful rolling woodlands approximately 6.5 miles west of historic downtown Hot Springs National Park.

Hours: Summer hours (Memorial Day Weekend through Labor Day Weekend): Daily, 9:30 A.M.–6 P.M. Winter hours (after Labor Day Weekend through weekend before Memorial Day): Tuesday–Sunday, 10 A.M.–5 P.M. Closed New Year's Day, Thanksgiving and Christmas Day.

Admissions: Exhibits only: under 2, free; youth (2–12), $7; military, $7; seniors (62+), $7; adult, $8. Laser Show $2; Simulator Ride, $3. Combo ticket for all 3, $11.

Nearby sites of interest: Aerospace Education Center, Arkansas Arts Center (offering 5 unique museums or historic sites), the Historic Arkansas Museum, Little Rock Zoo, Museum of Discovery (art and history), State Capitol, villa Marre, and the State Capitol.

For further information write to Mid-America Museum, 500 Mid America Blvd, hot Springs, AR 71913 or call (501) 767-3461. *www.midamericamuseum.org*

Museum of Discovery,
Arkansas' Museum of Science and History
Little Rock

Arkansas' Museum of Science and History offers "A world of discovery for all ages," with a mission of igniting a passion for science, technology and math in a dynamic, interactive environment. Boasting 3,000 sq. ft. of hands-on, interactive exhibits, permanent exhibits include "Arkansas Indians," "Bug Zoo," "Discovery Express," "Energy," "Health Hall," "Imagination Station," "Passport to the World," "World of the Forest," and "Zoom Zone." The museum also holds a number of collections, some of which are: "Kewpies," "Mummy Coffins," "Animal Collection," "Miss Kyoto" and "Masks." Several public programs are also offered throughout the year. The museum continues to grow: "Room to Grow" Phase I is now open. Phases II and III are expected to open in 2008.

Location: River market district of downtown Little Rock.

Hours: Monday–Saturday, 9 A.M.–5 P.M.; Sunday, 1 P.M.–5 P.M. Closed New Year's Day, Easter, Thanksgiving, Christmas Eve and Christmas Day, and Riverfest Weekend (last weekend in May).

Admissions: Under 1, free; children (ages 1–12), $7; seniors (65+), $7; adults (13–64), $8. Free and paid parking is available. Member AAM, ACM and ASTC.

Nearby sites of interest: Aerospace Education Center, Arkansas Arts Center (offering 5 unique museums or historic sites), the Historic Arkansas Museum, Little Rock Zoo, Museum of Discovery (art and history), State Capitol, Villa Marre, and the State Capitol.

For further information write to Arkansas' Museum of Science and History, 500 President Clinton Ave., Suite 150, Little Rock, AR 72201 or call (501) 396-7050 or Toll Free (800) 880-6475 or fax (501) 396-7054. *www.amod.org* E-mail: *jforrest@amod.org*

CALIFORNIA

A Special Place Children's Museum
San Bernardino

A Special Place Children's Museum has been operating at its present location for over 8 years, although they have been in business for more than 18 years. They recently completed extensive renovations and have created a new theme based on music, television, theatre and film. Exhibits include a mock TV studio, theatre playhouse, video gaming, music room, animation, costume dress up, face painting, an old-fashioned school house, and an outdoor play area.

The goal of the museum is to offer inexpensive entertainment to children while, at the same time, teaching tolerance and disability awareness. Visitors have the opportunity to examine an incubator, X-ray machine, crutches, braces and wheelchairs.

Info in brief: A hands-on museum especially for children from preschool to 5th grade, with an emphasis on disability awareness.

For further information write to A Special Place Children's Museum, 1003 East Highland Avenue, San Bernardino, CA 92404-4645 or call (909) 881-1201.

Bay Area Discovery Museum

Sausalito

The Bay Area Discovery Museum is an indoor/outdoor museum with exhibit centers in seven buildings, an ongoing schedule of workshops and classes, and other programs designed to make learning fun. Families with children 10 years of age and younger are the targeted audience.

The museum opened in its current location in a complex of historic buildings at East Fort Baker, at the northern end of the Golden Gate Bridge in 1991. It was awarded the National Historic Preservation Award in 1992 for its creative use of the facilities. After a couple of expansions, the museum now includes seven buildings with over 20,000 sq. ft. of exhibit space.

Exhibits offered in the galleries include: "San Francisco Bay" (underwater tunnel, a real boat, etc.); "Art Spot" (crafts, art projects, photography); "Architecture and Design"; "Powerhouse" (water power activities); "Discovery Hall" (changing exhibitions); "Science Lab" (with numerous discovery boxes); "Maze of Illusions" (mirrors, holograms and optical illusions); and more. The museum also offers nature walks and classes highlighting the area's indigenous wildlife.

Location: Northern end of the Golden Gate Bridge on National Park land in Fort Baker.

Hours: Tuesday thru Friday, 9 A.M.–4 P.M.; Saturday and Sunday, 10 A.M.–5 P.M. Closed most major holidays and the last two weeks of September.

Admissions: Under 1, free; children (1–17), $9; seniors (62+), $8; adults, $10. Memberships available.

Nearby sites of interest: The many San Francisco tourist attractions, such as San Francisco Bay, and Sausalito (a seaside town).

For further information write to Bay Area Discovery Museum, 557 McReynolds Road, East Fort Baker, Sausalito, California 94965, or call (415) 339-3900. *www.babykidsmuseum.org*

Boone Children's Gallery at LACMA *see* LACMA Boone Children's Gallery

The Bowers Kidseum

Santa Ana

The Bowers Kidseum is an extension of the Bowers Museum of Cultural Art which concentrates on pre–Columbian, Native American, Oceanic, African and Asian art. The Kidseum provides hands-on arts and cultural activities in the same areas for children ages 5 to 12 and their families. The interactive and hands-on exhibits feature masks, instruments, puppets and costumes for dress up from around the world. Little visitors can also go back in time in the Native American "Time Vault" and use grinding stones or learn about early Californians. A hands-on Art Lab offers a range of projects from creating an Asmat drum of New Guinea to designing your own African cloth.

Other special features in the museum include live storytellers on the weekends and ethnic design face painting. Kidseum artists adorn children's faces with traditional designs such as Aboriginal face design, Aztec symbols, Mehndi hand designs from India and more. Family festivals, teacher workshops, art camps and other special events are also offered at various times throughout the year.

Info in brief: Hands-on, interactive museum for children ages 5 to 12 and their caregivers.

Location: Two blocks south of the 5 Freeway.

Hours: Thursday–Friday, 10 A.M.–3 P.M. Saturday and Sunday, 11 A.M. to 4 P.M. The museum suggests visitors call ahead of time for a weekly update of scheduled times, prices and events.

Admissions: Under 5, free; children (5–12), $2; students (with ID), $4; adults, $6; seniors, $4. This price also includes same day admission to the Bowers Museum of Cultural Art at 2002 N. Main Street. Free parking is available.

Nearby sites of interest: Bowers Museum of Cultural Art, Discovery Science Center — Launch Pad, Disneyland and other California tourist attractions.

For further information write to The Bowers Kidseum, 1802 N. Main St., Santa Ana, California 92706, or call (714) 480-1520 or fax (714) 480-0053. *www.bowers.org*; E-mail: *info@bowers.org*

California Science Center
California Museum of Science and Industry
Los Angeles

The California Museum of Science and Industry became the California Science Center in 1998, and is still being developed under a 3-phase Master Plan. Phase I was completed in 1998, featuring: Creative World, World of Life, Science Plaza, IMAX Theater, Explora Store, and the renovation of the Armory Building and construction of the Science Center School and Amgen Center for Science Learning. Phases II and III are still in the planning stages, but are projected to contain the following features: World of Ecology, Exhibits, Programs and Outfitting of Science Center/Amgen Center, Air and Space Gallery, and finally, Worlds Beyond. When completed, the California Science Center will be the largest science center in the western United States.

Info in brief: An interactive, hands-on and technology-filled museum for the entire family. An IMAX Theater is also available.

Location: Exposition Park in Los Angeles.

Hours: Daily, 10 A.M. to 5 P.M. Closed Thanksgiving, Christmas and New Year's Day. IMAX Theater shows and prices are subject to change without notice, so be sure to contact the museum before visiting.

Admissions: (Exhibits) free. (IMAX Theater) under 3, free; children (4–12), $3.75; students (13+ with ID), $4.75; adults (18–59), $6.25; seniors (60+), $4.25. Evening discount is $3.75 per person from 6 P.M. to 9 P.M. Multiple show discounts are available. Parking, $6 per car, $10 for buses or oversize vehicles. Member ASTC.

Nearby sites of interest: Disneyland, Knott's Berry Farm, Universal Studio Tours, and the many other tourist attractions of Los Angeles.

For further information write to the California Science Center, 700 State Dr., Exposition Park, Los Angeles, California 90037, or call (323) SCIENCE (724-3623). IMAX Theater (213) 744-7400.

Castle Earth Children's Museum

Location: Ventura–East County

For further information write to Castle Earth Children's Museum, 77 Tierra Rejada Road, Simi Valley, CA 93065 or call (805) 583-5243.

Centennial Heritage Museum
The Discovery Museum of Orange County
Santa Ana

This history-centered discovery museum is an interactive learning environment where visitors can journey back to turn-of-the-century Southern California. Aspects of daily life, such as playing a pump organ, using a hand-cranked telephone, looking through a stereoscope, washing clothes on a washboard and wringer, wearing Victorian clothes, and much more are available for young and young-at-heart visitors to experience.

The museum is located in an area known as The Historical Plaza which contains the Kellogg House and three structures from the John Maag ranch (ranch house, carriage house and water tower).The heart of the museum is the fully-restored Kellogg House, originally built in 1898 and moved to its present location in 1980. Surrounding the Kellogg House is the Historic Plaza, which includes three buildings from the John Maag ranch. Although the ranch house, built in 1899, has not yet been restored, the carriage barn houses the museum offices, and the water tower contains a small child-oriented gift shop. An extensive rose garden, gazebo and several hundred citrus trees are also on the grounds.

Special demonstrations and events are offered throughout the year in and around the plaza. Be sure to contact the museum for exact details and schedules.

Info in brief: An 11-acre site which offers numerous activities, one of which is a hands-on children's historical museum.

Hours (Public Tours): Wednesday–Friday, 1 P.M. to 5 P.M.; Sunday, 11 A.M. to 3 P.M.

Admissions: Child, $4; adult, $5; seniors, $4. Memberships available.

Unique exhibitions: Seasonal Teas, Victorian fairies, and other special events scheduled well in advance.

Nearby sites of interest: Disneyland, Knott's Berry Farm, Discovery Science Center, Bowers Museum, Kidseum and other Orange County attractions.

For further information write to The Centennial Heritage Museum, 3101 W. Harvard St., Santa Ana, California 92704, or call (714) 540-0404. *www.centennialmuseum.org*

Chabot Space and Science Center
Oakland, California

Chabot Space and Science Center is a hands-on children's museum set amid 13 trail-laced acres of East Bay parkland, with beautiful views of San Francisco Bay and the Oakland foothills. A Mega-Dome Theater, Planetarium, Workshops, lectures and other events are also offered for visitors of all ages. Some of the exhibits include: Beyond Blastoff, Chabot Observatories: A View to the Stars, Solar-Go-Round, Destination Universe, and One Giant Leap: A Moon Odyssey. Free parking is also available nearby. The Center is a continuation and expansion of the public observatory that has been serving the area for more than 125 years (originally called The Oakland Observatory). After numerous improvements and a couple of moves, the new Science Center opened on August 19, 2000 as an 86,000 sq. ft. state-of-the-art science and technology education facility.

Info in brief: A hands-on "celebration of sights, sounds, and sensations."

Locations: Skyline Boulevard 1.3 miles from the Skyline Boulevard/Joaquin Miller Road signal light; 20 minutes from downtown San Francisco.

Hours: Regular hours (exhibits, planetarium and theater — Mid September–July 4): Wednesday and Thursday, 10 A.M.–5 P.M., Friday and Saturday, 10 A.M.–10 P.M., Sunday, 11 A.M.–5 P.M. The Center closes for maintenance for 2 weeks in September. Holiday hours: Open 10 A.M.–5 P.M. on MLK Day, Presidents Day, Memorial Day, Labor Day, Veterans Day and New Years Day. Closed July 4, Thanksgiving Day and Christmas Day.

Admissions: General admission (includes planetarium show): under 3, free; youth (3–12), $9; senior (65+) & student (with ID), $10; adult, $13. Mega-Dome Theater: youth, senior & student, $7; adult, $8. Sonic-Vision, Sky Tonight, Immersive Space: youth, senior & student, $7; adult, $8. Lunar Lounge Express (Fridays on a quarterly basis except where noted), youth, $10; senior & student, $10; adult, $15. Military discounts given. Member ASTC.

Nearby sites of interest: The Oakland Museum of California, The Oakland Zoo, Jack London Square, USS Hornet, Oakland Raiders, Golden State Warriors, Port of Oakland, and other Oakland and San Francisco attractions.

For further information write to Chabot Space and Science Center, 10000 Skyline Blvd., Oakland, CA 94619 or call (510) 336-7300 or fax (510) 336-7491. *www.chabotspace.org*

Chico Creek Nature Center
Chico

Chico Creek is more of a nature center than a hands-on children's museum, but is included as an entry in this book due to the interactive museum exhibits, the hands-on animal programs, and the exploratory nature hikes that are offered by the center. At the time of this publication, the Center was in the process of building a new facility directly behind the current Center — a 2,000 sq. ft. building that will offer more interactive displays.

Programs offered at the center include a summertime nature camp, animal adoption program and birthday parties. At the museum itself, interactive exhibits such as "A Walk Through Time" and "Air Aware" are offered at different times throughout the year. Be sure to contact the museum for the current exhibit on display.

Info in brief: A nature center with some activities geared toward children, especially children who love the outdoors and various aspects of nature.

Location: Northern Central Valley of California in Bidwell Park.

Hours: Year-round, Tuesday–Sunday, 10 A.M. to 4 P.M. Contact the Center for new hours.

Admissions: Free to the public. Special programs require special fees.

Unique characteristic: Chico Creek Nature Center is the only facility of its kind between Redding and Sacramento (approximately 200 miles).

Nearby sites of interest: Bidwell Park (the third largest municipal park in the country with over 3,000 acres of preserves and developed areas) and other attractions offered at California State University in Chico.

For further information write to Chico Creek Nature Center, 1968 E. 8th St., Chico, California 95928, or call (916) 891-4671 or fax (530) 891-0837. E-mail: *info@tidewellpark.org*

Children's Discovery Museum of San Jose
San Jose

As one of the largest facilities of its kind, the Children's Discovery Museum of San Jose offers more than 150 interactive and evolving exhibits and programs throughout the year. The mission of the museum is to place "emphasis on children's need to learn through concrete interactions," through exploration and play.

In 1990, the museum's unique purple gates opened to 42,000 sq. ft. of exhibit and office space designed by Mexico City–based architect Ricardo Legorreta. The exhibits themselves are designed around the intertwined themes of "Community, Connections and Creativity." Some of the exhibits include: "Streets of San Jose," "Step into the Past," "Doodad Dump," "Waterworks," "Early Childhood Resource Center," computer games/activities and more. Special workshops are also offered.

Location: Close to the heart of downtown San Jose near the San Jose McEnery Convention Center and Center for the Performing Arts.

Hours: Tuesday–Saturday, 10 A.M. to 5 P.M.; Closed — Monday, Thanksgiving and Christmas.

Admissions: Under 1, free; child (1–17), $8; adult (18–59), $8; senior (60+), $7. (Ask about Association of Youth Museums privileges.) Parking, $5 (limited)—museum suggests you use $1 and $5 bills only, in the machine. There is NO attendant on site.

Nearby sites of interest: Other California tourist attractions.

For further information write to Children's Discovery Museum of San Jose, 180 Woz Way, San Jose, California 95110-2780, or call (408) 298-5437 or fax (408) 298-6826. E-mail: *contactus@cdm.org*

Children's Discovery Museum of the Desert
Rancho Mirage

Founded in 1986, this private, non-profit museum offers an 18,000 sq. ft. complex where children are encouraged to use their natural curiosity and their right to self-expression in order to help them learn about themselves and the world around them. Permanent exhibits, traveling exhibits, classes, performances, birthday parties and outreach programs are offered in the Exhibit Gallery, while a multipurpose building (The Dinah Shore Center) offers an outdoor covered performance area/amphitheatre, horticultural gardens and "logo grove." Plans are currently underway for adding more facilities on recently donated acreage.

The Children's Discovery Museum of the Desert was the winner of the California Teachers Association State Gold Award in 1992.

Info in brief: Interactive, hands-on museum for youth, families, teachers, and community members. (No strollers are allowed in the museum.)

Location: 71-701 Gerald Ford Dr. in Rancho Mirage.

Hours: Monday–Saturday, 10 A.M. to 5 P.M.; Sunday 10 A.M. to 5 P.M.; Closed Mondays, May through December and some holidays.

Admissions: $8 per person. Memberships available.

For further information contact: Children's Discovery Museum of the Desert, 71-701 Gerald Ford Drive, Rancho Mirage, California 92270, or call (760) 321-0602 or fax (760) 321-1605.

The Children's Museum at La Habra
La Habra

Established in 1977 in an historic 1923 railroad depot building, The Children's Museum at La Habra now offers 7 galleries and 14 hands-on exhibits: a dinosaur fossil dig exhibit, live bees behind glass exhibit, dress-up theater, science demonstrations, mini grocery store, a carousel, model trains, preschool toys and games, workshops, outreach trunks, a changing exhibit gallery, and much more.

The Children's Museum at La Habra was the first children's museum to open west of the Rocky Mountains.

Info in brief: Children's museum exclusively for children and their caregivers.

Location: North Orange County.

Hours: Tuesday–Friday, 10 A.M. to 4 P.M.; Saturday, 10 A.M.–5 P.M.; Sunday, 1 P.M.–5 P.M. Closed all major holidays; first 2 weeks in September for annual renovation.

Admissions: Under 2, free; $5 for La Habra residents; all others, $8.

Unique Exhibits: "Operation M.A.C.K." (Museum Accessibility for Challenged Kids); "Puzzles of Places: A Kid's Eye View of Geography" (interactive puzzle exhibit).

Nearby sites of interest: Gene Autry Western Heritage Museum, Southwest Museum (Indians),

California Afro-American Museum, Los Angeles Children's Museum (see listing), Los Angeles Zoo, California Museum of Science and Industry, Natural History Museum of Los Angeles County, Disneyland and more. The Children's Museum at La Habra will send an excellent list of "Places to Go with Your Kids" at your request.

For further information write to The Children's Museum at La Habra, 301 S. Euclid St., La Habra, California 90631, or call (562) 905-9793.

Children's Museum of Los Angeles
Los Angeles

In 2004, the Children's Museum of Los Angeles celebrated its 25th anniversary. Housed in the Civic Center for 21 years, until the space became too small for the growing number of visitors, the museum will soon be located in a new, larger building at a new location at Hansen Dam Recreation Area. The new, 60,000 sq. ft. museum will continue to honor the founders' philosophy to educate, empower and entertain the children who visit the museum and the adults who care for them. There will be an indoor-outdoor feeling, encouraging visitors to easily move between the environments. Exhibit areas will include a city library, a colorful, inviting maze entrance, and a garden-discovery place of flora and fauna native to the northeast Valley.

Info in brief: Hands-on, participatory museum exclusively for children.

Location: Hansen Dam Recreation Area.

Hours and Admissions: Information were not yet available at the time of publication, as the museum was not yet open. Please be sure to contact the museum before visiting.

Nearby sites of interest: Japanese-American National Museum, the Geffen Contemporary Museum and the many other Los Angeles attractions.

For further information write to Children's Museum of Los Angeles, 11800 Foothill Blvd, Lake View Terrace, California 91342, or call (818) 686-9280 or fax 686-9299. *www.childrensmuseumla.org*

Children's Museum of San Diego
Museo de los Niños
San Diego

Opened originally in 1981, the museum has a new facility in the heart of the vibrant Marina district. Located at the corner of First and Front Street and Island Avenue, the building occupies the former museum's site. With approximately 50,000 sq. ft., the new Museum spans three-stories—more than doubling its previous space.

Info in brief: A unique hands-on arts and humanities museum for children of all ages. While some of the permanent exhibits are similar to those found in other children's museums, this museum offers unique arts experiences in uniquely designed exhibit areas.

Location: 200 West Island Avenue in downtown San Diego.

Hours: Mon.–Tues., Fri.–Sat., 10 A.M.–4 P.M.; Thurs., 10 A.M.–6 P.M.; Sunday, noon–4 P.M.

Admissions: $10; 65 & older, $5.

Unique exhibitions: Most of the short and long-term exhibits are designed by different artists, who give each exhibit its own unique flair.

Nearby sites of interest: The San Diego Zoo, the Mexican border and its border towns, and the many tourist attractions in San Diego.

For further information write to Children's Museum of San Diego/Museo de los Niños, 200 W. Island Ave., San Diego, California 92101, or call (619) 233-8792 or fax (619) 233-8796. *www.think playcreate.org*

Children's Museum of Santa Barbara
Santa Barbara

The Children's Museum of Santa Barbara is still in the planning stages, with an estimated opening date of 2012. Plans call for a 12,000 sq. ft. Green building which will include 7,000 sq. ft. for interactive exhibits, 3,000 sq. ft. for lobby, store and a multipurpose room, along with 2,000 sq. ft. for office and other functions.

Location: Possibly lower State Street.

For further information write to Children's Museum of Santa Barbara, P.O. Box 4808, Santa Barbara, CA 93140 or call (805) 680-7235. *www.childrensmuseumsb.org* E-mail: *sbchildrensmuseum@ gmail.com* or *Sheila@childrensmuseumsb.org*

The Children's Museum of Stockton
Stockton

Opened in March 1989, The Children's Museum of Stockton was inspired by the tragic Cleveland School shooting of 1989. Five children were killed and 30 wounded, including one teacher, Janet Geng. Ms. Geng's goal became to offer a safe, violence-free place where children could learn and have fun.

The museum's permanent exhibit area, "Mini-City," offers children the chance to work some parts of a real police car, bus and fire engine, plus work in a post office, bank and more. Temporary exhibits are also offered along with visual and performing arts displays. A special area for tiny tots and toddlers is available, as well as special group and family tours.

Info in brief: A hands-on participatory children's museum inspired by the Children's Museum in Washington, D.C.

Location: Downtown Stockton, across the street from the historic waterfront warehouse.

Hours: Tuesday–Friday, 9 A.M. to 4 P.M.; Saturday, 10 A.M.–5 P.M.; closed Monday, New Year's Day, Easter, Thanksgiving and Christmas.

Admissions: Under 2, free; others, $4.50. Memberships available. Member of the American Youth Museum Network. (All children must be accompanied by an adult.)

Nearby sites of interest: The Haggin Museum (1201 N. Pershing Ave.) and the World Wildlife Museum and Studio (1245 W. Weber Ave.).

For further information write to The Children's Museum of Stockton, 402 W. Weber Ave., Stockton, California 95203, or call (209) 465-4386 or fax (209) 465-4394. *www.stocktongov.com/ childrensmuseum/*

Chula Vista Nature Center
Chula Vista

The Chula Vista Nature Center is a fully accredited museum with a mission to "educate the public about the importance of coastal resource conservation through interactive exhibits."

Approximately four school field trips are scheduled each day. The Nature Center also offers weekly adult and children's programs such as docent-led tours, composting classes, and arts and crafts. In 2006, the Nature Center opened their renovated Discovery Center, a series of exhibits featuring live fish, sharks, snakes, and other San Diego–native animals, as well as Turtle Lagoon, exhibiting endangered green sea turtles. Other exhibits include a walk-through shorebird aviary, Raptor Row, Shark and Ray Experience, over a mile of walking trails, and a composting demonstration area.

Info in brief: Good combination of nature center and hands-on exhibits of interest to the whole family.

Location: San Diego Bay approximately 7 miles south of downtown San Diego and 7 miles north of the international border.

Hours: Tuesday–Sunday, 10 A.M. to 5 P.M.; Be sure to visit their website for holiday hours.

Admissions: Adults, $6; seniors (55+), $5; students (18+ with ID), $5; juniors (12–17), $4; children (4–11) $3; children under 4, free. Memberships available.

Nearby sites of interest: San Diego Bay attractions, Pacific Coast beaches, Mexico, San Diego Zoo, and other California attractions.

For further information write to the Chula Vista Nature Center, 1000 Gunpowder Point Dr., Chula Vista, California 91910, or call (619) 409-5900 or fax (619) 409-5910. *www.ChulaVistaNatureCenter.org* E-mail: *mail@cvnc.us*

Coyote Point Museum
San Mateo

Founded in 1954, the Coyote Point Museum for Environmental Education offers visitors a multi-sensory overall view of the ecology of the Bay Area in the indoor environmental hall, along with outdoor theme gardens, an 8,000 sq. ft. walkthrough songbird aviary, and wildlife habitats. The goal of the museum is to inspire people of all ages to act responsibly toward, and have a healthy respect for our environment and the interdependence of people and nature. Family members of all ages will enjoy the displays and activities provided. From September to May, the second weekend of each month is designated as "Family Activity Day," with crafts, games, experiments, speakers and storytellers offered to all visitors. Other activities include wildlife shows, River Otter feedings, fox talks, toddler programs, Spring, Summer and Winter camps, and after school programs.

The Museum is accredited by both the American Zoo and Aquarium Association and the American Association of Museums.

Info in brief: Museum for the general public with designated displays and events of specific interest to children.

Location: Six miles south of San Francisco Airport, just off Highway 101.

Hours: Tuesday–Saturday, 10 A.M. to 5 P.M.; Sunday, noon to 5 P.M.; closed Mondays, except Monday holidays. Closed December 24, 25, 31.

Admissions: Under 3, free; children (3–12), $2; seniors & students (13–17), $4; adults, $6.

Nearby sites of interest: San Francisco attractions.

For further information write to the Coyote Point Museum for Environmental Education, 1651 Coyote Point Dr., San Mateo, California 94401-1095, or call (650) 342-7572, or fax (650) 342-7853. *www.coyoteptmuseum.org*

The Discovery Center,
Central Valley Science Museum
Fresno

The Discovery Center is a hands-on children's science museum. Established in 1956, the current 5-acre site now offers both indoor and outdoor scientific exploratory experiences for children ages 3 to 13.

Special workshops, events and presentations are also offered to the public, while school groups can ask for a field trip experience or a program from the "Suitcase Science" offerings.

Info in brief: A small hands-on science museum for children and their caregivers.

Hours: Tuesday–Saturday, 10 A.M. to 4 P.M.; Sunday, noon to 4 P.M.

Admissions: Small admissions charge. Memberships available.

Nearby sites of interest: Winery tours, and other sites of interest in and around Fresno.

For further information write to The Discovery Center, 1937 N. Winery, Fresno, California 93703, or call (209) 251-5533 or fax (559) 251-5531. E-mail: *office@thediscoverycenter.net*

The Discovery Center for Science and Technology
Westlake Village

Having offered a "Museum Without Walls" program for students in Ventura, Santa Barbara and western LA counties, plans are currently underway to build a 70,000 sq. ft. facility with exhibit galleries organized around these themes: "Soup-up" your Scientist Skills, How Information Travels, Intersections and Connections, How Do We Know Stuff? and Science City, a young children's discovery area. The facility will also include a 270-seat large-screen theater/auditorium and an outdoor science park. Situated in the "101 Technology Corridor," the Discovery Center personnel believe that America's economy is relying more and more on a work force proficient in science and technology, and that we should then engage children in learning, and should encourage their sense of discovery and exploration, as a means of increasing their ability to be successful in the future.

Info in brief: A hands-on science and discovery center with an emphasis on technology.

Location: Adjacent to the Civics Arts Plaza in Thousand Oaks.

Hours and Admissions: Not yet determined.

Uniqueness: "Verizon Sci-Tech Community Clubhouse, where children will create on-going science projects in labs with scientists from the technology corporations in the area."

For further information write to The Discovery Center for Science and Technology, 5655 Lindero Canyon Road, Suite 422, Westlake Village, CA 91362 or call (818) 879-2021. *www.discoverycntr.org* E-mail: *administrator@discoverycntr.org*

Discovery Science Center
Launch Pad
Santa Anna

Launch Pad in Costa Mesa, was the preview facility of Discovery Science Center, which is now open in Santa Ana. The Discovery Science Center is a 76,000 sq. ft. science learning facility featuring over 100 interactive exhibits emphasizing science, math and technology. A large format 3-D theater is also on the premises.

Location: West side of Main Street at the Santa Ana Freeway.

Hours: Daily, 10 A.M.–5 P.M.

Admissions: 2 & under, free; Children (3–17), $9.95; adults (18 & over) $12.95. Memberships are available. Member of ASTC.

For further information write to The Discovery Science Center, 2500 N. Main St., Santa Ana CA 92705 or call (714) 542-2823 or fax (714) 542-2828. *www.discoverycube.org*

The Exploratorium
San Francisco

According to *Newsweek* magazine, "There are two models for great American amusement centers ... Disneyland and the Exploratorium. This place feeds all the senses." The Exploratorium itself advertises as a museum of "science, art and human perception," meaning that creative thinking is encouraged as much as the critical thinking encouraged by most other museums.

The Exploratorium is one of the largest children's museums in the nation, with over 650 exhibits on the grounds. The building itself, part of the Palace of Fine Arts designed by architect Bernard Maybeck, is the only survivor of the Panama Pacific Exposition of 1915. Founded in 1969 by physicist Frank Oppenheimer, the museum now features a 50-ft.-high, 103,000 sq. ft. interior which houses permanent and temporary displays and exhibits, classrooms, machine, wood, electronics and welding shops (most open to the public for viewing), the 175-seat McBean Theater, a Life Science laboratory, a reference library/media center, the museum store and a cafe.

Limited space permits only a brief description of the many facets of this museum. Suffice it to say that the goal of the museum is to provide opportunities for learning which are not likely to be experienced elsewhere. The exhibits which encourage this learning fall into 13 broad categories: light, color, sound, music, motion, animal behavior, electricity, heat and temperature, language patterns, hearing, touch, vision, waves and resonance, and weather.

Info in brief: One of the largest (per sq. ft. and per exhibit) hands-on children's museums in the nation.

Location: Palace of Fine Arts, near the Golden Gate Bridge. Directions to the Museum (recording): (415) 561-0399.

Hours: Open Tuesday through Sunday, 10 A.M.–5 P.M. Open these Mondays: Martin Luther King Day, Presidents Day, Memorial Day and Labor Day.

Admissions: Under 3, free; children (4–12 yrs), $9; youth (ages 13–17), seniors, people with disabilities & students (18+ with ID), $11; adult (18–64), $14. Member of Association of Youth Museums. Member ASTC.

Unique exhibits: Many.

Nearby sites of interest: Golden Gate Bridge, Fisherman's Wharf and many other San Francisco attractions.

For further information write to The Exploratorium, 3601 Lyon Street, San Francisco, California 94123, or call (415) 563-7337 or (415) 567-0709 or fax (415) 561-0307. Internet: *lindad@explorato riun.edu*

Explorit Science Center
Davis

Since 1982, Explorit has encouraged the exploration of science, using familiar everyday things as well as the "real stuff" of science. Two floors of museum space feature a long-term exhibition about the science of motion as well as smaller exhibitions that change three times a year. The museum also has a Discovery Room, Animal Alcove, Closer Look Microscope Nook, Wet Lab and Challenge Center, all full of activities true to their motto of "Think it. Try it. Explorit."

The museum has been located in Mace Park since 1982, but opened a main site on 2nd Street in 2006. Explorit's 2nd Street facility contains the hands-on exhibits, a Discovery Room and a Wet Lab, and is open to the public on weekends and Tuesday through Friday afternoons.

The 5th Street branch is the site for nature-based programs and classes available by reservation only.

Info in brief: A hands-on exploratory science museum for children, teachers, and families.

Location: 2801 2nd St. (Main Public Site) and 3141 5th Street in East Davis, (Mace Park Branch).

Hours: Saturday–Sunday, 11 A.M. to 4:30 P.M.; Tuesday–Friday, 2 P.M. to 4:30 P.M. Closed major holidays and during exhibition change weeks. Call ahead for schedule.

Admissions: $4. Members, children 3 & under, and teachers with school ID are admitted free. Fourth Sunday of each month is free admissions for all visitors. Member ASTC.

For further information write to Explorit Science Center, P.O. Box 1288, Davis, California 95617, or call (530) 756-0191 or (530) 756-0191 or fax (530) 756-1227. *www.exploritsciencecenter.org*

Gulf Wings Children's Museum
Oxnard

Gulf Wings is a small museum with a number of rooms, each offering hands-on experiences for children. Some of the 15 exhibits include laser display, space shuttle, dress-up area, puppet show area, play kitchen and snack shack, and crafts area. It is the only children's museum in Ventura County, and their focus is on children ages 2 to 12.

Hours: Tuesday thru Saturday, 10 A.M.–5 P.M. Closed most holidays.

Admissions: Under 2, free; all others, $4.

For further information write to Gulf Wings Children's Museum, 418 West Fourth St., Oxnard, CA 93030 or call (805) 483-3005 or fax (805) 483-3226. *www.gulfwings.org* E-mail: *info@gulf wings.org*

Habitot
Berkeley

Designed especially for kids age 7 and under, Habitot currently offers a 7,000 sq. ft. exhibit space, where exhibits include: Waterworks, an infant toddler garden, a child-size store and cafe, drop-in art studio, rotating dramatic arts exhibit, wiggle wall, and a toy lending library. The community, in conjunction with the Emery Unified School District, decided that a larger facility needs to be built. Plans are now calling for a 20,000 sq. ft. facility with world class exhibits, a children's theater, Science and Media labs, an art studio, on-site food court, demonstration kitchen and Working Garden, and on-site parking, Projected opening date is 2009 or 2010.

Location: 2065 Street, near Shattuck

Hours: Tuesday thru Thursday, 9:30 A.M.–1 P.M.; Friday and Saturday, 9:30 A.M.–4:30 P.M. Sunday — Private parties only. Closed Thanksgiving, Christmas, New Year's Day and every Monday.

Admissions: Under 1, free; child, $7; adult, $6; 10% discount for seniors and disabled.

For further information write to Habitot, 2065 Kittredge St., Berkeley, CA 94704, or call (510) 647-1111. *www.ci.berkeley.ca.us/coolthings/Museums/habitot.html*

Hall of Health
Berkeley

The Hall of Health is sponsored by Children's Hospital and Research Center at Oakland. It is a community health-education museum and science center, with a goal of promoting wellness and individual responsibility for one's health. Interactive, hands-on exhibits help to teach about the workings of the body, the value of sound diet and exercise, and the destructive effects of smoking and drug abuse. Special events and family programs include health and safety festivals and Kids on the Block Puppet Shows on physical, mental, medical and cultural differences.

Info in brief: A health-education museum and science center.

Location: 2230 Shattuck Ave., lower level in Berkeley.

Hours: Tuesday thru Saturday, 10 A.M.–4 P.M. Most visitors tour the museum as part of a school group or family group, so be sure to contact the museum before visiting.

Admissions: $5 per person.

Nearby sites of interest: Numerous attractions in the Berkeley area.

For further information write to the Hall of Health, 2230 Shattuck Ave., Berkeley, CA 94704, or call (510) 549-1564. *www.hallofhealth.org*

Kidspace Museum
Pasadena

Kidspace is a hands-on, participatory children's museum targeting children from 2 to 10. Exhibits have been developed in the areas of art, science, music and communication. Exhibit titles include "Eco-Beach," "Vons Mini-Market," "International Mask Gallery," "Critter Caverns," "Mouse House," "KCBS Television Station," "Backstage," "Stargazer Planetarium," "Firestation Kidspace," and "Toddler Territory." Special events and programs are also offered periodically.

The museum recently relocated to a new facility at the former Fannie Morrison Center in Brookside Park. The new Kidspace features world-class exhibits and 2.2 acres of outdoor learning environments. Children can experience an earthquake, feed giant bugs, craft various art projects, climb 40-foot tall raindrops and more.

Info in brief: A hands-on, participatory museum for young children (ages 2–10) and their caregivers.

Location: Renovated historic Fannie Morrison Horticultural Center buildings at Brookside Park in the Arroyo Seco.

Hours: January thru May and September thru December: Tuesday thru Sunday, 9:30 A.M.–5 P.M. and most Monday holidays. June thru August: Daily, 9:30 A.M.–5 P.M.

Admissions: Under 1, free; all others, $8. Memberships available. Member AYM.

For further information write to Kidspace, 480 N. Arroyo Blvd., Pasadena, CA 91103 or call (626) 449-9144. *www.kidspacemuseum.org* E-mail: *info@kidspacemuseum.org*

Kidzone Museum
Sierra Nevada Children's Museum
Truckee

The Sierra Nevada Children's Museum, founded in 1992, has been the result of community members working together to provide educational resources to its children. These members continue to work together to build a new facility (KidZone), which includes an indoor play structure with multi-sensory exhibits. The museum is designed for families with children up to age seven. Permanent exhibits include a *Baby Zone* for infants to age 18 months, a *Jungle Gym* for toddlers and older children, and a *Creative Corner* where visitors have opportunities to create, paint, cut, draw, and sculpt.

Location: Truckee is a tourist town located about 15 miles north of Lake Tahoe and 35 miles from Reno, Nevada.

Hours: Summer hours (Memorial Day thru Columbus Day): Tuesday thru Sunday, 9 A.M.–1 P.M. Winter hours: Tuesday thru Saturday, 10 A.M.–5 P.M.; Sunday, 10 A.M.–3 P.M. Closed most holidays and during inclement weather.

Admissions: Non-residents: Under 1, free; child (ages 1–17), $7; adult (18–59) $3; senior (60+), $2. Residents: under 1 free; child, $5; adult, $3; senior, $2. Weekly membership (family of 8), $20; locals, first Tuesday, $1. Memberships available. Member ACM.

For further information write to KidZone Museum, 11711 Donner Pass Road, Truckee, CA 96161, or call (530) 587-KIDS (5437), or fax (530) 587-0200. *www.kidzonemuseum.org*

Launch Pad: Discovery Science Center *see*
Discovery Science Center

Lawrence Hall of Science
Berkeley

Originally established in 1968 on the University of California at Berkeley, Lawrence Hall of Science (LHS) is a hands-on science center for families, and a resource center for preschool through high school science and math education.

Location: Centennial Drive in the Berkeley Hills east of the University of California, Berkeley campus, above the UC Botanical Gardens.

Hours: Daily, 10 A.M.–5 P.M. Planetarium show: Saturdays, Sundays and Holidays, closed December 24.

Admissions: General admission: under 3, free; child (ages 3–6), $6; student/senior/disabled, $9; adult (19–61), $11. Planetarium Show: adult, $3; others, $2.50.

For further information write to the Lawrence Hall of Science, University of California #5280, Berkeley, CA 94720-5200 or call (510) 642-7771 or fax (510) 643-0309. E-mail: *gems@berkeley.edu*

Lindsay Wildlife Museum
Walnut Creek

More than 50 species of California live, non-releasable native California wildlife are on exhibit at this unique natural history and environmental education center, where the focus is on learning to live with and conserve nature. The motto here is "Connecting People and Wildlife." Visitors can listen to the cry of a red-tailed hawk, go eye-to-eye with a gray fox, and watch a bald eagle eat lunch.

Founded in 1955, the museum offers innovative children's programs, a unique pet library (which allows family members to "check out" pets), a wildlife rehabilitation hospital and a hands-on discovery room for toddlers year-round. Special events and festivals are also held periodically.

Info in brief: A nature center with a hands-on discovery room for very young children.

Location: Larkey Park in Walnut Creek.

Hours: All weekday morning hours during the school year are reserved for school and group tours only. Open 10 A.M. to 5 P.M. most days; contact the Museum before visiting.

Admissions: Under 2, free; children (2–17), $5; adults, $7; seniors (65+), $6. Memberships available. Member ASTC.

Above: *The eyes have it at the Lindsay Wildlife Museum.* Below: *A one-on-one at the Lindsay Wildlife Museum.*

Nearby sites of interest: Larkey Park, Walnut Creek, Model Train Society Model Railroad.

Unique attraction: "Pet Library."

For further information write to the Lindsay Wildlife Museum, 1931 First Ave., Walnut Creek, California 94597, or call (925) 627-2926 *www.wildlife-museum.org*

Long Beach Children's Museum
Long Beach

The Long Beach Children's Museum is a small hands-on museum for kids and their families.

Nearby sites of interest: Long Beach Aquarium of the Pacific, Earl Burns Miller Japanese Garden, Long Beach City Beach, El Dorado Nature Center, Long Beach Museum of Art, the *Queen Mary*, Museum of Latin American Art, Rancho Los Alamitos Historic Ranch and Gardens, Rancho Los Cerritos Historic Site, Skinny House, the Spruce Goose, and more in the Long Beach area.

For further information write to the Long Beach Children's Museum, 445 Long Beach Boulevard, Long Beach, CA 90802-2462 or call (562) 495-1163.

The Lori Brock Children's Discovery Center
Bakersfield

One of the Kern County Museums, the Lori Brock Children's Discovery Center offers hands-on experiences for children ages eight and under. Current exhibits include: Kid City, Lewis and Clark: Journey Across America; Art Safari and Rope 'Em, Ride 'Em.

Location: Downtown Bakersfield.

Hours: Monday thru Saturday, 10 A.M.–5 P.M.; Sunday, noon–5 P.M., Closed holidays.

Admissions: Under 3, free; child (3–5), $5; students (6–12), $6; students (13–17), $7; seniors (60+), $7; adults, $8. Memberships available.

Nearby sites of interest: Opened in 1976, the Kern County Museum contains over 50 historic structures and exhibits depicting the history of Kern County, California and the West.

For further information write to Kern County Museum, 3801 Chester Avenue, Bakersfield, CA 93301, or call (661) 852-5000 or fax (661) 322-6415.

My Jewish Discovery Place *see*
Zimmer Children's Museum

Orange County Natural History Museum
Laguna Niguel

The Orange County Natural History Museum is committed to the preservation, exhibition, and interpretation of Orange County's natural history. Both paleontological and archeological artifacts are on display, along with native animals. The museum recently acquired a building in Santa Ana that is being renovated to house the current museum displays, new exhibits and additional classrooms.

Hours: Wednesday thru Sunday, 11 A.M.–5 P.M.

For further information write to Orange County Natural History Museum, 28373 Alicia Parkway, Laguna Niguel, CA 92677-1355 or call (949) 831-3287. *www.ocnhm.com*

Palo Alto Junior Museum and Zoo
Palo Alto

The Palo Alto Junior Museum and Zoo is a small children's museum operated by the Department of Community Services in the City of Palo Alto. The museum offers a variety of hands-on educational opportunities which encourage children to touch, look, and listen as they learn by discovery.

Permanent displays include "PlaySpot," an interactive play area for preschoolers and their caregivers; "Starlab," an inflatable planetarium; and the Zoo, located adjacent to the museum. Other temporary exhibits are made available throughout the year. Other educational opportunities offered include classes, workshops, interpretive programs and science outreach programs. At the time of this publication, The Friends of the Palo Alto Junior Museum and Zoo are planning a number of improvements and renovations to this facility.

Info in brief: Hands-on, exclusively for children ages 2 to 12 and their caregivers.

Location: 1451 Middlefield Road in Palo Alto, just north of the intersection of Embarcadero Road.

Hours: Tuesday–Saturday, 10 A.M. to 5 P.M.; Sunday, 1 P.M. to 4 P.M.

Admissions: No admissions charge, but donations are appreciated.

Nearby sites of interest: Museums in Palo Alto and other California tourist attractions.

For further information write to the Palo Alto Junior Museum and Zoo, City of Palo Alto, Dept. of Community Services, 1451 Middlefield Road, Palo Alto, California 94301, or call (650) 329-2111. *www.city.palo-alto.ca.us*

Pretend City, the Children's Museum of Orange County
Irvine

Pretend City is a non-profit organization designed to stimulate and nurture the intellectual and creative curiosity of children in an innovative community environment. Designed as a small city, exhibits include a grocery store, construction site, art studio, house, café, bank, emergency services, health center and farm. Opportunities are provided in which children ages infant through 8 years of age will develop problem-solving and critical thinking skills and will be provided an opportunity to develop creativity and a love of learning. Projected opening date is 2009.

Hours and Admissions: Not established at time of printing.

Nearby sites of interest: Numerous Orange County, California attractions.

For further information write to Pretend City, The Children's Museum of Orange County, 17752 Sky Park Circle, Suite 280, Irvine, CA 92614 or call (949) 428-3900 or fax (949) 428-3908. *www.pretendcity.org* E-mail: *info@pretendcity.org*

The Randall Museum
San Francisco

The "Junior Museum" first opened in 1937 in the city's old jail on Ocean Avenue. In 1951, the museum reopened in its current location on a 16-acre park overlooking San Francisco Bay with the new name, The Josephine D. Randall Junior Museum, or The Randall Museum. The philosophy of the museum was and is to "be a place that would foster a love of science, natural history, and the arts."

The Randall Museum currently houses several permanent exhibits, 3 changing exhibits, a live animal collection, woodworking shop, ceramics room, darkroom, lapidary workshop, and an art room. An auditorium and several classrooms are available along with picnic facilities outside. The Golden Gate Model Railroad Club also houses their train layout on the grounds of the museum.

Info in brief: An educational, program-based museum for children and their families.

Location: Corona Heights Park, in the geographic center of the city.

Hours: Tuesday–Saturday, 10 A.M. to 5 P.M.; Closed most major holidays. The Golden Gate Model Railroad Club's train layout is open Saturdays from 10 A.M. to 4 P.M.

Admissions: No admissions fees charged; small charge for some events and classes; donations are appreciated.

Nearby sites of interest: Golden Gate Park, Buena Vista Park, and other San Francisco tourist attractions.

For further information write to The Randall Museum, 199 Museum Way, San Francisco, California 94114, or call (415) 554-9600.

Reuben H. Fleet Space Theater and Science Center
San Diego

The Space Theater and Science Center is operated by the San Diego Space and Science Foundation. Programs are offered in two main areas—the Space Theater and the Science Center. In the Space Theater, visitors can experience an Omnimax/IMAX film or planetarium program. (In fact, the term Omnimax was coined by the Space Theater founders for the giant tilted dome screen and fish-eye effect created by the projection of the new IMAX films onto their tilted dome screen.) The museum is proud to be the first and only IMAX Theater in San Diego. In the Science Center, more than 60 interactive exhibits in the 7 exhibit galleries allow visitors to experience science.

Conceived in 1957, the museum opened on a small scale with a unique model planetarium in 1965. This area now offers both planetarium and IMAX Theater presentations. The Science Center facility opened to the public in 1973. Several traveling exhibits, special programs and special events are offered throughout the year. A simulator ride has also been added to activities available at the Center.

Info in brief: A hands-on museum for children, plus a planetarium/IMAX Theater and motion simulator ride.

Location: Prado in Balboa Park, two blocks south of the San Diego Zoo on Park Blvd. Physical address: 1875 El Prado, San Diego, CA 92101.

Hours: Posted on a calendar at *www.rhfleet.org/site/imax/Calendar_08.cfm*

Admissions: Under 3, free to all activities. (Galleries) juniors (3–12), $6.75; adults, $8; seniors (65+), $6.75. (Galleries & 1 IMAX) juniors, $9.75; adults, $12.50; seniors, $9.75. (Galleries & 2 IMAX) juniors, $13.75. Motion Simulator Ride, $4. Member ASTC.

Nearby sites of interest: San Diego Zoo and other San Diego tourist attractions.

For further information write to the Reuben H. Fleet Space Theater and Science Center, Balboa Park, P.O. Box 33303, San Diego, California 92163-3303, or call (619) 238-1233 (TDD 238-2480) or 232-6866 or fax (619) 685-5771. Website: *www.rhfleet.org*

Sacramento Children's Museum
Sacramento

As of the date of this publication, The Sacramento Children's Museum has not yet opened. The desire to build a children's museum has encouraged local educators, parents, physicians, attorneys and others to join the rank of those working to get the museum open. In 2006, the Junior League of Sacramento adopted the museum as a signature project, bringing more hope to those involved. No projected date has been published at this time.

When completed and opened, the museum will include hands-on exhibits, a child-size amphitheater, a parent's resource room/classroom, an edible children's garden, classes and special programs, a party room, retail store and café. All exhibits and activities will be designed for children from birth to eight years. An early childhood exhibit space will be specially designed to meet the needs and interests of children three years of age and younger.

For more information write to The Sacramento Children's Museum, P.O. Box 13303, Sacramento, CA 95813 or call (916) 952-6852. *www.sacramentochildrensmuseum.org* E-mail: *info@sackids.org*

San Luis Obispo Children's Museum
San Luis Obispo

The new 8400 sq. ft. museum offers a unique kind of "town square" setting where "play inspires life-long learning." Previously serving a younger audience, SLO now offers new exhibits for ages 10 to 13, and will offer a larger toddler space. At the date of this publication, two of the three floors are open.

Info in brief: A hands-on museum for toddlers thru 13-year-olds.

Location: Downtown near the creek walk.

Hours: Monday, closed; Tuesday thru Friday, 10 A.M.–4 P.M.; Saturday, 10 A.M.–5 P.M.; Sunday, 11 A.M.–5 P.M.

Admissions: Adults and children, $8; children under 2, free; check the website for discounts and multi-day passes.

Nearby sites of interest: Numerous California attractions.

For further information write to San Luis Obispo Children's Museum, 1010 Nipomo St., San Luis Obispo, CA 93401 or call (805) 545-5874 E-mail: *jeller@slokids.org*

Tech Museum of Innovation
San Jose

The Tech Museum offers visitors an expansive variety of interactive exhibits focusing on innovations in technology. More than 132,000 sq. ft. of exhibit space are divided among themed galleries on innovation, the internet, the human body, and exploration. Exhibit titles are "Spirit of American Innovation," "Life Tech," "Innovation," "Exploration," Green by Design," "View from Space," "What's New," "IDEA house," "Silicon Workshop Genetics," and "Technology with a Twist." Also on site are a domed IMAX theater, an educational center for workshops, etc., and a retail store. It has become a landmark for visitors interested in the latest high-tech gizmos and gadgets.

Location: Silicon Valley area.

Hours: Exhibits are open daily, 10 A.M. to 5 P.M. except Thanksgiving and Christmas. IMAX films are updated daily.

Admissions: Museum + 1 IMAX, $8; additional IMAX tickets, $4; IMAX DMR Feature Film, $10.

Nearby sites of interest: Children's Discovery Museum of San Jose and many other California attractions.

For further information write to Tech Museum of Innovation, 201 South Market Street, San Jose, CA 95113 or call (408) 294-8324 or fax (408) 279-7167. E-mail: *webmaster@thetech.org*

World of Wonders (WOW)
Lodi

WOW will be a hands-on science museum in Downtown Lodi. Expected opening date is 2009. Current plans call for a 12,000 sq. ft. building with 800 sq. ft. for retail sales, 1000 sq. ft. for a hands-on classroom, office, storage and, mainly, room for 30–40 major exhibits. WOW is also partnering with the Exploratorium in San Francisco, which will provide them with 30–35 visiting exhibits each year.

Location: 2 North Sacramento St., Downtown Lodi, CA 95240.

Hours and Admissions: Not yet determined.

For further information write to World of Wonders, P.O. Box 1671, Woodbridge, CA 95258 or call (209) 327-6369. E-mail: *sally@wowsciencemuseum.org*

Youth Science Center
Hacienda Heights

The Youth Science Center was established in Fullerton, California in 1962 but relocated to Hacienda Heights in 1984. Besides the many exhibits, classes, and lectures, field trips are offered with an aim to increase children's interest in science and to increase their appreciation and respect for the environment. Visitors can experiment with exhibits involving volcanoes, astronomy, weather, the body, insects, reptiles and liquid crystals. Several Macintosh computers with CD-ROM drives are also available for use, and a digital StarLab portable planetarium was added in 2007.

Currently, 24 instructors offer classes during a six-week summer science camp. Five of these 24 have been honored as "Teacher of the Year" or "Teacher of the Month" in their districts. Even though the main emphasis is placed on school groups, the museum is open to the public three days a week during the school year. Summer hours allow visitors to visit five days of the week.

Info in brief: A small hands-on children's museum with a target audience of elementary school-aged children.

Location: Wedgeworth Elementary School on Wedgeworth Drive in Hacienda Heights.

Hours: (School year) Tuesday and Friday, 1 P.M. to 4 P.M.; Saturday, 11 A.M. to 3 P.M.; (summer) Monday–Friday, 8:30 A.M. to 12 P.M. Be sure to contact the museum for other program information.

Admissions: Free (donations accepted).

Nearby sites of interest: Hsi Lai Buddhist Temple (largest Buddhist temple in North America), La Habra Children's Museum, Knott's Berry Farm (Buena Park) and other California tourist attractions.

For further information write to Youth Science Center, 16949 Wedgeworth Dr., Hacienda Heights, California 91745, or call (626) 854-9825. *www.youthsciencecenter.org*

Zeum
San Francisco

Zeum is an interactive, multi-generational (encouraging ages 3 thru adult), and ADA accessible museum with exhibits that focus heavily on five core arts and media subjects: Animation, Video Production, Sound Production, Performance and Visual Arts. The museum has two floors with six major exhibit galleries to explore: Animators Studio, Digital Workshop, Spiral Walkway, Main Gallery, Music Production Lab and The Roundabout.

Location: Corner of 4th and Howard St. in Yerba Buena Gardens in downtown San Francisco.

Hours: Wednesday thru Friday, 1 P.M.–5 P.M.; Weekends, 11 A.M.–5 P.M.

Admissions: 2 & under, free; youth (ages 3–18), $6; students/seniors, $7; adults, $8. Memberships available.

Nearby sites of interest: Include the many sites of San Francisco.

For further information write to the Zeum, 221 Fourth Street, San Francisco, CA 94103 or call (415) 820-3320 or fax (415) 820-3330. E-mail: *info@zeum.org*

Zimmer Children's Museum
Los Angeles

Now in its 18th year, the Zimmer Children's Museum is a hands-on museum featuring Jewish cultural themes. The 10,000 sq. ft., 2-level museum features an actual airplane where chil-

A world of wonder awaits behind the door of the Zimmer Discovery Children's Museum.

dren are encouraged to play, a theatre with costumes, and "Zimmer Main Street," which features the Blue Bagel Café, where children can make their own food creations and ring up their customers on an old fashioned cash register. Bubbie's Book Store offers books for reading and blocks for building. Other exhibits include a bouncy room for children 2 and under, a model synagogue, a home and a marketplace, a life-size ambulance, a water table and the world's largest known Tzedakah Pinball Machine.

The mission of the museum is to promote values that help make a better society by emphasizing the ideals of respect for others, generosity of heart, helping those in need, accepting differences and celebrating uniquenesses. These values are taught through interactive learning, creative self-expression, and art experiences.

Info in brief: Hands-on, exploratory children's museum.

Location: Lobby level of the Jewish Federation Building in Los Angeles.

Hours: Tuesday–Thursday, 12:30 P.M. to 5 P.M.; Wednesday, 10 A.M. to 5 P.M.; Friday, 10 A.M. to 12:30 P.M.; Sunday, 12:30 P.M. to 5 P.M. Group tours available by appointment.

Admissions: Under age 3, free; ages 3 & above, $5; adults, $8.

Unique feature: All exhibits focus on Jewish life.

Nearby sites of interest: The many tourist attractions of Los Angeles.

For further information write to Zimmer Children's Museum, 6505 Wilshire Blvd., Suite 100, Los Angeles, California 90048, or call (323) 761-8910, or fax (323) 761-8990. *www.zimmermuseum.org*

COLORADO

The Children's Museum of Denver
Denver

Since 1973, the Children's Museum of Denver has offered innovative, hands-on exhibits, educational programs, theater performances and special events encouraging children "to explore, create, discover and imagine themselves in the world around them." The museum continues to ignite and foster a love of learning. Their mission is to create a community where children and their grownups learn through play, thereby helping them to prepare for their future.

The museum offers 11 interactive Playscapes, year-round special events, and daily educational programming.

Info in brief: An interactive museum for children, ages newborn to 8 years, and their caregivers.

Location: I-25 and 23rd Ave. in the Platte River Valley close to downtown Denver.

Hours: Tuesday–Sunday, 10 A.M. to 5 P.M.; open Monday, June–August only; toddler hours, Tuesday and Thursday, 9 A.M. to 10 A.M.

Admissions: Under 1, free; age 1, $5.50; ages (2–59), $7.50; seniors (60+), $5.50. Free admission on the first Friday of every month.

Other sites of interest nearby: The Colorado Railroad Museum, Forney Transportation Museum, Rio Grande Ski Train, Elitch Gardens theme park, skiing attractions and other Denver tourist attractions.

For further information write to The Children's Museum of Denver, 2121 Children's Museum Dr., Denver, Colorado 80211, or call (303) 561-0111.

Many museums, including the Children's Museum of Denver now have specific areas for toddlers.

The Children's Museum of Denver.

Discovery Science Center Museum
Fort Collins

The Discovery Science Center Museum is northern Colorado's only hands-on science and technology center, offering 120 interactive exhibits for children of all ages and their families. Besides the hands-on exhibits, the museum offers events, educational programs, and traveling exhibitions, to promote critical thinking and problem-solving skills for its visitors.

Hours: Tuesday thru Saturday, 10 A.M.–5 P.M., plus Mondays through the middle of May; Closed Sundays, New Years Day, Independence Day, Thanksgiving Day, and Christmas Day.

Admissions: Under 3, free; children (3–12 years), $5; seniors (60+), $5.50; adults (13–59), $7. Member ASTC.

For further information contact: Discovery Center Science Museum, 703 E. Prospect, Fort Collins, Colorado 80525, phone: (970) 472-3990. *www.discoverysciencecenter.org*

Sangre de Cristo Arts and Conference Center & Buell Children's Museum
Pueblo

The Sangre de Cristo Arts Center opened in 1972. The original two-building complex did not contain a children's museum, but two expansions have now added, among other attractions, a 7,500 sq. ft. interactive gallery, a theater, a café and a gift shop dedicated to the Buell Children's Museum.

Info in brief: A 3-building complex, one of which is the Buell Children's Museum.

Hours: Tuesday thru Saturday, 11 A.M.–4 P.M.

Admissions: Arts Center and Children's Museum: children, $3; adults, $4. Free adjacent parking. Memberships available.

For further information write to the Sangre de Cristo Arts & Conference Center, 210 N. Santa Fe Ave., Pueblo, CO 81003. *www.sdc-arts.org*

University of Colorado Museum
Boulder

The University of Colorado Museum is a natural history museum for people of all ages. Inside the Museum, however, is a hands-on "Discovery Corner" for kids. In the "Discovery Corner" children can try on a turtle shell, weave on a Navajo loom, piece together a buffalo skeleton, view dinosaur remains, and more. An annual "Museum in the Dark" program is also offered for children and their families, along with many special events, changing traveling exhibits, lectures and trips.

Info in brief: An adult museum with one section specifically designated as a hands-on museum for children.

Location: Boulder campus in the Henderson Building at 15th and Broadway.

Hours: Monday–Friday, 9 A.M. to 5 P.M.; Saturday, 9 A.M. to 4 P.M.; Sunday, 10 A.M. to 4 P.M. Closed all university holidays.

Admissions: No admissions fee. Suggested donations, $1–$3. Be sure to contact the museum about parking space and fees before visiting, as some programs require a small fee.

For further information write to the University of Colorado Museum, Campus Box 218, Boulder, Colorado 80309-0218, or call (303) 492-6892.

Western Colorado Math & Science Center
Grand Junction

The Western Colorado Math & Science Center is a non-profit, hands-on facility whose goal is to "create enthusiasm and excitement for math and science" for all ages. Basic elements of science are placed on tables with descriptions so that children and adults can investigate on their own. More than 160 hands-on exhibits dealing with math and science concepts are provided, along with the "Riverview Science Park" for outdoor learning.

Info in brief: A hands-on Math & Science center.

Location: Northeast corner of Palisade Street and Unaweep Avenue in the New Emerson School Building.

Hours: Wednesday thru Saturday, 10 A.M.–4 P.M.

Admissions: $1 per person.

For further information write to the Western Colorado Math & Science Center, 2660 Unaweep Ave., Grand Junction, CO 81503 or call (970) 254-1626.

World of Wonders
Lafayette

World of Wonders opened in 1996, becoming a non-profit organization in 1997. The museum offers an 8,000 sq. ft. area that includes educational and dramatic play exhibits geared for children ages 1 to 11 years of age. Exhibits include art displays, arts and crafts, music, dance, theater, wind energy, air and gravity, dinosaurs, a pirate ship and lighthouse, trains, play house, grocery store credit union, sand castle, built-it-yourself house, bubbles, ball maze and more. WOW was ranked as one of the top 50 children's museums in the country by *Child Magazine* in February of 2002.

Info in brief: Specifically for toddlers and school age children and their families, with interactive and informative educational and creative exhibits and programs.

Hours: Fall/Winter/Spring hours: Tuesday thru Wednesday, 9 A.M.–5 P.M., Toddler hour (5 and under), Tuesday & Wednesday, 9 A.M.; Thursday thru Saturday, 10 A.M.–6 P.M.; Sunday, noon–4 P.M.; Summer hours vary — be sure to contact the museum before visiting.

Admissions: 14 months & under, free; adults, free; $7 per child. Memberships available.

For further information write to World of Wonders Children's Museum, 110 North Harrison Ave., Lafayette, CO 80026 or call (303) 604-2424. *www.wowmuseum.com*

CONNECTICUT

Children's Museum
West Hartford

The Museum is the largest in the state. It is comprised of a science-curriculum based preschool; the state's largest space theater, the Glengras Planetarium; wildlife; and a nature center in Canton.

Hours: Tuesday–Saturday, 10 A.M.–5 P.M.; Sunday, noon–5 P.M.

Admissions: 1 & younger, free; 2–62, $11; 63 & older, $10.

For further information write to the Children's Museum, 950 Trout Brook Drive, West Hartford, CT, or call (860) 231-2824; www.thechildrensmuseumct.org

Children's Museum of Southeastern Connecticut
Niantic

The goal of this museum is to educate the children and families of southeastern Connecticut "by developing their awareness of the world around them through exploration of the arts, sciences, culture and history." Exhibits are interactive and celebrate the cultural diversity found in the area. In the February 2002 issue of *Child Magazine*, the Children's Museum of Southeastern Connecticut was ranked 27th out of more than 200 children's museums in the United States, and it was the smallest museum to receive the honor. As with many older museums, CMSC has plans for renovating several areas of the museum in the near future.

Info in brief: Small hands-on museum for children and their families.

Hours: Tuesday thru Saturday, 9:30 A.M.–5 P.M.; Fridays until 8 P.M.; Sunday, noon–5 P.M.; open Mondays during school vacations and in the summer. Open New Year's Eve, 9:30 A.M.–5 P.M.

Admissions: Under 1, free; others, $6. Memberships available.

For further information write to the Children's Museum of Southeastern Connecticut, 409 Main St., Niantic, CT 06357 or call (860) 691-1111. *www.childrensmuseumsect.org*

Connecticut Children's Museum
New Haven

Eight thematic and community-inspired rooms shape the Connecticut Children's Museum into a hands-on, interactive experience for children and their families. The museum houses three programs, interwoven in philosophy and purpose: Creating Kids Child Care Center, Creating Curriculum Child Care Providers Training Programs, and the Connecticut Children's Museum itself. Each is inspired by psychologist Howard Gardner's Theory of Multiple Intelligences, inspiring exhibits like: Musical Room, Bodily-Kinesthetic Room, Logical-Mathematical Room, Linguistic Room, Spatial Room, Interpersonal Room, Intrapersonal Room, and Naturalist Room. The museum is designed to be a place full of color, whimsy and wisdom.

For further information write to the Connecticut Children's Museum, Creating Kids, Creating Curriculum Children's Building 22 Wall St., New Haven, CT 06511 or call (203) 562-5437 or fax (203) 787-9414. *www.thechildrensbuilding@snet.net*

Connecticut Science Center
Hartford

The mission of the Connecticut Science Center is to inspire "lifelong learning through interactive and innovative experiences that explore our changing world through science," with the hope of inspiring the next generation of researchers, discoverers, healers, teachers, inventors and well-informed citizens in general. The Center will offer high-impact learning in a green, clean, bright and stimulating environment. Exhibits will include: Forces in Motion,

Planet Earth, Exploring Space, The Picture of Health, Smart Energy, Sight & Sound Experience, Sports Lab, Invention Dimension, A River of Life, KidSpace and AT&T Learning.

Hours & Admissions: Not yet set at time of publication. It is opening in Spring 2009.

For further information write to Connecticut Science Center, 50 Columbus Blvd., Suite 500, Hartford, CT 06106 or call (860) 727-0457 or fax (860) 727-0850. *www.ctsciencecenter.org*

Discovery Museum, Inc.
Bridgeport

The Discovery Museum has three floors of hands-on activities that encourage visitors to manipulate mechanical exhibits on electricity, electronics, computers, sound, light, magnetism and energy. A Planetarium and a Challenger Learning Center are also on site, along with traveling exhibits, classrooms and more. The Challenger Learning Center is one of 49 such centers in the U.S. State-of-the-art innovative two-room simulators, consisting of a Space Station and Mission Control, give visitors experience in being astronauts, engineers, and scientists in order to complete their "mission."

For more information write to Discovery Museum, Inc., 4450 Park Avenue, Bridgeport, CT 06604 or call (203) 372-3521 or fax (203) 374-1929.

Imagine Nation
Bristol

Imagine Nation is an indoor and outdoor museum for children and their families. Among other exhibits, Imagine Nation offers a number of IBM–donated toddler workstations, and exhibits with names like: Waterplay, Greenhouse, Jungle Theme, and Playscape. Three floors of exhibit space also offer classrooms, a birthday party room, and, at the time of the printing of this book, a temporary exhibit on the third floor entitled "Dark Room." Plans call for other temporary/visiting exhibits to occupy this space periodically.

Hours: Wednesday thru Friday, 9:30 A.M.–5 P.M.; Saturday, 11 A.M.–5 P.M.; Sunday, noon–5 P.M. The first Friday of each month the museum is open until 8 P.M.

Admissions: Under 1, free; others, $5.

For further information write to Imagine Nation, One Pleasant Street, Bristol, CT 06010 or call (860) 314-1400. *www.imaginenation.org* E-mail: *info@imaginenation.org*

Lutz Children's Museum
Manchester

The Lutz Children's Museum is located in a former school house and serves children 2–10 and their families. Services include hands-on exhibits, live animals, classes, concerts, trips, and special events. The museum also offers an extensive school outreach program and operates a nature center located nearby.

Info in brief: Hands-on activities, nature walks, live animal exhibits and visual displays for children and adults.

Location: Downtown Manchester, Connecticut (Exit 3 off I-384).

Hours: Tuesday thru Friday, 9 A.M. to 5 P.M.; Saturday and Sunday, noon to 5 P.M. Closed Mondays and major holidays.

Admissions: Under 1, free; others, $5. Memberships are offered.

Unique exhibits or exhibitions: An Alaskan Brown Bear, and an area where children can display their own collections.

For further information write to Lutz Children's Museum, 247 South Main Street, Manchester, Connecticut 06040, or call (860) 643-0949. *www.lutzmuseum.org* E-mail: *reckert@lutzmuseum.org*

The Maritime Aquarium of Norwalk
Norwalk

The Maritime Aquarium consists of the Aquarium area, an IMAX Theater and Maritime Hall. A multi-phase expansion is being planned — the first phase was an Environmental Education Center which opened in 2001.

The aquarium area of the museum features 20 habitats stocked with more than 125 species indigenous to the Long Island Sound. The entire Aquarium is one of a few in the country solely devoted to one body of water. In Falconer Hall, where the aquarium begins and ends, harbor seals live in a special indoor-outdoor tank, where visitors can watch them being fed three times daily. Several videos and a touch tank are also offered here.

The IMAX Theater at the Maritime Aquarium is the only IMAX Theater in Connecticut. (IMAX is short for "Image MAXimum.") More than two dozen films focusing on natural history and science have been offered here. Film titles change frequently, so it is best to contact the aquarium for current titles before visiting.

The Maritime Hall is a two-story building which features a new series of hands-on displays explaining what a fish is and how it works. A new Shark Touch Pool is also available for visitors to experience. Interactive displays also provide activities which teach about navigational procedures and boatbuilding.

Info in brief: An aquarium, IMAX theater and hands-on children's science center of interest to the whole family.

Location: A few minutes off I-95, at Exit 14 northbound and Exit 15 southbound.

Hours: Daily, 10 A.M. to 5 P.M.; open until 6 P.M. July 1–Labor Day. Closed Thanksgiving and Christmas Day.

Admissions: General admission (aquarium and special exhibits), under 2, free; children (2–12), $9; adults, $11; seniors (62+), $10. IMAX Theater admission: under 2, free; children, $6.50; adults, $9; seniors, $8. Combination (aquarium and IMAX): children, $12.50; adults, $16.50; seniors, $15. Other combination tickets are available. SpongeBob SquarePants Simulated 3D ride is an extra cost. Member ASTC.

Unique exhibitions: All exhibits, touch tanks, etc. focus on species indigenous to the Sound.

Other sites of interest nearby: Essex Steam Train & Riverboat Ride, Valley Railroad Company, The Connecticut Valley Line (Essex); Railroad Museum of New England (Essex); Lake Compounce Amusement Park (Bristol), and Quassy Amusement Park (Middlebury).

For further information write to The Maritime Aquarium at Norwalk, 10 N. Water St., Norwalk, Connecticut 06854, or call (203) 852-0700 or fax (203) 838-5416. *www.maritimeaquarium.org* E-mail: *info@maritimeaquarium.org*

The New Britain Youth Museum &
New Britain Youth Museum Hungerford Park
Kensington

Founded in 1956, the New Britain Youth Museum and the New Britain Youth Museum at Hungerford Park are non-profit educational institutions dedicated to enhancing the learning environment for children, young adults, and adults in central Connecticut. Through the collection, preservation, care and exhibition of material culture, natural history collection, plants and live animals, the museum endeavors to create a greater understanding of the arts, the humanities, natural history, and science. Activities include a puppet theater, construction toys and games, and the Dinosaur Room.

Two museum sites have been established which support this mission. The New Britain Youth Museum in downtown New Britain offers school programming outreach, exhibits and special events that focus on history, art and the cultural heritage of the diverse peoples of central Connecticut. The museum at Hungerford Park, Kensington, offers educational programming, exhibits and special events that relate to science, natural history, the environment and other issues confronting today's society.

Info in brief: The Youth Museum is a hands-on, participatory museum especially for children and their caregivers. The Hungerford Park site is a hands-on nature center.

Hours: (Youth Museum) Tuesday, 10 A.M. to 5 P.M.; Wednesday–Friday, Noon–5 P.M.; Saturday, 10 A.M. to 4 P.M., Craft Program at 2 P.M.; Closed Sunday and Monday. (Hungerford Park) Tuesday–Saturday, 10 A.M.–4:30 P.M. Saturdays, Public Animal Programs at 11 A.M., 1:30 P.M., and 3:30 P.M.; Closed Sunday and Monday.

Admissions: Youth Museum, free. Hungerford Park, under 2, free; child $2; senior, $3; adult, $4.

Other sites of interest nearby: New Britain Industrial Museum, New Britain Museum of American Art, New Britain Chorale, Musical Club, Opera, Symphony, Hole in the Wall Theater, and the Repertory Theater of New Britain.

For further information write to The New Britain Youth Museum, 30 High Street, New Britain, Connecticut 06051, or call (860) 225-3020. For Hungerford Park write to The New Britain Youth Museum at Hungerford Park, 191 Farmington Ave., Kensington, Connecticut 06037, or call (860) 827-9064. *www.newbritainyouthmuseum.org*

Stepping Stones Museum for Children
Norwalk

Stepping Stones features interactive, hands-on exhibits and educational programs for children ages ten and under and their families. More than 100 exhibits are available in the four main galleries and special toddlers-only gallery. The museum has received two special awards: one of "America's Top 50 Children's Museums" and a unique building. Upon arrival, the whimsical tower draws the attention of visitors. Its windows are eyes, ears and a mouth. Its nose is a sundial. Its hat is a birdcage with a "feathervane" in honor of the local folk hero, Yankee Doodle Dandy. Exhibits in the museum proper include: Healthyville, Waterscape, Rainforest Adventure, In the Works, Toddler Terrain, Color Coaster, Bubbles, and Traveling Exhibits.

Info in Brief: Hands-on museum for families with children 10 and under.

Location: Mathews Park.

Hours: Winter: Tuesday, 1–5 P.M.; Wednesday thru Sunday, 10 A.M.–5 P.M. Closes at 3 P.M. on July 4, Thanksgiving Eve and New Year's Eve. Summer (July 1–Labor Day): Daily, 10 A.M.–5 P.M. Closed Easter, Thanksgiving, Christmas Eve, Christmas, and New Year's Day.

Admissions: Under 1, free; seniors (62+), $7; others, $9. Seniors admitted for free from 5–8 P.M. on the last Thursday of every month. Memberships available. Free parking.

For further information write to Stepping Stones Museum for Children, 303 West Ave., Norwalk, CT 06850 or call (203) 899-0606 or fax (203) 899-0530. *www.steppingstones.org*

FLORIDA

The Bailey-Matthews Shell Museum
Sanibel Island

The Bailey-Matthews Shell Museum is the only museum in the United States which is devoted solely to shells. More than just a "display" museum, the museum offers the visitor opportunities to increase his scientific knowledge of shells and to learn about the relationship between shells and the web of life.

The museum hosts the second largest library in Florida (in this scientific field) and conducts lectures and seminars throughout the year. Touch Tables are available for children along with special paper "games" that children can play as they tour the exhibits.

Info in brief: Although this museum is not specifically for children, the Touch Tables and impressive displays offer a unique opportunity for children to learn about something that is, for most of them, fascinating.

Location: Physical Address— 3075 Sanibel-Captiva Rd., Sanibel, FL 33957.

Hours: Daily, 10 A.M. to 4 P.M.

Admissions: Under 7, free; youth (5–16 yrs.), $4; adults, $7.

Unique exhibits: Over 200 species of shells.

Other sites of interest nearby: Thomas Edison and Henry Ford homes, Imaginarium children's museum, Gulf Coast beaches.

For further information write to The Bailey-Matthews Shell Museum, P.O. Box 1580, Sanibel, Florida 33957, or call 1-888-679-6450 or (239) 395-2233 or fax (239) 395-6706. *www.shellmuseum. org*

The Brevard Museum, Inc.
Cocoa

The Brevard Museum employs two full-time and four part-time staff who, along with the more than 100 volunteers, help to keep the programs and exhibits running smoothly. More than 12,000 sq. ft. of floor space is devoted to permanent exhibits in ornithology, paleontology, marine biology, archaeology, geology, the Spanish Period, Seminole Indians and pioneer history. A 22-acre nature center is also on the grounds.

Both interpretive and hands-on exhibits are available, with a special "Discovery Room" (all hands-on activities) offered especially for kindergartners through third graders. Puppet shows and a walking tour of historic Cocoa Village are also of special interest to children.

Info in brief: Interpretive museum of interest to the entire family, but with a number of hands-on displays specifically for children.

Hours: Monday thru Saturday, 10 A.M.–4 P.M.

Admissions: Under 5, free; children (5–16), $4.50; adults, $6.

Unique exhibitions: The entire museum concentrates on Florida history, culture, and flora and fauna.

Other sites of interest nearby: Numerous Florida tourist attractions, such as Kennedy Space Center.

For further information write to the Brevard Museum, Inc., 2201 Michigan Ave., Cocoa, Florida, 32926, or call (407) 632-1830. *www.brevardmuseum.org*; E-mail: *bmhs@brevardmuseum.org*

Challenger Learning Center
Tallahassee

The Challenger Learning Center is a 32,000 sq. ft. outreach facility of the Florida A&M University–Florida State University College of Engineering, with a mission of providing students in grades K–12 with high-quality hands-on educational experiences in science and engineering through the use of high-fidelity aerospace simulators. The facility offers state-of-the-art, large-format and domed digital theaters to accomplish this mission through exhibiting thematically related films and planetarium programs. The facility intends to motivate students to pursue careers in math, science and technology.

Info in brief: A hands-on science museum, planetarium and observing museum for children of all ages.

Location: Kleman Plaza in downtown Tallahassee.

Hours: Monday thru Thursday, 10 A.M.–7 P.M.; Friday & Saturday, 10 A.M.–Midnight; Sunday, 1–6 P.M.

Admissions: IMAX only: under 3, free; children (3–12), $5.50; seniors (55+) & students w/ID, $6.50; adults, $7. Combo tickets: under 3, free; children, $9; seniors & students, $10.50; adults, $11.50. Public parking garages are located close by.

For further information write to the Challenger Learning Center, 200 South Duval St., Tallahassee, FL 32301 or call (850) 645-7788 or fax (850) 645-7784. *www.challengertlh.com* For IMAX show times call (850) 645-4629.

Children's Museum of the Highlands
Sebring

A small museum especially for young children and their families, the Children's Museum of the Highlands offers a multitude of hands-on exhibits and a gift shop. Exhibits include a grocery store, doctor's office, weather station, fire station, face painting, puppet theater, stage, and a number of science and creativity areas.

Location: Downtown Sebring.

Hours: Tuesday thru Saturday, 10 A.M.–8 P.M.; Thursday, 10 A.M.–8 P.M.

Admissions: $3 per person; "Thrifty Thursday," after 5 P.M., $1 per person.

Other sites of interest nearby: Sebring 500, run annually.

For further information write to Children's Museum of the Highlands, 219 N. Ridgewood Dr., Sebring, FL 33870 or call (863) 385-KIDS (5437). *www.childrensmuseumhighlands.com*

Children's Museum of the Treasure Coast
Stuart

Located in a renovated former chapel/auditorium building in Indian Riverside Park in Jensen Beach/Stuart, this new 12,000 sq. ft. facility has a mission to offer children and their families a place to explore and learn through hands-on, interactive activities. Most exhibits are designed to reflect and teach about Florida's unique character, especially in, around, and under the water. The first phase of the museum is projected to be opened in early 2008, with other phases to follow. The floor plan is divided into two distinct sections—for permanent and traveling exhibits. Space is also available for classrooms, a gift shop, a parent resource area and offices. Planned exhibits include an eighteenth century Spanish galleon ship, an interactive exhibit about the indigenous Ais Indians, a Florida Cracker house, a river/water play area, a child-sized city, and more.

Location: Indian Riverside Park, Jensen Beach (mailing address is Stuart), 10 miles east of I-95.

Hours: Monday–Wednesday, Friday 9 A.M.–5 P.M., Thursday 9 A.M.–8 P.M., Saturday 10 A.M.–4 P.M., Sunday noon–4 P.M. Closed: New Year's Day, Easter Sunday, Thanksgiving and Christmas day.

Admissions: Under 12 months, free; 12 months to 2, $3; 2–12, $6; adults, $6.

Other sites of interest nearby: Florida beaches, Lake Okeechobee, Flagler Museum in Palm Beach

For further information write to The Children's Museum of the Treasure Coast, P.O. Box 2147, Stuart, FL 34995 or call (772) 225-7575. *www.childrensmuseumtc.org*

The Children's Science Center
Cape Coral

The Children's Science Center in Cape Coral is a hands-on exploratory science museum and outdoor nature trail. Science and technology areas explored include holograms, optical illusions, electricity, space, mazes, Calusa Indian technology, fossils and dinosaurs, bubbles, telescope viewing (January–April), bug hunting and more.

Info in brief: Hands-on exploratory museum for children, even on the nature trail.

Location: 2915 NE Pine Island Road.

Hours: Weekdays, 9:30 A.M. to 4:30 P.M.; weekends, noon to 5 P.M.

Admissions: Under 2, free; children (3–16) $2; adults, $4. Member ASTC.

Unique exhibits: Outdoor exploratory nature trail.

Other sites of interest nearby: Calusa Nature Center and Planetarium, Sun Splash Family Waterpark, Six Mile Cypress Slough Preserve, Marine Science Center, Corkscrew Swamp Sanctuary, Thomas Edison and Ford homes (Ft. Myers), Florida beaches.

For further information write to The Children's Science Center, 2915 NE Pine Island Road, Cape Coral, Florida 33909-6513, or call (941) 997-0012.

Children's Science Explorium
Boca Raton

The Children's Science Explorium offers hands-on, interactive science exhibits primarily designed for ages 5 to 12 and their families. These exhibits, both permanent and traveling, primarily challenge and enhance children's understanding of how physical science impacts their everyday lives. Exhibits allow children to explore electricity, rocketry, weather, and other aspects of science.

Info in brief: Hands-on science museum for children from kindergarten thru 6th grade.

Location: Sugar Sand Park, Boca Raton (the park includes 132 acres of recreation facilities, including a Community Center, Willow Theatre, Field House, baseball/softball fields, in-line roller hockey rink, Science Playground, and picnic pavilions as well as the Explorium.

Hours: Monday thru Friday, 9 A.M.–6 P.M.; Weekends & Holidays, 10 A.M.–5 P.M.; Closed Thanksgiving and Christmas.

Admissions: Free; $1 per person to ride the Sugar Sand Park Carousel. Member ASTC.

Other sites of interest nearby: Sugar Sand Park facilities, Florida Atlantic University cultural events.

For further information write to the Children's Science Explorium, 300 South Military Trail, Boca Raton, FL 33486 or call (561) 347-3913. E-mail: *explorium@myboca.us*

Dinosaur World
Plant City

Dinosaur World in Florida has over 150 life-size dinosaur models as well as fossil digs, a museum, boneyard, classrooms, playground, caves and more.

Info in brief: One of three in the U.S.—others in Kentucky and Texas.

Location: Off I-4, Exit 17 in Plant City, approximately 20 minutes from Tampa and 1 hour from Orlando.

Hours: February thru November, Daily, 9 A.M.–6 P.M.; December & January, 9 A.M.–5 P.M.

Admissions: Under 3, free; children (3–12), $9.75; adults, $12.75.

Other sites of interest nearby: Busch Gardens in Tampa and the many attractions in Orlando.

For further information write to Dinosaur World, 5154 Harvey Tew Road, Plant City, FL 33565 or call (813) 717-9865. *www.dinoworld.net*

Explorations V,
Polk County's Children's Museum
Lakeland

Polk County's Children's Museum is a hands-on museum where visitors can pilot a space shuttle, pretend shop at a grocery store, make news at a miniature TV station, learn about banking and more at the permanent exhibits. Rotating exhibits and creative workshops are also offered.

Info in brief: Hands-on, participatory museum for children.

Location: Downtown historic Lakeland, Florida.

Hours: Monday thru Saturday, 9 A.M. to 5:30 P.M.

Admissions: Under 2, free; all others, $5. Free and metered parking available.

Other sites of interest nearby: Cypress Gardens, other Florida attractions within an hour's drive.

For further information write to Explorations V Children's Museum, 109 N. Kentucky Ave., Lakeland, Florida 33801, or call (863) 687-3869 or fax (963) 680-2357. E-mail: *info@explorationsv.com*

Fantasy of Flight
Polk City

Opened in 1995, Fantasy of Flight is an aviation-theme attraction featuring more than 40 rare vintage aircraft, a full-scale realistic diorama of a World War II bombing mission aboard a B-17 Flying Fortress, and flight simulator experiences. Most of the aircraft are a part of the largest private collection of vintage aircraft in the world, belonging to founder Kermit Weeks. The "History of Flight" chronicles air travel from the beginnings of man's attempts at flight to the jet era in realistic displays. Visitors can virtually control a Corsair Fighter atop a simulated aircraft carrier as well as tour hangers and the real working restoration facilities of the "world's largest aircraft collection." Some of these impeccably restored planes include the legendary World War II B-26 Marauder and the B-17 Flying Fortress, and the actual plane used in the Spielberg movie, *Indiana Jones and the Temple of Doom*. Also on the property are a multimedia exhibit dedicated to the courageous Tuskegee Airmen of World War II and an inter-active "Fun with Flight" center which features state of the art hang glide and hot air balloon simulators.

The 300-acre site also houses two private grass runways, a seaplane base and support facilities, hangars used for restoration, maintenance and storage, a gift shop and an Art Deco–style restaurant. Guided tours are offered throughout the day, and daily aerial demonstrations are performed.

Info in brief: Unique access to flight simulators, not available at many other locations. The world's largest private collection of vintage airplanes.

Location: Mid-way between Tampa and Orlando on Interstate 4 at Exit 44.

Hours: Open 363 days a year from 10 A.M. to 5 P.M. Closed Thanksgiving and Christmas.

Admissions: Under 5, free; children (5–15), $14.95; adults (13–59), $28.95. Hot air balloon rides start at $175 per person, plus applicable tax. Bi-plane rides are $64.95 plus tax in the "New Standard" or $229 plus tax in the 1942 Boeing Stearman PT-17.

Unique exhibits: Flight simulators, vintage aircraft.

Other sites of interest nearby: All the Orlando/Kissimmee/St. Cloud attractions.

For further information write to Fantasy of Flight, P.O. Box 1200, Polk City, Florida 33868-1200, or call 863-984-3500 *www.fantasyofflight.com*

Florida Adventure Museum
Punta Gorda

This hands-on, interactive museum is designed to educate people of all ages about the history, culture, and natural surroundings of Florida, especially Charlotte County. The main exhibit changes every 10 to 12 weeks, with a wide variety of educational and outreach programs and special events offered throughout the year.

Other sites of interest nearby: Roger's Christmas House Village, Max Stringer Heritage Museum, Pioneer Florida Museum in Dade City, Homosassa Springs, and others.

Hours: Monday to Friday, 10 A.M. to 5 P.M.; Saturday, 10 A.M. to 3 P.M.; Sunday, closed.

Admissions: Ages 12 & under, $1; adults, $2. Member ASTC.

For further information contact Florida Adventure Museum, 260 W. Retta Esplanade, Punta Gorda, Florida 33950, phone: (239) 639-3777, or fax (239) 639-3505.

Glazer Children's Museum
Tampa

With a projected opening date of fall 2009, the Glazer Children's Museum advertises itself as a museum that will be a place "Where children learn to play & play to learn!" Little information was available at the time of publication of this book.

For further information write to Glazer Children's Museum, 1107 E. Jackson, #101, Tampa, FL 33602.

Great Explorations, The Children's Museum
St. Petersburg

An entire wing of Great Explorations is dedicated to educating children about nutrition, exercise and the importance of leading a healthy lifestyle. Other exhibits include: I Can Construct, Engine Company 15 — The Fire House, The Veterinary Office — Be a Great Pet Vet, Puppets on Parade, Bernoulli Station, Laser Harp, Magnetic Hotplates, Touch For Sound, Gears, Great Balancing Act, Demo Platform and more than 25 others.

Info in brief: A hands-on, interactive museum for children of all ages.

Location: Near Sunken Gardens in downtown St. Petersburg.

Hours: Monday thru Saturday, 10 A.M.–4:30 P.M.; Sunday, noon–4:30 P.M.; Closed Easter, Thanksgiving, Christmas Day and New Years Day.

Admissions: 11 months & under, free; seniors, $8; all others, $9.

Other sites of interest nearby: Sunken Gardens, Busch Gardens, St. Petersburg beaches, Historic forts.

For further information write to Great Explorations, 1925 Fourth St., N., St. Petersburg, FL 33704 or call (727) 821-8992. *www.greatexplorations.org*

G.WIZ (Gulfcoast Wonder & Imagination Zone)
Sarasota

G.WIZ began as the Gulf Coast World of Science in December of 1990. After several expansions, and a move to a new permanent home, the new hands-on science and technology center was opened in May of 1998. The facility contains 33,000 sq. ft. of exhibit and education space.

Location: Former Selby Library building in downtown Sarasota, on Sarasota's bay front.

Hours: Monday thru Thursday, 9 A.M. to 7 P.M.; Friday & Saturday, 9 A.M.–8 P.M.; Sunday, 10 A.M.–6 P.M.

Admissions: General admissions: under 3, free; children (3–18), $6; senior (65+), $8; adults (19–64), $9. Additional rates are charged for special exhibits. Be sure to contact the museum before visiting. Member ASTC.

Other sites of interest nearby: The Blivas Science & Technology Center, Florida beaches, historic sites.

For further information write to G-WIZ, 1001 Boulevard of the Arts, Sarasota, FL 34236, or call (941) 309-4949 or fax (941) 906-7292. *www.gwiz.org*

Hands On Children's Museum
Jacksonville

Located in a castle-like building, the Hands On Children's Museum of Jacksonville offers playful, interactive exhibits for children and their families. Exhibits include: The Winn-Dixie Little Grocery Store, the Kids Main Bank, Little Post Office, the Bubble Room, and a "First Adventures" room and playhouse for ages 3 and under.

Hours: Monday thru Saturday, 9:30 A.M.–5 P.M.

Admissions: Under 1, free; children (1–3), $3.50; adults, $5.50.

Other sites of interest nearby: Jacksonville Beaches, and more.

For further information write to Hands On Children's Museum, 8580 Beach Blvd., Jacksonville, FL 32216-4615 or phone (904) 642-2688. *www.handsonchildrensmuseumjax.com*

Imaginarium
Fort Myers

Opened in July 1995, the Imaginarium is an interactive, hands-on learning center emphasizing science, the humanities and the uniqueness of the surrounding geographical region. The 4 acre sight is dedicated to a variety of indoor and outdoor hands-on exhibits in science. More than 13 theme exhibit areas are offered to visitors. Exhibits include a tropical retreat housing iguanas, turtles, finches, chameleons, and tortoise corral; the "Fisheye Lagoon" featuring turtles, ducks, swans, and freshwater fish; and "Sea to See" touch tanks which allow children to encounter barbless stingrays, horseshoe crabs, hermit crabs, marine snails, sea stars, and urchins. A 100-seat full surround sound system theater offers various programs. A 1,000 sq. ft. programming area (the "Dr. James A. Adams Orientation Center") hosts exhibits, programs and special events. "The Imagination Station" is a 460 sq. ft. area which houses various self-directed activities, art classes, parties and special events. The Museum Store and a 1,300 sq. ft. pavilion area complete the services available.

Info in brief: A hands-on, interactive children's museum which will house several aquariums.

Location: Built on the site of the Fort Myers Water Treatment Plant at the corner of Cranford Avenue and Martin Luther King, Jr. Boulevard in downtown Fort Myers.

Hours: Monday–Saturday, 10 A.M. to 5 P.M.; Sunday, noon to 5 P.M. Open every day but Christmas and Thanksgiving.

Admissions: Under 3, free; children (3–12), $5; adults (13–54), $8; seniors (55+), $7. All children must be accompanied by an adult. Free parking available. Memberships available. Member of ASTC, AAM, FAM (Florida Association of Museums), and FAA (Florida Attractions Association).

Other sites of interest nearby: Thomas Edison's Home, Henry Ford's Winter Home, Fort Myers beaches and other South Florida attractions.

For further information write to the Imaginarium, 2000 Cranford Ave., Ft. Myers, FL 33916, or call (239) 337-3332 or fax (239) 337-2109. *www.cityftmyers.com/imaginarium*. E-mail: *imaginarium@cityftmyers.org*

Junior Museum of Bay County
Panama City

The Junior Museum of Bay County, established in 1967, is a hands-on, interactive museum focusing on science, history and culture. Permanent exhibits include the Natural Trail (through a hardwood swamp), Once Upon a Time (history exhibit), Imagine Me Room (theater), Engine 904 (real engine), Pioneer Homestead (authentic buildings), Discovery Depot (for toddlers), Body Works, Nature Corner and Hands On Science. Other temporary and or rotating exhibits are put on display in the museum building itself several times each year.

Info in brief: A village museum and a children's hands-on interactive museum on the same grounds.

Location: 1731 Jenks Avenue, approximately five minutes from Panama City Mall.

Hours: Monday–Friday, 9 A.M. to 4:30 P.M.; Saturday, 10 A.M. to 4 P.M.

Admissions: $5.

Other sites of interest nearby: Gulf Coast beaches and the Miracle Strip amusement park.

For further information write to The Junior Museum of Bay County, 1731 Jenks Ave., Panama City, Florida 32405, or call (850) 769-6128 or fax (850) 769-6129. *www.jmuseum.org*

Kennedy Space Center Visitor Complex
Kennedy Space Center

The Visitor Complex at the Space Center offers many experiences, including live action theatrical shows, tours of the base, a walk-through of a full-size Space Shuttle mock-up, numerous exhibits and hands-on experiences. Flight simulators, two giant IMAX theaters and numerous historic artifacts are on display.

Location: 45 minutes east of Orlando, on the Space Coast.

Hours: Daily, 9 A.M.–5:30 P.M., except for Christmas Day and certain launch days. The Astronauts Hall of Fame stays open one full hour later.

Admissions: Program prices vary. The best way to get information is to visit their web-site, then click on "Contact us."

Other sites of interest nearby: Port Canaveral, Island Boat Lines, Indian River Cruises, Police Hall of Fame, The Space Coast, Cocoa Beach, Daytona Beach, and the many Orlando attractions.

For further information write to the Kennedy Space Center, SR 405 — Mail Code: DNPS, Kennedy Space Center, FL 32899 or call (321) 449-4444. *www.kennedyspacecenter.com* For ticket information and purchasing: *www.ksctickets.com*

KID CITY, The Children's Museum of Tampa
Tampa

The Mission of KID CITY is to inspire children and families "by creating learning opportunities through community, creativity, curiosity, discovery, diversity, friendliness, fun, imagination, and innovative play." Sixteen recently renovated exhibit buildings hold experiences like: Fire House, Bank, Grocery Store, Fast Food Restaurant, Verizon Telecommunications Center, Safety First Stations, International Travel Agency, Library, Puppets, Pediatric Urgent Care Clinic, Post Office, City Hall & Courthouse, TECO Children's Art Gallery, Music School House, Café, and more. Pre-school exhibits include "Under the Sea" and "By the SeaShore."

Location: Off I-275, approximately ¼ mile past the Lowry Park Zoo.

Hours: Wednesday & Friday, 9:30 A.M.–2 P.M.; Saturday, 9:30 A.M.–4 P.M.

Admissions: Under 1, free; all others, $5. Free parking.

Other sites of interest nearby: Lowry Park Zoo, St. Petersburg beaches, Busch Gardens, and more.

For further information write to KID CITY, 7550 N. Boulevard, Tampa, FL 33604 or call (813) 935-8441 or fax (813) 915-0063. *www.kidcity.org*

Miami Children's Museum
Miami

Founded in 1983, the Miami Children's Museum moved to its current site in 2003. The 56,500 sq. ft. facility holds 12 galleries, classrooms, parent/teacher resource center, Kid Smart educational gift shop, a 200-seat auditorium and Subway restaurant.

The Miami Children's Museum is a strictly hands-on, exploratory museum where children can discover the fun and facts about real-life roles through hundreds of permanent and changing special interactive exhibits. A few of the exhibits include playing at becoming a police officer, fire fighter, or other uniformed worker, driving a child-sized model of a Metro-Dade police car or fire truck, shopping at a Publix Supermarket, visiting a dentist's office, starring in the NBC-

6 Newsroom news, and more. Exhibits and programs are intended to emphasize arts, culture, community and communication. Special workshops and classes are also offered.

Info in brief: Hands-on, interactive, participatory museum for children and their caregivers.

Location: Watson Island.

Hours: Monday–Saturday, 10 A.M. to 6 P.M.

Admissions: Under 1, free; all others, $10. 50% Discount for Miami residents. MCM Member. Parking $1 per hr.

Other sites of interest nearby: Miami Museum of Science, Vizcaya and the Seaquarium (all within 5 miles), plus the many other tourist attractions in Miami.

For further information write to the Miami Children's Museum, 980 MacArthur Cswy, Miami, Florida 33132, or call (305) 373-5437. *www.miamichildrensmuseum*

MOSI, Museum of Science & Industry
Tampa

MOSI, the Museum of Science and Industry, is the result of 52 years of change and growth. The basic mission of the museum, however, has remained the same—"to make a difference in people's lives by making science real for people of all ages and backgrounds." The Museum was first opened in 1962 under the name of the Museum of Science and Natural History. A few name changes, location changes and extensive renovations later, the current structure in North Tampa was opened as "The Museum of Science & Industry." In 1987, an intensive study of the Museum's mission, goals and facility produced a 15-year, long-range, three-phase Master Plan. In 2000, the final parcel of land was purchased and construction of the 190,000 sq. ft. science center began. MOSI now contains extensive permanent and temporary exhibition galleries, a planetarium, public library, Nature Center, Disasterville (featuring WeatherQuest), a Science Works Theater, "Kids in Charge! The Children's Science Center," and more, making MOSI the largest science center in the southeast and the 5th largest in the nation.

Info in brief: One of the largest children's museums in the nation is just one of the features of MOSI.

Location: North Tampa, across from the USF Sun Dome and just one mile from Busch Gardens.

Hours: Monday thru Friday, 9 A.M.–5 P.M.; Saturday & Sunday, 9 A.M.–6 P.M. Open 365 days per year.

Admissions: Under 2, free; general admission (includes MOSI, Kids In Charge, and one standard IMAX film): under 2, free; child (2–12), seniors (60+), $18.98; adults (13–59), $20.95. Additional charges for other programs. Member AAM and ASTC. Free parking.

For further information write to MOSI, 4801 E. Fowler Ave., Tampa, Fl33617 or call (813) 987-6100 or fax (813) 987-6310. *www.mosi.org*

Museum of Discovery & Science & AutoNation IMAX Theater
Ft. Lauderdale

The Museum of Discovery & Science in Ft. Lauderdale, like most children's museums, started on a small scale in a house on the river. Today, the larger new facility includes an IMAX 3D Theater along with hundreds of hands-on exhibits. Visitors can hang out with bats (and explore Florida's Everglades), be charmed by a 12-foot snake or hundreds of bees, pet a green iguana, wrap themselves in a giant bubble or become a human hurricane.

Info in brief: A hands-on science museum and IMAX 3D Theater targeting children of all age ranges and their caregivers.

Location: Downtown Ft. Lauderdale.

Hours: (Museum) Monday–Saturday, 10 A.M. to 5 P.M.; Sunday, noon to 6 P.M. (IMAX 3D Theater shows) Monday–Saturday, 10 A.M., 11:30, 12:45 P.M., 2, 3:15, 4:30, 5:45, 7, 8:15, 9:30 and 10:45 (Friday and Saturday only); Sunday, noon, 1:15, 2:30, 3:45, 5, 6:15, 7:30, and 8:45 P.M. Open everyday except Christmas.

Admissions: (Exhibits) under 3, free; children (3–12), $5; adults, $6; seniors (65+), $5. (IMAX 3D Theater) children, $9; adults, $8; seniors, $7. (Combo tickets) children, $10.50; adults, $12.50; seniors, $11.50. Member ASTC.

Unique exhibits: IMAX 3D Theater.

Other sites of interest nearby: South Florida beaches, Miami tourist attractions, and more.

For further information write to the Museum of Discovery & Science, 401 S.W. Second St., Ft. Lauderdale, Florida 33312, or call (954) 713-0915, or fax (954) 467-0046. *www.mods.org*

My Jewish Discovery Place
Plantation

This is a hands-on, interactive museum dealing specifically with Jewish history, culture and values in this multi-cultural world. Some exhibits include Pieces for Peace, Archaeological Digs, Immigration: Journey to a new Life, Kibbutz Discovery, The Little Market, Home for the Holidays, Traditions, 3-2-1— Blast Off!, Hadassah Hospital, Jerusalem's Western Wall, Noah's Ark and more.

Info in brief: Children's museum dedicated to teaching about the Jewish life.

Location: Soref JCC Campus in Plantation.

Hours: Tuesday–Friday, 10 A.M.–4 P.M.

Admissions: Under 2, free; ages 2 to 6, $3; ages 7 to adult, $4; family maximum, $12.

Other sites of interest nearby: Davie Schoolhouse Children's Museum, Boynton Beach Children's Science Explorium, and many other Florida attractions.

For further information write to My Jewish Discovery Place, 6501 West Sunrise Blvd, Plantation, FL 33313, or call (954) 792-6700. *www.sorefjcc.org*

The Orlando Science Center
Orlando

The $44 million Orlando Science Center opened its doors in February of 1997. This huge four-story structure is filled with hands-on exhibits, interactive performance areas, science experiments, and more. Visitors can watch a large-format film, see a planetarium show or watch a laser light show at the $1.5 million Dr. Phillips CineDome. The other major area is the Darden Adventure Theater, where a performing arts company performs various full-scale theater productions throughout the day.

Visitors enter the complex through a glass skywalk from the 600-space parking deck. The main lobby that greets them is open to all four floors and houses a natural habitat with trees, birds and aquatic wildlife.

The first floor (ground floor) offers KidsTown for toddlers through elementary ages with numerous rooms designed for kids to see at their own eye-level. Exhibits include water play, a tree to climb, a bubble machine, phones, see-through fire hydrant and more.

The second floor contains NatureWorks, an exhibit of more than 100 native Floridian wildlife. Guides give continuous talks on the wildlife in the area.

The third floor contains The Cosmic Tourist, an area where visitors can discover how much their suitcases would weigh on every planet, and more.

The fourth floor contains an observatory and The BodyZone, where visitors enter through a giant mouth and step on a squishy tongue to explore how the body works. Tech Works, also on this floor, gives visitors a look at light power and how scientists and filmmakers use animation and models to find out how dinosaurs moved or what people looked like 100 years ago.

Info in brief: One of the largest children's museums in the country. Plan to spend most of a day here.

Location: Princeton St., off I-4 in Loch Haven Park, across from the Orange County Historical Museum, the Orlando Museum of Art and the Civic Theatres of Florida.

Hours: Sunday thru Thursday, 10 A.M.–6 P.M.; Friday & Saturday, 10 A.M.–9 P.M. Closed Easter, Thanksgiving, Christmas Eve & Day. Observatory hours— Friday & Saturday, 6–9 P.M.

Admissions: Full Experience — 2 & under, free; students (wID), $21; youth (3–11), $18; adults, $25; seniors (55+), $21. Parking, $4. Member ASTC.

Other sites of interest nearby: Church Street Station sites, Disney World and the Disney World theme areas, Sea World, Wet 'n Wild, and other Orlando tourist attractions.

For further information write to The Orlando Science Center, 777 E. Princeton St., Orlando, Florida 32803, or call 1-888-OSC-4FUN or (407) 514-2114. *www.osc.org* E-mail: *info@osc.org*

The School Board of Seminole County Student Museum and Center for the Social Studies
Sanford

The Student Museum is supported and operated by the Seminole County Public Schools. The emphasis is on a total approach to social studies education through hands-on experiences. The main exhibit theme areas are the Lobby (containing a photographic essay of Seminole County), the Pioneer Room, the Native American Room, a Turn of the Century Classroom, and Grandma's Attic.

The building itself was erected in 1902 and is the fourth oldest school in continuous use in Florida. It is one of the few surviving examples in Florida of Victorian school architecture at the turn of the century, and was placed on the National Register of Historic Places in 1984.

Info in brief: A hands-on children's museum with an emphasis on historic artifacts and events in Seminole County.

Hours: Open to the public — weekdays, 8 A.M. to 4 P.M. Closed when school groups are scheduled. Be sure to contact the museum before visiting.

Admissions: No admissions charge.

Other sites of interest nearby: Disney World, Sea World, and other Orlando tourist attractions, the Sanford Museum, the Seminole County Historical Museum, Geneva Museum, Lawton House in Oviedo, the Central Florida Zoo, and more.

For further information write to the Seminole County Public School Student Museum, 301 W. Seventh St., Sanford, Florida 32771-2505, or call (407) 320-0580 or fax (407) 320-0511.

Schoolhouse Children's Museum
Boynton Beach

Learn about the history of Florida in this hands-on, interactive children's museum.

Hours: Tuesday thru Saturday, 10 A.M.–5 P.M.

Admissions: Under 2, free; 2 and over, $3; adults, $5; grandparent accompanied by grandchild, $6 for both admissions. Member ACM and FAM.

For further information write to the Schoolhouse Children's Museum, 129 E. Ocean Ave., Boynton Beach, FL 33435 or call (561) 742-6780 or fax (561) 742-6781. *www.schoolhousemuseum.org*

Science Center
St. Petersburg

Established in 1959, the Science Center was one of the first of its kind in the U.S., with a vision to "inspire interest in and understanding of science." Hands-on, interactive exhibits teach students of all ages how to "hypothesize, discover, investigate, interpret and evaluate." Exhibits include permanent exhibits, traveling exhibits, a 600-gallon Marine Touch Tank, a replica of a 16th century Indian village and a state-of-the-art planetarium.

Location: Built on 7 acres in west St. Petersburg, approximately ½ mile west of the Tyrone Square Mall.

Hours: Monday thru Friday, 9 A.M.–4 P.M. and Friday at 3 P.M. for Planetarium shows.

Admissions: $5 per person. Memberships available.

For further information write to Science Center, 7701 22nd Ave., N., St. Petersburg, FL 33710 or call (727) 384-0027. *www.sciencecenterofpinellas.com*

South Florida Science Museum
West Palm Beach

The South Florida Science Museum is a hands-on museum for kids. At the same site, but under separate admissions fees, is the Dreher Park Zoo. Other educational and fun activities include an aquarium, planetarium, laser show and Galaxy Golf.

Hours: Monday thru Friday, 10 A.M.–5 P.M.; Saturday, 10 A.M.–6 P.M.; Sunday, noon–6 P.M.

Admissions: (Museum only) under 3, free; children (3–12), $6; adults, $9; seniors (62+), $7.50. ADDITIONAL PROGRAMS—Planetarium: children, $2; adults, $4. Laser Matinee, $5. Galaxy Golf, $2. Memberships available. Member ASTC, AAM & FAM.

For further information write to the South Florida Science Museum, 4801 Dreher Trail North, West Palm Beach, Florida 33405, phone: (561) 832-1988 or fax (561) 832-0551. *www.sfsm.org*

Young at Art Children's Museum
Plantation

Young at Art is a unique art-centered hands-on museum that features an ever-changing number of educational exhibits and activities. Four permanent displays offer children (and their caregivers) opportunities to explore using a computer: "Earthworks," Global Village 1, Global Village 2, and Kenny Scharf's Closet. Other areas include the Toddler Playspace, Darkroom, Masterworks Gallery, and the Annenberg Satellite School Classroom.

Gallery features and changing exhibits add to the variety of art experiences available. School tours, outreach programs, art classes and workshops are also offered at the museum.

Location: Fountains Shoppes of Distinction in Plantation, Florida.

Hours: Monday–Saturday, 10 A.M. to 5 P.M.; Sunday, noon to 5 P.M.; closed some Mondays; closed Thanksgiving, Christmas Day, New Year's Day, and Easter.

Admissions: Under 2, free; senior (62+), $7.50; others, $8. Memberships available.

Other sites of interest nearby: Atlantic Ocean beaches, other Florida tourist attractions.

For further information write to the Young at Art Children's Museum, 11584 W. State Road 84, Davie, Florida 33325, or call (954) 424-0085, or fax (954) 370-5057. *www.youngatartmuseum.org*

GEORGIA

Georgia's Agrirama
Tifton

Georgia's Agrirama depicts Georgia's culture in the years between the Civil War and the early 1900s. Visitors can "experience" life through hands-on displays in this 95-acre living history museum. The "museum" is divided into five areas: a traditional farm community of the 1870s; a progressive farmstead of the 1890s; an industrial complex with water-powered grist mill, steam-powered train and sawmill; an early 1900s rural town with a drugstore containing a marble top soda fountain that sells Coca-Cola floats, a print shop, a commissary, a cotton gin and more; and The Shepherd Barn which houses the metal, fuel-powered peanut combine developed by James L. Shepherd. There are more than 35 restored structures on the site, staffed by costumed interpreters. Many of these buildings are used in the hands-on education programs.

Be sure to contact the museum before visiting, as many special events are held throughout the year.

Info in brief: A village museum or "living history museum" with items of particular interest to children. Most hands-on experiences are directed by the interpreters, and not all children will be able to enjoy such an experience, unless they are part of a group or special tour. The barnyard animals and many of the farmyard buildings are "explorable," however.

Location: I-75 Exit 20 in Tifton.

Hours: Tuesday thru Saturday, 9 A.M.–5 P.M. Closed Labor Day, Veterans Day, Thanksgiving (Thursday & Friday). Christmas Holidays (December 22–January 1).

Admissions: Under 4, free; children (5–16), $4; seniors (55+), $6; adults, $7. Annual passes available. Group rates available.

Other sites of interest nearby: Liberty Farms Animal Park (Valdosta); Crystal Beach & Water Park (Irwinville); Presidential Pathways region; Macon attractions such as Georgia Music Hall of Fame, Ocmulgee National Monument and "Lights on Macon" (a self-guided historic homes tour); Georgia's Stone Mountain; Six Flags Over Georgia (Atlanta), and more.

For further information write to Georgia's Agrirama, P.O. Box Q, Tifton, Georgia 31793, or call (912) 386-3344. *www.agrirama.com* E-mail: *market@agrirama.com*

The National Science Center (NSC)
Augusta

Fort Discovery is the National Science Center's children's hands-on museum area. NSC is a unique partnership between the National Science Center, Inc and the U.S. Army. The mission of NSC is to be a catalyst to exciting America's young people about math, science and technology through hands-on experiences in the sciences. Over 128,000 sq. ft. of exhibit area hold 250 hands-on exhibits, custom digital theater programs, portable planetarium, educational work-shops and demonstrations, a depository for an array of national educational outreach programs.

Some of the exhibits offered in the two-story facility include: Martian Towers (a 22-foot tall, space-themed climbing structure), Math, Motion and Momentum Gallery, Power Generation Gallery, Everyday Technologies Gallery, Robotics Gallery, Space Technologies Gallery, Communications Gallery and the Imaging and Perception Gallery.

Info in brief: A large hands-on museum for children of all ages, especially ages 7 and up.

Location: Scenic Riverwalk in downtown Augusta.

Hours: Monday–Saturday 10 A.M.–5 P.M.; Sunday noon–5 P.M. Closed: Easter, Thanksgiving, Christmas Day, and New Year's Day.

Admissions: Under 4, free; 4–17, $6; seniors (+55) & active military, $6; adults, $8.

Other sites of interest nearby: Many historical sites.

For further information write to The National Science Center, One 7th Street, Augusta, GA 30901, or call 800-325-5445. *www.nscdiscovery.org*

SciTrek
Atlanta

SciTrek is one of Georgia's few interactive science and technology centers, with over 150 permanent exhibits, a specially designed area for young children ages two to seven, science shows and traveling exhibits. People of all ages are encouraged to do, see, touch, play and think. Science areas to be explored include light and color, perception and illusion, simple machines, and more.

Info in brief: Hands-on museum for children of all ages and their families.

Location: Next to the Atlanta Civic Center. Physical address: 395 Piedmont Ave., NE, Atlanta, GA 30087.

Hours: Monday thru Saturday, 10 A.M.–5 P.M.; Sunday, noon–5 P.M.; Closed Easter, Thanksgiving, Christmas and New Year's Day.

Admissions: Under 3, free: children (ages 3–17) and military, $7.50; seniors, $6; adults, $9.50. Memberships available.

Other sites of interest nearby: Stone Mountain, Roswell-Archibald Smith Plantation Home, Six Flags American Adventure, Six Flags White Water Atlanta, Kennesaw-Southern Museum of Civil War and Locomotive History, Woodruff Arts Center, the Margaret Mitchell House, World of Coca Cola, Underground Atlanta, the Atlanta Zoo and more.

For further information write to SciTrek, P.O. Box 54248, Atlanta, GA 30087. *www.inusa.com/tour/ga/atlanta/scitrek.htm*

HAWAII

Children's Discovery Center
Honolulu

Founded in 1985 as a not-for-profit, community organization, the museum did not officially open its doors until 1990 at its temporary site in the Dole Cannery Square in Lwilei under the name of the Hawaii Children's Museum. The 5,000 sq. ft. hands-on museum is a successful step toward a permanent location which is projected to open soon. The new 37,000 sq. ft. facility will be the first of its kind to open as part of a waterfront redevelopment plan and is currently under construction. More than 200 exhibits will be available for exploration.

The new facility will use a staff of 12 full-time employees, and plans call for around 200 volunteers to work at least four hours a day. Currently, only the director and secretary are on staff.

Info in brief: Both the old and new facilities are hands-on science and humanities museums for children.

Location: Across from the Kakaako Waterfront Park in downtown Honolulu on the island of Oahu.

Hours: Tuesday–Friday, 9 A.M. to 1 P.M.; Saturday and Sunday, 10 A.M. to 3 P.M. Closed most major holidays. Open Labor Day. Closed the two weeks after Labor Day.

Admissions: Under 2, free; ages 2–17, $6.75; senior (62+), $5; others, $8.

Other sites of interest nearby: The many tourist attractions in Hawaii.

For further information write to Children's Discovery Center, 111 Ohe St., Honolulu, Hawaii 96813, or call (808) 524-KIDS (5437) or fax (808) 524-5400. *www.discoverycenterhawaii.org* or email: *info@discoverycenterhawaii.org*

IDAHO

The Discovery Center of Idaho
Boise

The Discovery Center of Idaho is a children's science museum with over 150 hands-on exhibits, the beginning of the scaled Solar System Walk along the greenbelt in Boise, Science Saturday classes, summer camps, demonstrations, special exhibitions and lectures, and more. A portable STARLAB is also sponsored by the Center and travels throughout the state. Exhibit areas include: Mapping: Contraptions A to Z; Discovery Market; Teeth, Robots, Rovers and Puppets; Rodeo Gyro; Under Your Skin; as well as several visiting exhibits each year.

The Solar System Walk begins at the Discovery Center, where the model sun sets the scale for both the planet sizes and the distances through the entire model. Each planet appears on one of nine bronze plaques placed in various Boise parks. The museum provides visitors with a written tour guide for "visiting" the planets.

Info in brief: Large hands-on science museum for children and their caregivers.

Location: 131 Myrtle Street, between Broadway and Capitol Boulevard.

Hours: (Summer — May 31–Aug. 31) Monday–Friday, 9 A.M. to 5 P.M.; Saturday, 10 A.M. to 5 P.M.; Sunday, noon to 5 P.M. (Winter — September–May) Tuesday–Friday, 9 A.M. to 5 P.M.; Saturday, 10 A.M. to 5 P.M.; Sunday, noon to 5 P.M. Closed Mondays, Thanksgiving, Christmas and New Year's Day.

Admissions: Under 2, free; children (3–17), $4; adults, $6.50; seniors (60+), $5.50. Memberships available. Member ASTC.

Unique exhibits: Solar System Model Walk (see information above).

Other sites of interest nearby: Boise Zoo, MK Nature Center, Old Idaho Penitentiary, Boise Art

Museum, World Center for Birds of Prey, Museum of Mining & Geology, Idaho Museum of Military History, Idaho Botanical Garden, The Basque Museum, and the Idaho Historical Museum.

For further information write to The Discovery Center of Idaho, 131 Myrtle St., Boise, Idaho 83702, or call (208) 343-9895 or fax (208) 343-0105. *www.scidaho.org*

Museum of Idaho
Idaho Falls

The Museum of Idaho is dedicated to preserving and showcasing the natural and cultural history of Idaho and the Intermountain West. Traveling exhibits permanent exhibits, programs, presentations, and a reading and reference library are on the site. Specifically for children, is the Children's Discovery Room, where children are encouraged to touch, listen to, and explore the artifacts on display, and even play with pioneer toys in a log cabin.

Info in brief: A cultural history museum with one room set aside specifically for hands-on experiences for children.

Location: The Children's Discovery Room is located inside the Museum of Idaho.

Hours: Monday & Tuesday, 9 A.M.–8 P.M.; Wednesday thru Sunday, 9 A.M.–5 P.M. (Closed on most Sundays or open only from noon to 5 P.M.

Admissions: Under 4, free; youth (4–18), $4; seniors (62+), $5; adults, $6. Memberships available.

Other sites of interest nearby: Snake River Territory Convention & Visitors Bureau, Willard Arts Center & Colonial Theater, Art Museum of Eastern Idaho, Tautphaus Park Zoo, and more.

For further information write to the Museum of Idaho, 200 N. Eastern Ave., Idaho Falls, ID 83402, or call (208) 522-1400. *www.museumofidaho.org*

ILLINOIS

The Art Institute of Chicago
Chicago

Besides being a world-renowned destination for art, The Art Institute of Chicago offers programs and spaces designed to enhance the museum experience for children and their families. Experiences include family gallery walks, studio programs, interactive exhibitions and workshops for families to learn about art together. Interactive exhibitions present a select group of the highest quality objects from the Art Institute collections in an installation made accessible through interpretive environments, didactic displays, and interactive computer programs. The Illustrators' Gallery exhibits works of art by renowned children's book illustrators. The Family Room houses award-winning picture books, puzzles for children, and several cozy corners for browsing. Also offered in this space are Readings from children's books on selected weekends, and book signings by children's illustrators. Family programs are free with museum admission and feature registration-based and drop-in programs for all ages. For a complete listing of upcoming programs, check the museum's website.

Plans call for a May 2009 opening of the Renzo Piano designed Modern Wing where families will be able to enjoy expanded programming in the new Ryan Education Center. This new center will provide visitors with an introduction to the Art Institute through state of the art technology and expanded programming.

Info in brief: An art museum/institute which offers special hands-on art experiences for children. Other special children's activities are also offered year-round at the Ryan Education center.

Location: Corner of Michigan and Adams in Chicago's famous downtown Loop.

Hours: Monday thru Friday, 10:30 A.M. to 5 P.M. (Thursday evenings until 8 P.M.) Saturday and Sunday, 10 A.M. to 5 P.M. Summer hours: Thursday and Friday evenings until 9 P.M.

Admissions: Children under 12, free; students, $7; adults, $12; seniors, $7. Thursday evenings from 5–8 P.M. are free. Closed Thanksgiving, Christmas, and New Year's Day.

For further information write to The Art Institute of Chicago, 111 S. Michigan Ave., Chicago, Illinois 60603-6110, or call (312) 443-3600 (TDD 443-3890). *www.artic.edu/aic*

Bronzeville Children's Museum
Chicago

The Bronzeville Children's Museum was founded in 1993 by a group of people who wanted a child-friendly museum that would increase literacy and encourage children, especially underserved African American children, to develop a love of learning, while increasing their hope and self-esteem. It is the first and only African-American children's museum in the country. Interactive exhibits and program are provided for hands-on learning in the areas of the arts, humanities, and sciences.

Info in brief: The first and only African-American children's museum in the U.S.

Location: (New in 2007) 9301 South Stony Island Avenue.

Hours: Tuesday thru Saturday, 10 A.M.–4 P.M.; tour schedule: 10 A.M., 1 P.M., 2 P.M., and 3 P.M.

Admissions: Under 3, free; all others, $5.

Other sites of interest nearby: Museum of Science and Industry, Spertus Museum, many other Chicago attractions.

For further information write to the Bronzeville Children's Museum, 9301 S. Stony Island Ave., Chicago, IL or call (708) 636-9504 or fax (708) 636-9543. E-mail: *Bronzeville@aol.com*

Chicago Children's Museum
Chicago

Exhibits at the Chicago Children's Museum focus on newsgathering or medical technology (hospital exhibit). Permanent exhibits include: The Allstate Foundation's Play It Safe, Artabounds Gallery, BIG Backyard, Dinosaur Expedition, Inventing Lab, Kids on the Fly, Kids Town, Kovler Family Climbing Schooner, My Museum, Skyline, Treehouse Trails, and Water Ways.

Location: Physical address— 435 E. Illinois St.

Hours: Sunday thru Wednesday & Friday, 10 A.M.–5 P.M.

Admissions: Under 1, free; children, $9; adults, $9; seniors, $8. Target *Free* 1st Mondays for ages 15 & under. Kraft *Free* Family Night, Thursday, 5–8 P.M. Member ASTC.

For further information write to the Chicago Children's Museum, 700 E. Grand Ave. #127, Chicago, Illinois 60611 or call (312) 527-1000 or fax (312) 527-9082. *www.chicagochildrensmuseum.org*

Children's Discovery Museum
Normal

With three floors of hands-on exhibits, children of all ages will find exciting things to explore. Some of the exhibits include: AgMazing!, Paint Wall, a two-story Luckey Climber, Main Street Market, Toddler Backyard, and more. The mission of the museum is to inspire the love of learning through the power of play. The building itself was built with the health of its visitors and employees in mind — it was the first children's museum in the country to achieve LEED Certification.

Info in brief: An interactive, hands-on museum for children of all ages and their families.

Location: Uptown Normal.

Hours: Tuesday, Wednesday & Saturday, 9 A.M.–5 P.M.; Thursday & Friday, 9 A.M.–8 P.M.; Sunday, 1 P.M.–5 P.M. Check with museum before planning a holiday visit.

Admissions: Under 2, free; all others, $4.

For further information write to Children's Discovery Museum, 101 E. Beaufort, Normal, IL 61761 or call (309) 433-3444. *www.childrensdiscoverymuseum.net*

Discovery Center Museum
Rockford

The Discovery Center is a participatory museum designed to provide hands-on learning experiences for visitors of all ages. The targeted audience is preschool through junior high ages, and the caregivers are encouraged to participate with their children.

Founded in 1980, the museum moved into its current 26,000 sq. ft. facility in 1991, where it shares the Riverfront Museum Park building with five other cultural organizations. The museum was visited by Elizabeth Dole in 1996.

Permanent exhibits explore the areas of sound (a walk-on piano is featured here), newscasting (a state-of-the-art news studio is here), and art (one gallery is devoted to color and light experimentation and includes a video art exhibit, prisms, bubbles and more). Other permanent exhibits include "Body Shop," where families can learn about bodies and how they function, nutrition, genetics, fingerprinting and agility. In "Tot Spot," preschoolers are offered role-playing and tactile experiences. The "Space" exhibit includes a planetarium, space photographs, a gravity well, Geochron clock, a Bernoulli blower and a collection of NASA photos. Rock River Discovery Park is an outdoor play and exploration area offering a cave, locks and dams, Newton's cradle, automated kinetic ball towers, pendulum swings and whisper dishes. In May of 1992, it was listed by *Child Magazine* as one of the ten best outdoor facilities of its kind in the nation.

Info in brief: A sophisticated hands-on museum and outdoor play and exploration area especially for children.

Location: Riverfront Museum Park, a cultural center along the Rock River in downtown Rockford, approximately 90 minutes northwest of Chicago off I-90.

Hours: Regular hours— Monday thru Saturday, 10 A.M. to 5 P.M.; Sunday, noon to 5 P.M.; open Mondays on school holidays. (Summer) Monday–Wednesday & Friday & Saturday, 10 A.M. to 5 P.M.; Thursday, 10 A.M.–7 P.M.; Sunday, noon to 5 P.M.

Admissions: Under 2, free; children, $5; adults, $6. Memberships available. Member ACM.

For further information write to Discovery Center Museum, 711 N. Main St., Rockford, Illinois 61103, or call (815) 963-6769. *www.discoverycentermuseum.org*

Discovery Depot Children's Museum
Galesburg

Discovery Depot is an interactive children's museum offering exhibits on community activities. Children ages 3 to 10 will enjoy exhibits such as Depot Grocery, climbing rock wall, train play, weather station, and more.

Location: Downtown Galesburg.

Hours: Labor Day thru Memorial Day: Tuesday–Saturday, 10 A.M.–5P.M.; Sunday, 1 P.M.–5 P.M. Extended hours on the third Friday of each month (until 7 P.M.).

Admissions: $3.50 per person; "Thrifty Thursday" (last Thursday of each month), $1. Memberships available. Member ACM.

For further information write to Discovery Depot Children's Museum, 128 S. Chambers, Galesburg, IL 61401 or call (309) 344-8876. *www.discoverydepot.org*

DuPage Children's Museum
Naperville

The DuPage Children's Museum is a three-story building with a variety of different exhibit "neighborhoods."

Each neighborhood has numerous exhibits that encourage children to "explore art, math, science and how they work together in the world." Three "Young Explorers" neighborhoods are designed especially for children two years and younger. Some of the exhibit areas include: Build It, AirWorks, Young Explorers, Make It Move, Creativity Connections, Math Connections, WaterWays, Bubbles, The Gallery, and more.

Info in brief: Large, multifaceted museum for children of all ages and their families.

Hours: Monday, 9 A.M.–1 P.M.; Tuesday, Wednesday, Friday & Saturday, 9 A.M.–5 P.M.; Thursday, 9 A.M.–8 P.M.; Sunday, noon to 5 P.M. DCM is also open from 9 A.M. to 5 P.M. on select Mondays that are also school holidays.

Admissions: Under 1, free; seniors (60+), $6.50; all others, $7.50. Memberships available. Free parking available.

For further information write to DuPage Children's Museum, 301 N. Washington St., Naperville, IL 60540 or call (630) 637-8000 or fax: (630) 637-1276. *www.dupagechildrensmuseum.org*

Kohl Children's Museum
Wilmette

The Kohl Children's Museum opened in 1985, building on the success of its predecessor, the Kohl Teacher Center, a pioneer Chicago resource since 1973. The museum encourages hands-on learning as one of the most effective modes of learning, and caters to children ages 1 to 8 years of age. Imaginative play is greatly emphasized.

Besides the museum proper and its exhibits, Kohl offers field trips, focused programs, summer camps, workshops, seminars, special events, after-school programs, free daily art, cultural and science activities, and more.

Some of the 17 current exhibits include "Adventures in Art," "All About Me," "City on the Move," "Cooperation Station," "Discovery Maze," "Habitat Park," "Hands on House," "Music Makers," "Nature Explorers," and "Water Works." Temporary Exhibits are also offered throughout the year.

Info in brief: Hands-on, interactive, imaginative experiences for children ages birth to 8.

Location: Intersection of Patriot Boulevard and West Lake Avenue on The Glen in Glenview.

Hours: Monday, 9:30 A.M. to 12 P.M.; Tuesday–Saturday, 9:30 A.M. to 5 P.M.; Sunday, noon to 5 P.M. Members only, Monday–Saturday, 9–9:30 A.M.

Admissions: Under 1, free; grandparents & seniors (55+), $6.50; adults & children, $7.50. Memberships available.

Other sites of interest nearby: The many Chicago tourist attractions.

For further information write to Kohl Children's Museum, 2100 Patriot Boulevard, Glenview, Illinois 60026, or call (847) 832-6600.

The Lederman Science Center
Batavia

The Lederman Science Center is a hands-on experience where visitors can learn about how Fermilab physicists understand and work with "natures' secrets." The Center was named for Nobel Laureate and former Fermilab Director Leon M. Lederman.

Location: Fermilab, approximately 35 miles west of Chicago.

Hours: Monday thru Friday, 8:30 A.M.–4:30 P.M.; Saturday, 9 A.M.–3 P.M. (Call ahead for holiday hours.)

Admissions: Students are free.

Other sites of interest nearby: Many attractions in Chicago.

For further information write to The Lederman Science Center, Box 500, Batavia, Illinois 60510, or call (630) 840-8258 or fax (630) 840-2500.

Museum of Science and Industry
Chicago

Although the Museum of Science and Industry would not strictly be called a hands-on museum, there are so many exhibits that are designed for the interest of children, that this museum is well worthy of a visit. Opened in 1933, the Museum of Science and Industry in Chicago is the oldest science museum of its kind in the Western Hemisphere, and is one of the top seven most visited museums in the U.S. It is the largest science museum in a single building in the Western Hemisphere, with over 800 exhibits and over 2,000 interactive units located in over 350,000 sq. ft. of exhibit space. It was the first museum in North America to develop the idea of hands-on, interactive exhibits. Children who are especially interested in interactive displays can walk through a cantilevered Boeing 727, communicate with others in the Whispering gallery, go inside a Human heart model (nearly 20-ft. tall walk-through model), and more. Other displays that are especially interesting to families with young children include a World War II captured German submarine (listed on the National Register of Historic Places), a working coal-mine shaft elevator from 1933, a 3,500 sq. ft. model railroad, a baby-chick hatchery, an Apollo 8 Spacecraft and 3 other crafts from the space program, a Texaco Racer Plane (broke Charles Lindbergh's transcontinental speed record in 1930), a 999 Empire State Express steam locomotive, a 1914 Ford Model T, and so much more.

The museum has received several awards: named one of the country's top 50 family attractions by Zagat Survey (2004), featured in the 2005 World Almanac for Kids, voted best museum in Chicago by users of Citysearch.com (2003), named one of the best destinations for travelers by Lets Go Publications (2003), and voted best museum in Chicago by Citysearch.com

(2002). One of the most visited museums in the world, the Museum of Science and Industry has ties to two World's Fairs. Inspired by a visit to the Deutches Museum in Munich, Julius Rosenwald determined to build a museum in America where visitors could interact with the exhibits and still receive "industrial enlightenment." He restored and converted the Palace of Fine Arts, the last major remaining structure from the 1893 World's Fair. Then, in 1933, the Museum of Science and Industry opened to the public at the same time as the Century of Progress Exposition.

The Museum of Science and Industry also is a repository for collections, with approximately 50,000 artifacts, and offers several quality on-line exhibits. New exhibits are being added regularly. There is something for everyone to see and do!

Info in brief: A large, family-oriented museum with both visual and hands-on exhibits.

Location: 57th Street and Lake Shore Drive.

Hours: Monday thru Saturday, 9:30 A.M.–4 P.M.; Sunday, 11 A.M.–4 P.M. Special extended hours are offered throughout the year. Be sure to check with the museum before visiting. Open every day except Christmas.

Admissions: Museum: under 3, free; child (3–11), $9; senior (65+), $12; adult, $13. Museum & Omnimax: child, $14; senior, $19; adult, $20. The U-505 Submarine Optional On-Board tour: (required general admission, not included): $5. Members and Chicago residents receive a discount. Parking, $14 per vehicle. Member AAM, & ASTC.

Other sites of interest: Spertus Museum, lake views, and many other Chicago attractions.

For further information write to The Museum of Science and Industry, 5700 S. Lake Shore Dr., Chicago, IL 60637 or call (773) 684–1414. *www.msichicago.org*

Orpheum Children's Science Museum
Champaign

Located in the 1914 Orpheum Theater, The Children's Museum, aims to provide children of all ages the chance to explore and learn about science in a fun, informal setting. The theater closed in 1986. In 1994, it was purchased by the Discovery Place, Inc., which renovated 6,750 sq. ft. for a hands-on science demonstration museum. In 1996, the name was changed to the Orpheum Children's Science Museum. Both indoor and outdoor exhibits are available. Indoor exhibits include: Waterworks, Giant Lever, and SS Ackermann Tugboat. Outdoor exhibits are closed in the winter, but include Critter Corner & Biology, Whisper Dishes, and a simulated 15' × 30' paleontological dig. A second phase added a vestibule, lobby and mezzanine. Planning is currently underway for Phase III, which calls for renovation of the auditorium and stage.

Info in brief: A hands-on children's science museum.

Location: The old Orpheum Theater on the north end of downtown Champaign.

Hours: Tuesdays thru Fridays, 10 A.M.–4 P.M.; Saturdays & Sundays, 1 P.M.–5 P.M.

Admissions: Child (2–18 years), $2; adult, $3. Memberships available.

For further information write to the Orpheum Children's Science Museum, 346 N. Neil, Champaign, IL 61820-3614 or call (217) 352-5895 or fax (217) 352-8160. *www.m-crossroads.org/orpheum*

The Science Center
Carbondale

The Science Center in Carbondale is a small hands-on, interactive children's museum with exhibits that allow visitors to experience the wonders of science.

Info in brief: Hands-on and interactive children's museum.

Hours: Monday–Saturday, 10 A.M. to 9 P.M.; Sunday, noon to 5:30 P.M.

Admissions: $2.50. Member ASTC.

For further information contact: The Science Center, 1237 East Main St., #C2, Carbondale, Illinois 62901-3148, phone: (618) 529-5431.

SciTech, Science and Technology Interactive Center
Aurora

In 1989, a 7,000 sq. ft. building in Naperville was donated for the temporary housing of a science museum. By the following year, SciTech signed a 10-year lease with the City of Aurora for the use of its former post office in downtown Aurora (listed on the historic register). The museum now hosts more than 200 exhibits on physics, chemistry and mathematics, going from a strictly volunteer-run organization to a 44-employee-plus-volunteers museum.

Sci-Tech's mission is to "provide a cultural resource focusing on science and technology for a broad general audience." One aspect of this mission is to encourage children to participate in many of the exhibits. This is done through activities at the museum and in the community.

In the community, SciTech offers "Museum in a School," traveling chemistry demonstrations and the "Hook 'Em While They're Young" program. Museum programs include the "Student Explainer Program," "Discover & Explore," SciTech clubs for girls, field trips and focused field trips, science camps and classes, along with more than 200 permanent exhibits. Three science activity rooms, an auditorium and a solar telescope are also in-house.

Info in brief: Strictly a science museum with a broad range of hands-on activities for children.

Location: Historic district on Stolp Island in downtown Aurora, in the old Post Office building.

Hours: Monday thru Saturday, 10 A.M.–5 P.M.; Sunday, noon–5 P.M.

Admissions: 3 & under, free; seniors (60+), $7; all others, $8. Member of the Association of Youth Museums. Member ASTC.

Unique exhibitions: Large number of science participatory experiment-type exhibits.

Other sites of interest nearby: Fermi National Accelerator Laboratory, Illinois Mathematics and Science Academy, Blackberry Farm, and Red Oak Nature Center.

For further information write to SciTech, 18 W. Benton, Aurora, Illinois 60506, or call (830) 859-3434 or fax (830) 859-8692. *www.scitechmuseum.org* E-mail: *joyce@scietechmuseum.org*

Spertus Museum
Chicago

The Spertus Museum reexamines Jewish culture in order to celebrate, challenge, and advance modern Jewish identity. Spertus aims to demonstrate the endlessly powerful and reciprocal effect between Jewish and broader culture by reaching visitors of every generation and background and kindling their active pursuit of learning.

The museum's collections-based display presents over 1,500 objects in a viewable storage facility. Ranging from ritual objects to fine art, historical artifacts to ephemera, the collection demonstrates the depth and breadth of Jewish artistic expression.

Spertus' Gray Children's Center houses an interactive, hands-on space for children to

The Spertus Museum in Chicago reexamines Jewish culture (photograph by William Zbarren).

encounter and explore the magic and mystery of language and stories. Designed in partnership with Jim Lasko, artistic director of Redmoon Theater, the Children's Center provides an engaging space in which to play with letters and words to stretch their imaginations and create new worlds.

Spertus also features changing exhibitions of fine art and material culture that explore a range of questions surrounding identity, social issues, and contemporary cultural production.

Info in brief: The museum is basically an historical and art museum with items specifically for children, but of interest to all ages.

Location: 610 S. Michigan Ave., Chicago.

Hours: Sunday–Wednesday, 10 A.M. to 6 P.M.; Thursday, 10 A.M.–7 P.M.; Friday, 10 A.M. to 3 P.M.; closed Saturday.

Admissions: Adults, $4; students & seniors, $5; members & children under 5, free. Free hours: Tuesday, 10 A.M.–noon and Thursday, 3 P.M.–7 P.M.

Unique exhibits: Most comprehensive Judaic collection in the Midwest.

Other sites of interest nearby: Many Chicago tourist attractions.

For further information write to the Spertus Museum, 610 S. Michigan Avenue, Chicago, Illinois 60605, or call (312) 322-1747. *www.spertus.edu* E-mail: *museum@spertus.edu*

Wonder Works
Oak Park

Wonder Works is a 6,400 sq.ft. museum for kids up to 10 years of age. Originally founded in 1991, the museum lost its lease. In 2001, they purchased a building in Oak Park which then opened in 2001 as Wonder Works children's museum. It now offers four permanent exhibits and several temporary exhibits. A long-range fundraising plan calls for ever-increasing additions.

Location: Corner of Elmwood and North, just a few blocks west of Ridgeland Avenue in Oak Park.

Hours: Wednesday–Saturday, 10 A.M.–5 P.M.; Sunday, noon–5 P.M. Closed July 4, Thanksgiving, Christmas Day, New Year's Day, Memorial Day and Labor Day. Open noon–5 P.M.: Martin Luther King, Jr., Day; President's Day; Columbus Day; Veterans Day; Christmas Eve; New Year's Eve; and days when school is not in session.

Admissions: Under 1, free; all others $5.

For further information write to Wonder Works, 6445 W. North Avenue, Oak Park, Illinois or call (708) 383-4815.

INDIANA

The Children's Museum of Indianapolis
Indianapolis

As of January 1, 1997, the Indianapolis Children's Museum was the largest children's museum in the world. From its beginnings in a small carriage house in 1925, the museum aimed to encourage children to enrich their lives through learning and exploring. The current 356,000 sq. ft. museum now houses ten major galleries which offer exhibits in the physical and natural sciences, history, foreign cultures and the arts, continuing the original mission.

The present site offers an IWERKS CineDome Theater, an Outdoor Festival Park and Clowes Garden Gallery, a Welcome Center, and hundreds of hands-on permanent and changing exhibits. The galleries are connected by a sky-lit open core, with zig-zagging ramps rising 70 feet to the top level. Some of the exhibits on permanent display include a Victorian railway depot, "Space-Quest Planetarium," "What If...," "Mysteries in History" (which includes an authentic 1830s cabin and a 1900s downtown street on the fourth level of the museum), and the Eli Lilly Center for Exploration, to name a few. The Eli Lilly Center is the museum's largest gallery with 15,000 sq. ft. of exhibits and explorations especially for children ages 10 to 18. On the fifth level is an actual working carousel (50¢ charge) along with other toys and play activities.

Besides the more than 110,000 artifacts at the museum, special outreach programs, workshops and events are also sponsored by the museum. More than 180 full-time and 200 part-time staff members, along with more than 850 volunteers, help to keep the museum running smoothly.

Location: On 13 acres of land in Indianapolis' central city.

Hours: (Labor Day–February) Tuesday–Sunday, 10 A.M. to 5 P.M.; (March–August) open daily, 10 A.M. to 5 P.M.; first Thursday of each month, 5 P.M. to 8 P.M., free of charge. Free admissions on Martin Luther King and Presidents' days. Closed Thanksgiving and Christmas Day.

Admissions: Under 2, free; children, $8.50; adults, $13.50; seniors (60+), $12.50. Memberships are available. Member of ASTC and AYM.

Unique characteristic: Largest children's museum in the world; working carousel on the fifth level.

For further information write to The Children's Museum, 3000 N. Meridian St., Indianapolis, Indiana 46208-4716, or call 1-800-208-KIDS or (317) 924-5431. *www.childrensmuseum.org*

College Football Hall of Fame
South Bend

The College Football Hall of Fame opened in South Bend, Indiana, in August of 1995 and advertises itself as one of the most interactive sports museums in the nation. The Hall offers an innovative 360-degree "Stadium Theater" which surrounds the viewer with the sights and sounds of a college game. Other exhibits include the "Hall of Champions," with memorabilia and artifacts; "Pigskin Pageantry," where the traditions that accompany the game are celebrated; "The Training Center," where visitors can test their football skills through a series of interactive, fun-filled challenges and activities; and "Record Breakers," containing artifacts from record-breaking games. Also at the museum is a 43-foot-high sculpture — "Pursuit of a Dream," a football resource library, the Gridiron Plaza (19,000 sq. ft. area) in front of the museum (available for rent), and the Press Box (4,300 sq. ft. also available for rent).

Info in brief: A collections museum with lots of interactive exhibits and a few actual hands-on activities for kids.

Location: Downtown South Bend.

Hours: Thanksgiving–Memorial Day: Daily, 10 A.M.–5 P.M. Memorial Day–Thanksgiving: Monday thru Thursday, 10 A.M.–5 P.M.; Friday & Saturday, 9 A.M.–6 P.M.; Sunday, 9 A.M.–5 P.M. Hall hours are extended on University of Notre Dame home football weekends. Closed Christmas, New Year's and Thanksgiving Day.

Admissions: 4 & under, free; children (5–12), $5; adults, $12; adults (St. Joseph County residents), $8; seniors, $8. Free parking available.

Unique exhibits: Largest collection of historic college football artifacts anywhere in the world; also, possibly the most interactive sports museum in the United States.

Other sites of interest nearby: The Northern Indiana Center for History.

For further information write to the College Football Hall of Fame, 111 S. St. Joseph St., South Bend, Indiana 46601, or call 1-800-440-FAME (3263) or (574) 235-9999 or fax (574) 235-5720. *www.col legefootball.org/*

Hannah Lindahl Children's Museum
Mishawaka

This hands-on museum is designed with kids in mind. Many scientific and historical items are exhibited at a kid's eye level and are placed so that young hands can handle and examine them. Children (and their caregivers) are invited to touch fossils, rocks, geodes, mastodon bone, tools and clothing from the mid–1800's, Native American artifacts, old musical instruments, firefighting equipment, period furniture and more. Gallery Hall begins the journey, with a beautiful mural depicting northern Indiana from the glacier period to the 1800's. Visitors are then lead on a winding brick street of Mishawaka as it may have looked in the 1800's. Displays along this street include a dental office, a toy store, a general store, the Charles Mish Clothing Store, a furnished two-room house, a post office, train station, old fashioned church and a one-room schoolhouse. Various Native American artifacts are also exhibited along the way. Finally, visitors step through the "Japanese culture gate" where a traditional Japanese house and garden have been recreated. These recreations are indicative of those one could see in Mishawaka's Sister City, Shiojiri, Japan.

Info in brief: A hands-on cultural and historical children's museum.

Hours: School year: Tuesday thru Friday, 9 A.M.–noon and 1 P.M.–4 P.M.; Closed weekends, Mondays and during school vacations. June hours: Tuesday thru Thursday, 10 A.M.–2 P.M.

Admissions: 1 & under, free; ages 2–4, $1; ages 5 & up, $2. Memberships available.

Unique exhibits: Japanese house and garden recreations.

Other sites of interest nearby: College Football Hall of Fame, Healthworks! Kids' Museum, Northern Indiana Center for History, South Bend Chocolate Company's Chocolate Museum, The Snike Museum of Art, South Bend Regional Museum of Art, Studebaker National Museum, Notre Dame.

For further information write to the Hannah Lindahl Children's Museum, 1402 South Main Street, Mishawaka, IN 46544 or call (574) 254-4540, or fax (574) 254-4585. *www.hlcm.org* E-mail: *pmarker @hlcm.org*

Healthworks! Kids' Museum
South Bend

Visitors can explore the digestive system, the cigarette butt chair and the brain theatre. HealthWorks! is a hands-on, interactive health education center for children ages 5 to 12.

Hours: Monday thru Friday, 9 A.M.–4 P.M.; Saturday, noon–4 P.M.

Admissions: Children, $3; adults, $5.

Other sites of interest nearby: College Football Hall of Fame, Hannah Handahl Children's Museum, Northern Indiana Center for History, South Bend Chocolate Company's Chocolate Museum, The Snike Museum of Art, South Bend Regional Museum of Art, Studebaker National Museum, Notre Dame.

For further information write to HealthWorks! Kids' Museum, 111 West Jefferson Blvd, Suite 200, South Bend, IN 46601 or call (574) 287-5437. *www.qualityoflife.org/healthworks*

Imagination Station
Lafayette

Imagination Station is a hands-on children's museum where exhibits are designed to give children a chance to "explore science and technology in an interactive and supportive environment." The museum is a 2-story brick building, offering two main galleries: First Floor, where mechanical science is taught with decommissioned flight simulators, an historic fire truck, two micro cars, and opportunities to take apart old everyday electronics like computers, amplifiers, phones and more; and the Second Floor, where visitors can observe more natural science exhibits like African Clawed Frogs, dinosaurs, rocks, water cycle displays, human body displays and more.

Location: Corner of Fourth and Cincinnati Streets in the Greater Lafayette area.

Hours: Wednesday & Thursday, 9 A.M.–1 P.M.; Friday & Saturday, 9 A.M.–5 P.M.

Admissions: Age 2 & under, free; children (3–12), $3; adults (13+), $4.

Other sites of interest nearby: Historic landmarks; Purdue University cultural events.

For further information write to Imagination Station, 600 N. 4th St., Lafayette, IN 47901, or call (765) 420-7780 or fax (765) 420-8260. E-mail: *info@imagination-station.org*

kidscommons
Columbus

Kidscommons is a children's museum that encourages children to explore, create and collaborate. Three floors of exhibits are offered. The first floor features "Our House" (lifestyles, cultures and traditions of another country), "Early Childhood Garden" (a child-size camper, hollow sycamore tree and sights and sounds of Indiana wildlife), "Columbus Works" (a changing interactive imaginary city space), and "Kids-At-Art Studio" (arts & crafts area). The second floor features "Climbing Wall," "Bubblology," "ExploraHouse" (lets visitors explore the "ins and outs" of a house). The third floor features "Storytelling Kiosk," "Community Planning," "Giant Chess," and "Power Outlet" (a special computer center). Other exhibits are added periodically, and traveling exhibits are rotated regularly.

On June 11, 2007, kidscommons' giant toilet (from the ExploraHouse exhibit) was featured on the Jay Leno Show.

Info in brief: A children's hands-on museum featuring a variety of types of exhibits.

Hours: Tuesday thru Saturday, 10 A.M.–5 P.M.; Sunday, 1 P.M.–5 P.M.

Admissions: Under 1, free; ages 1–99, $6.

For further information write to kidscommons, 309 Washington St., Columbus, IN 47201 or call (812) 378-3046. *www.kidscommons.org*

kidsfirst Children's Museum
South Bend

The Northern Indiana Center for History is located on a ten-acre site in the historic West Washington District in South Bend. kidsfirst Children's Museum is an interactive history museum where children can experience a farmer's field as it might appear to an earthworm, participate in a demonstration of the basic food groups, work in an archaeology dig, sit in a wigwam or canoe, run a printing press or computer, and more. The other museums offer a variety of exhibits and collections mainly focusing on the St. Joseph River Valley history and geology. For further information on each of these museums, write to the Center (see Northern Indiana Center for History information below).

Info in brief: Kidsfirst is a hands-on museum for children and their caregivers.

Location: West Washington Historic District in downtown South Bend.

Hours: Tuesday–Saturday, 10 A.M. to 5 P.M.; Sunday, noon to 5 P.M.

Admissions: Small admissions charge for each museum —contact the Center for exact details.

For further information write to kidsfirst Children's Museum, Northern Indiana Center for History, 808 W. Washington, South Bend, Indiana 46601, or call (219) 235-9664 or fax (219) 235-9059.

Koch Family Children's Museum of Evansville
Evansville

A newly renovated CMOE opened in the fall of 2006 in the former downtown Central Library with 18,000 sq. ft. of exhibit space. Four main galleries are offered: "Work Smart" which focuses on engineering skill development and encourages children to build and create; "Live Big" which showcases the human body and promotes the freedom to make choices; "Speak Loud" which encourages the freedom of self-expression through the arts; and, "Quack Factory" which water play and large-muscle activities to promote the freedom to explore. A fifth area is the multimedia theater entitled the "Freedom Gallery," which includes a performance stage for storytellers, small musical groups and other performance artists.

Info in brief: An interactive museum for children and their caregivers.

Location: Downtown Evansville in the renovated former Downtown Central Library building. Physical address: 22 S.E. Fifth Street.

Hours: Tuesday thru Saturday, 10 A.M.–5 P.M.; Sunday, noon–5 P.M.; closed Mondays, except for some Monday holidays.

Admissions: Under 18 months, free; all others, $6. Memberships available.

Unique exhibits: A Mark Twain talking head lets visitors play with words and sentences, and frequently "spouts bits of wisdom" from Mr. Twain.

For further information write to the Children's Museum of Evansville, P.O. Box 122, Evansville, IN 47701 or call (812) 464-CMOE (2663) or fax (812) 477-4339. *www.cmoekids.org* E-mail: *info@cmoekids.org*

Muncie Children's Museum
Muncie

The Muncie Children's Museum, originally opened in the early 1970s, opened a new facility in July 1996. The new facility has 24,000 sq. ft. of exhibit space and employs about 15 people on staff.

A wide variety of exhibits are available, including: "Digging into the Past" (paleontology); "Don't Be a Drip, Go with the Flow" (water activities); "Guts and Stuff" (a Stuffee soft sculptured doll featuring removable internal organs); "Learn Not to Burn"; "Under Indiana" (the geology of Indiana); "Middletown" (variety of changeable storefronts for role-playing); "Garfield Theater" (allows children to interact with Garfield in a cartoon using blue screen technology); and more. An outdoor learning center, a computer lab, a reading loft, a giant locomotive, an actual semi-tractor, and a model train layout are also available for the visitor's use.

Info in brief: A hands-on, participatory museum for children and their caregivers.

Hours: Tuesday–Saturday, 10 A.M. to 5 P.M.; Sunday, 1 P.M. to 5 P.M.

Admissions: $6, ages 1–100.

Unique exhibits: As Jim Davis, Garfield's creator, lives in Muncie; he has been instrumental in establishing the Garfield exhibit — the only one of its kind in the nation.

For further information write to the Muncie Children's Museum, 515 S. High St., Muncie, Indiana 47305, or call (317) 286-1660. *www.munciechildrensmuseum.com*

Northern Indiana Center for History
South Bend

This combination history, cultural, living-history and children's museum is located in a scenic site that showcases an elegant 38-room Victorian mansion, a charming 1930's cottage, a local history gallery, a gallery of Notre Dame history, and a Children's Museum (see kidsfirst Children's Museum above).

Info in brief: Unique combination of "museums" located on one campus.

Location: West Washington Historic District in Downtown South Bend.

Hours: Monday thru Saturday, 10 A.M.–5 P.M.; Sunday, noon–5 P.M.

Admissions: Students, $5; seniors, $6.50; adults, $8.

Other sites of interest nearby: College Football Hall of Fame, Hannah Handahl Children's Museum, South Bend Chocolate Company's Chocolate Museum, The Snike Museum of Art, South Bend Regional Museum of Art, Studebaker National Museum, Notre Dame.

For further information write to Northern Indiana Center for History, 808 W. Washington St., South Bend, IN 46601 or call (574) 235-9664. *www.centerforhistory.org*

Science Central
Fort Wayne

Science Central is a hands-on science museum with more than 120 exhibits for school-aged children and their caregivers. All exhibits focus on the skills that scientists use: measurement, observation, prediction, classification and inference. Visitors are encouraged to ask questions and participate in all activities and experiments. Exhibits offer instruction about weather, the ocean, earth forces, and more. The main changing exhibits gallery offers new exhibits approximately four times a year.

Info in brief: A hands-on science museum offering the "real stuff" of science to be explored, offering sophisticated equipment and technology.

Location: Downtown Fort Wayne.

Hours: (School Year) Wednesday thru Saturday, 10 A.M.–5 P.M.; Sunday noon–5 P.M. (Summer) Tuesday thru Saturday, 10 A.M.–5 P.M.; Sunday, noon–5 P.M. Closed Thanksgiving, Christmas Eve & Day, New Year's Day, and Easter.

Location: 2 and under, free; all others, $7.

Other sites of interest nearby: Historic Fort Wayne, Fun Spot Amusement Park in Angola, Indiana Beach in Monticello.

For further information write to Science Central, 1950 N. Clinton St., Fort Wayne, Indiana 46805-4049, or call (260) 424-2400 or 1-800-4HANDS-ON or fax (260) 422-2899. *www.sciencecentral.org*

Terre Haute Children's Museum
Terre Haute

The Terre Haute Children's Museum, an interactive science and technology museum for children and their caregivers, originally opened in 1988 in the basement of Central Christian Church with 1,500 sq. ft. of exhibit/activity space. In 1991, it moved to its present location in downtown Terre Haute, doubling its exhibit space. Current plans call for another move in mid-late 2008 to a facility offering 35,000 sq. ft., of which 10,000 sq. ft. will be specifically for exhibits. Projected use of exhibit space will include: Toddlers Gallery, One changing exhibits gallery, 3 Immersive Galleries for permanent exhibits, 3 exploration labs, space for traveling exhibits, and an outdoor amphitheatre.

With a mission to build a place where children can explore, test, and create through participatory learning, the museum has plans to name their galleries/exhibits as follows: Dinosaur Dig, Secret Tree House, Animal Hospital, Toddler Space, Construction Zone, Sailing Ships, The Reef, Technology Station and 3 as yet unnamed learning labs.

Info in brief: A hands-on science and technology children's museum.

Location: Downtown Terre Haute.

Hours: Tuesday thru Friday, 10 A.M.–5 P.M.; Saturday, 10 A.M.–3 P.M.

Admissions: Under 3, free; child (3–12), $3; seniors, $3; adults, $3.75. Member ASTC.

Other sites of interest nearby: Indiana State University, Hulman Civic Center, the Swope Museum and the Clabber Girl Museum.

For further information write to the Terre Haute Children's Museum, 523 Wabash Ave., Terre Haute, IN 47807 or call (812) 235-5548. *www.cstm.org* Email: *tjacks@terrehautechildrensmuseum.com*

WonderLab Museum of Health, Science & Technology
Bloomington

In 1998, WonderLab opened as a small museum on the Bloomington Court House square, with the intention of establishing a larger, permanent museum as soon as funds allowed. In 2003, that intention came to fruition as a larger (two stories), newer WonderLab opened its doors with a mission to provide opportunities for "people of all ages, especially children, to experience the wonder and excitement of science, through hands-on exhibits and programs that stimulate curiosity, encourage exploration, and foster lifelong learning." In the few years of its existence, the museum has won more than a dozen awards of excellence.

Some of WonderLab's permanent exhibits include opportunities to explore the following: bubbles, magnetism, electricity, light, sound, air, kinetic energy, gravity, cosmic rays, health and the human body, nature and live animals, including microorganisms, reptiles, amphibians, insects and fish. A dramatic two-story climbing maze and a special exhibit area specifically for very young children, are also on site.

Info in brief: A hands-on museum for children and families, including a special area for the very young.

Location: Downtown Bloomington.

Hours: Tuesday thru Saturday, 9:30 A.M.–5 P.M.; Sunday, 1 P.M.–5 P.M.; Closed some major holidays.

Admissions: Under 1 year, free; child (1–17), $6; adult, $7. Memberships available. Member Alliance of Bloomington Museums. Member ASTC. Some free on-street parking; metered parking close by.

Other sites of interest nearby: Indiana University cultural activities, the Convention Center, and several other museums in the area.

For further information write to WonderLab, 308 W. 4th St., Bloomington, IN 47404 or call (812) 337-1337, or fax (812) 330-1337. *www.wonderlab.org*; E-mail: *writeus@wonderlab.org*

IOWA

Bluedorn Science Imaginarium, The Grout Museum
Waterloo

The Grout Museum is a combination of four unique attractions on one campus: the Grout Museum of History & Science, Bluedorn Science Imaginarium, Rensselaer Russell House Museum, and the Snowden House. Each of these attractions would be of interest to older children, but the Imaginarium is the official children's museum on site. The Carl A. and Peggy J. Bluedorn Science Imaginarium was opened in 1993 due to an increasing interest in the Grout's science programs. It is an interactive, hands-on children's science museum with exhibits that encourage children to examine how science affects our everyday lives. Opportunities are provided for experimenting with physics, light, sound, momentum and other scientific concepts. Live biological specimens and science demonstrations are also featured.

Info in brief: A children's hands on science museum.

Location: Campus of The Grout Museum complex.

Hours: (for Grout Museum of History & Science and the Imaginarium) Tuesday thru Saturday, 9 A.M.–5 P.M.; (Planetarium Shows and Science Demos) September thru May: Saturday 11 A.M., 1:30 P.M. & 3 P.M. June thru August: Tuesday thru Saturday 11 A.M., 1:30 P.M. & 3 P.M.

Admissions: General admission on all sites: child, age 12 and under, $3; adult, $4.50. Explorer Pass (admission to all 3 sites in one day): child, $7; adult, $9.50. Explorer Pass (Grout Museum & Imaginarium — available only when the Rensselaer Russell House Museum is closed): child, $5; adult, $7.50.

Other sites of interest nearby: The other museums in the Grout Museum complex.

For further information write to Grout Museum, 503 South St., Waterloo, Iowa 50701 or call (319) 234-6357 or fax (319) 236-0500. *www.groutmuseumdistrict.org*

Family Museum of Arts and Science
Bettendorf

A proposal written in 1990 by a manager of arts programming for the City of Bettendorf called for a complex near the center of the community where residents could have access to library facilities, art and dance classes, a hands-on museum, and more in the proposed "center for learning," now retitled "The Learning Campus." In a few short years, the museum opened (1997) and now offers five main in-house hands-on exhibits in its 9,600 sq. ft. of gallery space, as well as outreach programs in science, and the visual and performing arts. More exhibits are already in the process of being built. The museum is a department of the City of Bettendorf.

The five interactive exhibits currently on display are "The Homestead" (touch a 10-foot-tall tornado, create a lightning bolt, control soil erosion, climb a tree house, etc.); "Kinder Garten" (a pre-schoolers area which celebrates the strong German heritage of the area); "Heartland" (Heartbeat Cafe, Cardiac Cruiser, Hemobile, and more); "Rhythm Alley" (activities with sound, music and a psychedelic shadowbox encourage visitors to explore and create); "Brainstorms" (examples of the inventive genius of dreamers and doers).

The Family Museum has received many awards and honors, including the 1998 Iowa Attraction of the Year by the Travel Federation of Iowa, 1999 Consumer Brochure of the Year for their general brochure, and many local awards.

Info in brief: A hands-on museum with activities for pre-schoolers through middle-schoolers and their families.

Location: Learning Campus Drive in the 2900 Block of 18th St., next to Bettendorf Public Library and Information Center.

Hours: Monday–Thursday, 9 A.M. to 8 P.M.; Friday and Saturday, 9 A.M. to 5 P.M.; Sunday, noon to 5 P.M.

Admissions: Under 1, free; visitors (2–59), $5; seniors (60+), $2. Member ASTC, AAM, ACM and others.

For further information write to the Family Museum of Arts and Science, 2900 Learning Campus Drive, Bettendorf, Iowa 52722, or call (563) 344-4106 or fax (563) 344-4164. *www.familymuseum.org*

The Imaginarium Grout Museum of History and Science *see* Bluedorn Science Imaginarium

The Iowa Children's Museum
Coralville

One of the largest cultural attractions in Iowa, the Iowa Children's Museum aims is to "celebrate and nurture the power and potential of every child while promoting lifelong learning that is serious fun." Over 28,000 sq. ft. of playground interactive exhibits provide opportunities for children ages birth to twelve to interact with their caregivers. Exhibits include: Indonesia, Land of Diversity; Cityworks; Notion of Motion; Imaginacres; Under Construction; Spin Me a Story; Growing up in Iowa; Block Party; Puppet Kingdom; and Wild About Animals. Space for changing exhibits is also offered.

ICM was the recipient of two ICKY awards—for Best Children's Programming and Best Collaboration.

Info in brief: A two-story, 28,000 sq. ft. facility with interactive children's exhibits.

Hours: Tuesday thru Thursday, 10 A.M.–6 P.M.; Friday & Saturday, 10 A.M.–8 P.M.; Sunday 11 A.M.–6 P.M. Closed most Mondays, except for Monday school holidays.

Admissions: Under 1, free; seniors (60+), $5; children & adults (ages 1–59), $6. Memberships available.

For further information write to The Iowa Children's Museum, Coral Ridge Mall, 1451 Coral Ridge Ave., Coralville, IA 52241 or call (319) 625-6255. *www.theicm.org*

Rensselaer Russell House Museum
Waterloo

The Grout Museum has grown into a facility with three unique and separate properties—The Grout Museum of History and Science, the Rensselaer Russell House Museum and the Carl and Peggy Bluedorn Science Imaginarium.

The Grout Museum emphasizes the cultural and natural history of the region. It features permanent and changing exhibits, daily planetarium shows and the interactive "Discovery Zone" with hands-on activities for children.

The Rensselaer Russell House is one of the oldest dwellings in Black Hawk County, having been built in 1861. The house is listed on the National Register of Historic Places. Tours are offered to the public all year round.

The Imaginarium is strictly a hands-on science museum with dozens of exhibits for children. Visitors can grab the controls of the laser spirograph and create a laser show; participate in a bubble race, shoot a ring of air across the room with an air cannon, ride a life-size gyroscope, spin on a turntable platform, and more. Live science demonstrations and experiments are also offered daily.

Info in brief: Three separate museums, two of which offer hands-on experiences for children. The Imaginarium is a strictly hands-on museum for children and their caregivers. The Grout Museum has one area, "The Discovery Zone," with hands-on experiences for young children.

Location: The Grout Museum District—off South Street in Waterloo. Grout Museum, 503 South St.; Rensselaer Russell House Museum, 520 W. 3rd St.; Imaginarium, 322 Washington St.

Hours: Grout Museum and Imaginarium—(June–August) Tuesday–Saturday, 10 A.M. to 4:30 P.M.; (September–May) Tuesday–Friday, 1 P.M. to 4:30 P.M.; Saturday, 10 A.M. to 4:30 P.M. Imaginarium also open Sunday, 1 P.M. to 4:30 P.M. Russell House Museum—(April–May and September and October) Tuesday–Saturday, 1 P.M. to 4:30 P.M. (September and October) Tuesday–Friday, 10 A.M. to 4:30 P.M.; Saturday, 1 P.M. to 4:30 P.M.

Admissions: Under 3, free to all museums. Museum District Pass (includes 3 museums)—children, $4; adults, $6. Museum District Pass (includes 2 museums)—all visitors, $4. General admission at both the Grout and Imaginarium, $2.50. Russell House admissions—child, $1; adult, $2.50. Memberships available. Member ASTC.

Other sites of interest nearby: Cedar Rapids attractions.

For further information write to The Grout Museum of History & Science, 503 South St., Waterloo, Iowa 50701. You may also call Grout Museum, (319) 234-6357; Russell House, (319) 233-0262; or Imaginarium, (319) 233-8708.

Science Station
Cedar Rapids

Science Station has celebrated many anniversaries since its opening in 1986. The City of Cedar Rapids vacated the original brick Central Fire Station in 1985, and the Junior League of Cedar Rapids, Inc., turned the building into a hands-on science museum. Three years later, the League turned it over to the community, and it was expanded in 2000, and again in 2001 to accommodate the many exhibits that meet the mission of the Science Station. The Science Station is a science and technology center which provides entertaining learning experiences that inspire and stimulate the imagination.

Three floors of hands-on galleries provide an exhibit environment for children and adults to learn together. Exhibits cover areas such as Bubbles, Space, Music, Sense & Perceptions, Light & Illusions, Nutrition, with major new permanent exhibits for pre-schoolers, a new weather exhibit plus a new science of news exhibit to be opened in 2008–2009.

Info in brief: A hands-on museum for children and their caregivers.

Location: Historic, 1917 brick fire station in downtown Cedar Rapids, across from the public library.

Hours: Tuesday–Saturday, 10 A.M. to 5 P.M.; Sunday, noon–5 P.M. Closed Mondays.

Admissions: Under 3, free; children (3–12), $4.50; students (ages 12–22), $5.50; adults (19–62), $7.50; seniors, $5.50. Member ASTC.

For further information write to Science Station, 427 First St., S.E., Cedar Rapids, Iowa 52401-1808, or call (319) 363-4629. *www.sciencestation.org*

KANSAS

The Children's Museum of Kansas City
Kansas City

Incorporated in 1984, The Children's Museum of Kansas City moved into its permanent location in 1990. The museum is committed to reaching children of all backgrounds. Its mission is to provide "interactive, educational and entertaining exhibits and programming in a professional manner, aiming to unfold a learning journey that stimulates imagination and creative thinking."

The more than 40 hands-on exhibits are built around the themes of machinery, light, energy, science exploration and art. The targeted age range is children from 3 to 10 and their families. Touching and exploring are encouraged.

The museum also provides educational experiences in the community. Museum "teachers" visit classrooms, take field trips, and offer workshops to various groups through outreach programs such as "The Magic School Bus," youth afterschool programs and "Hands On Science Outreach" programs.

Info in brief: Hands-on, interactive, directed and nondirected activities for children and their caregivers.

Location: Lower level of Indian Springs Marketplace in Kansas City.

Hours: Tuesday–Saturday, 9:30 A.M. to 5 P.M.; Sunday, 1 P.M. to 5 P.M.; closed Monday. Open Mondays, June through August. Special Sundays, $4 + tax.

Admissions: Under age 2, free; all others, $5. Memberships available.

Other sites of interest nearby: Kansas City Museum, Nelson-Atkins Museum of Art, Kansas City Zoo, Leavenworth County Historical Museum, Wyandotte County Museum, Worlds of Fun and more.

For further information write to The Children's Museum of Kansas City, 4601 State Ave., Kansas City, Kansas 66102, or call (913) 287-8888. *www.kidmuzm.org*

Exploration Place
Wichita

Exploration Place is a $62 million 98,500 sq. ft. science center, which, along with an adjacent park area, offer enrichment and entertainment for all ages. Four main exhibit areas include activities about flight, health and human life, people, and places and environments of Kansas. State-of-the-art shows are offered in the CyberDome Theater and in the Simulation Center. More than 40 exhibits are offered in the Kids Explore area alone, while the park also offers a miniature golf area.

Info in brief: Hands-on museum especially for children.

Location: Banks of the Arkansas River in the scenic downtown Wichita Museums on the River district.

Hours: Tuesday–Sunday, 9 A.M. to 5 P.M.; summer hours— Mondays and longer Sunday hours.

Admissions: Under 2, free; ages 2–4, $3; ages 5–15, $6; ages 16–64, $8; ages 65+, $7.50. CyberDome Theater shows for all ages 2 & up, $2. Memberships available.

Other sites of interest nearby: Omnisphere and Science Center, Sedgwick County Zoo, Wichita Boathouse & Arkansas River Foundation, Wichita Greyhound Park, Wichita International Raceway, Wichita Thunder Hockey, Wichita Wings, and more.

For further information write to Exploration Place, 300 N. McLean Blvd., Wichita, Kansas 67203, or call (316) 263-3373, *www.exploration.org*

Kansas Cosmosphere & Space Center
Hutchinson

Although the Kansas Cosmosphere & Space Center was not originally a hands-on museum, special 5-day-long camps called "Future Astronaut Training Programs" were offered to chil-

Visitors are treated to real space vehicles at the Kansas Cosmosphere and Space Center in Hutchinson.

More space vehicles are on display at the Kansas Cosmosphere and Space Center.

dren during the summer. Participants trained on sophisticated space simulators, built and launched model rockets, learned flight techniques and experienced other activities which taught them what it's like to be an astronaut or work in the space program. Now, along with the "Future Astronaut Training Program" in the summer, all patrons can ride a g-force simulator and test other astronaut-training simulators year-round.

The Cosmosphere has become an internationally-known staple of the space science community, which, in depth and size, is second only to that of the Smithsonian Air and Space Museum in Washington, DC. It also holds the largest collection of Russian space artifacts outside of Moscow. This Hall of Space Museum is one of only three museums in the world to display flown spacecraft from all three early-manned space programs—Mercury (Liberty Bell 7), Gemini (Gemini 10), and Apollo (Apollo 13).

Several documentaries and movies have been made at the Cosmosphere, most notably, the Cosmosphere built the replica spacecrafts used in the movie *Apollo 13*, starring Tom Hanks.

The Cosmosphere holds the Hall of Space museum, one of the most significant collections of U.S. and Russian space artifacts in the world; the Carey IMAX Dome Theater, the 12th IMAX Dome theater built in the world, and astronaut training camps for all ages.

Info in brief: A Space Center, Planetarium and summer camp location, education center, museum, and IMAX dome theater.

Hours: Monday–Saturday, 9:30 A.M. to 9 P.M.; Sunday, noon to 8 P.M. Open every day except Thanksgiving, Christmas and Easter. Contact the Space Center for Planetarium and Omnimax Theater showtimes. The museum may close early for special events.

Admissions: 2 & under, free; children (3–12) & seniors (60+), $8; adults, $8.50; all-day admission includes one IMAX film, one planetarium show, Dr. Goddard's Lab & Hall of Space Museum: 2 & under, free; children & seniors, $13; adults, $15.

Unique exhibits: The Hall of Space Museum contains the world's largest and most comprehensive collection of space suits.

Other sites of interest nearby: Kaleidoscope (Kansas City), Toy and Miniature Museum (Kansas City), Jesse James historic sites, Kansas City Zoo, NCAA Hall of Champions, American Royal Museum & Visitors Center and other Kansas City attractions.

For further information write to Kansas Cosmosphere & Space Center, 1100 N. Plum, Hutchinson, Kansas 67501, or call (620) 662-2305 ext. 359.

McPherson Museum
McPherson

Although not a hands-on museum, the McPherson Museum offers children an opportunity to learn about things of special interest to the young. Located in the historic three-story 1920s Vaniman house, the museum is packed with historic and scientific artifacts in a relaxed, friendly atmosphere. Some of the artifacts on display and of special interest to children include a large collection of fossils and ice-age artifacts, the original M-G-M lion's skin (first seen live on the M-G-M movie screen in July 1928), the first synthetic diamond, and much more. Several special events are hosted by the museum throughout the year, including the Old Fashioned Fall Harvest Festival in September which features many demonstrations of old time crafts (children can participate in some of these crafts).

The museum now has a dedicated Learning Center on the 3rd Floor featuring many hands-on items as well as the doll and toy collections, school and music displays.

Info in brief: A collections-based museum with many artifacts of special interest to children, and others of special interest to adults.

Hours: Tuesday–Saturday, 1 P.M. to 5 P.M. Closed Sundays, Mondays and holidays. Tours are available upon request.

Admissions: Free (donations accepted).

Unique exhibit: Many unique artifacts on display such as the M-G-M lion skin.

Other sites of interest nearby: Historic City of Lindsborg (its strong Swedish influence draws tourists from around the world), the Maxwell Game Preserve (buffalo habitat tours available), the Mennonite museum in Gossell and the Mennonite museum in Newton.

For further information write to the McPherson Museum, 1130 E. Euclid St., McPherson, Kansas 67460, or call (620) 241-8464. *www.mcphersonmuseum.com*

The Omnisphere & Science Center
Wichita

Founded in 1975, The Omnisphere & Science Center is both a hands-on children's science museum and a planetarium. Live science shows are also offered, with scheduled shows changing seasonally. A model railroad is on display Saturdays only.

In the Science Center are approximately 80 hands-on science exhibits, including the antigravity mirror, the harmonograph (which makes spirographical designs), a VanDeGraaff Generator, and plenty of telescopes and microscopes to allow visitors to study the stars, crystal structures, tiny insects, and other microscopic life.

Info in brief: A hands-on children's museum which also offers live demonstrations, planetarium shows and a model railroad display.

Location: Housed in the old 1915 Carnegie Library building in downtown Wichita.

Hours: Science Center — Tuesday–Friday, 8 A.M. to 5 P.M.; Saturday and Sunday, 1 P.M. to 5 P.M.

Model railroad open on Saturday only. Planetarium and science shows schedules vary, usually at 1 P.M., 2 P.M. and 3 P.M., but be sure to contact the museum before visiting for exact scheduling details.

Admissions: Contact the museum for current charges.

Other sites of interest nearby: Sedgewick County Zoo, Sportsworld, Wichita Greyhound Park, Wichita International Raceway, Wichita Thunder Hockey, Wichita Wings, Wichita Wranglers, Wichita Center for the Arts, Wichita Children's Theatre and Dance Center, Children's Museum of Wichita (see listing) and more.

For further information write to Omnisphere & Science Center, 220 S. Main, Wichita, Kansas 67202, or call (316) 337-9174.

Wonderscope Children's Museum
Shawnee

Wonderscope Children's Museum is an inter-disciplinary museum, featuring exhibits and programs in both the arts and sciences. They are committed to encouraging a serious life-long love of learning in children through the fun of play. Exhibit areas include: Lego Ocean Adventure, City of Wonder, Crater City, Artworks, Nature & Science Lab, Raceways, Healthy Kids, Small Wonders, and Express Yourself. Performance areas and indoor picnic area are also available. The targeted audience includes children aged 10 and under.

Info in brief: Both an arts and a science hands-on museum for children and their caregivers.

Location: Shawnee.

Hours: Tuesday thru Saturday, 10 A.M.–5 P.M.; Sunday, noon–5 P.M. (Closed on Monday from September through February.)

Admissions: Under 1, free; 1 & 2 year olds, $3; seniors (64+), 64; ages 3–63, $6.

Other sites of interest nearby: Johnson County Museum of History, Shawnee Town, Power Play family entertainment center, Theatre in the Park, CUBE (Center for Understanding the Built Environment), and more.

For further information write to Wonderscope Children's Museum, 5705 Flint, Shawnee Mission, KS 66203 or call (913) 268-8130. *www.wonderscope.org* E-mail: *info@wonderscope.org*

KENTUCKY

Dinosaur World
Cave City

Over 100 life-sized dinosaurs are on exhibit. See "Dinosaur World," Plant City, Florida for more information on exhibits.

For further information write to Dinosaur World, 711 Mammoth Cave Rd., Cave City, KY, or call (270) 773-4345 or fax (270) 773-5308.

Explorium
Lexington

The Explorium is a history and heritage children's museum. Visitors can become a student in a nineteenth century classroom or a patient or doctor in the medical world of that time, visit the two generation family of Billy Ray Cyrus, create their own music at the Karaoke Korner stage or at the Music Quilt, or pay tribute to soldiers of the twentieth century. A special play area for toddlers is featured. Older children can play in a flight simulator, an actual towboat, a treehouse, or on a front porch, where games, puzzles and puppets entertain. Revolving exhibits are also featured, showcasing sports, regional art, textiles and quilts.

Info in brief: A cultural/historical hands-on children's museum.

Location: Downtown Ashland.

Hours: Tuesday thru Saturday, 10 A.M.–5 P.M.; Closed Sunday & Monday.

Admissions: Under 2, free; children 2 & over, $4.50; seniors, $4.50; adults, $5.50. Memberships available. Member ASTC.

Other sites of interest: Kentucky Horse Farm.

For further information write to the Explorium, 1620 Windhester Ave., Ashland, KY 41101, or call (606) 329-8888 or fax (606) 324-3218. *www.highlandmuseum.com* E-mail: *highlandsmuseum@yahoo.com*

Louisville Science Center
Louisville

Founded in 1871 as a part of the Public Library System of Kentucky, the Louisville Science Center is one of the oldest children's museums in the country. Following a few name and location changes, the museum is now located in five restored 19th-century cast-iron warehouse buildings on Louisville's historic Main Street, and has become Kentucky's largest hands-on science center. Three floors of permanent and temporary exhibits are on display, teaching visitors about science and natural history topics. An IMAX Theater, a Space Science Gallery with space missions artifacts, a mummy's tomb (including a 3,400-year-old mummy), and "A Show of Hands" (a multi-disciplinary exhibit that explores the human hand) are also on display. Interactive science demonstrations and mini-plays are presented daily.

The Center adopted a new mission statement along with its new name in 1994. Visitors can expect to see several changes and improvements to the site over the next few years.

Info in brief: A hands-on and interactive science and natural history museum for children and all members of the family.

Location: Downtown Louisville's historic Main Street, in five restored 19th-century cast-iron warehouse buildings.

Hours: Monday–Thursday, 10 A.M. to 5 P.M.; Friday and Saturday, 10 A.M. to 9 P.M.; Sunday, noon to 5 P.M.

Admissions: (Science Center only) children (2–12), $4.25; adults, $5.25; seniors (60+), $4.25. (Science Center & IMAX Theater) children (2–12), $5.50; adults, $7; seniors (60+), $5.50. Memberships available. Member ASTC.

Other sites of interest nearby: Louisville Slugger Museum, Kentucky Derby Museum, Kentucky Kingdom amusement park, Louisville Zoo, and Fall of the Ohio Interpretive Center.

For further information write to the Louisville Science Center, 727 W. Main St., Louisville, Kentucky, 40202-2681, or call (502) 561-6103 or fax (502) 561-6145. *www.louisvillescience.org*

LOUISIANA

Children's Museum of Acadiana
Lafayette

The Children's Museum of Acadiana is a hands-on museum that offers real-life experiences like an operating room, an ambulance, a television newsroom, a bank and more.

Hours: Tuesday thru Saturday, 10 A.M.–5 P.M.

Admissions: Under 1, free; all others, $5.

Other sites of interest nearby: Evangeline Downs, Cajun French Music Association, Maison du Codofil, Alexandre Mouton House, Lafayette Museum and Downtown Lafayette.

For further information write to the Children's Museum of Acadiana, 201 E. Congress St., Lafayette, LA 70501-6919 or call (337) 232-8500 or fax (337) 232-8167. *www.childrensmuseumofacadiana.com*

The Children's Museum of Lake Charles
Lake Charles

Incorporated in 1988, the Children's Museum of Lake Charles was housed in an unused school building. After a couple of moves, the museum is finally located in its present location — 2-story facility, with more than 40 exhibits in a 7,000 sq. ft. area. Hundreds of volunteers help the two full-time and three part-time staff in maintaining the facility, setting up exhibits and staffing special events.

Exhibits encourage visitors to explore the social sciences, science and technology, and the visual and performing arts. Although the targeted age range is 3 to 14 years of age, the hands-on, participatory exhibits are of interest to all ages.

Info in brief: A hands-on exploratory museum for children of all ages and their caregivers.

Location: Near the Charpentier Historic District in Lake Charles.

Hours: Monday–Saturday, 10 A.M. to 5 P.M. (Other hours are for tours only.)

Admissions: Under 2, free; children & adults, $6; seniors (55+), $4. Free parking is available.

For further information write to The Children's Museum of Lake Charles, 327 Broad St., Lake Charles, Louisiana 70601, or call (337) 433-9420. *www.child-museum.org*

Louisiana Children's Museum
New Orleans

At the Louisiana Children's Museum, explorations in math, science and physics have been the main focus since 1986. Originally situated in 8,000 sq. ft. of a 134-year-old building in New Orleans' historic warehouse district, the museum has continued to add square footage to its area, until finally purchasing the entire building in 1992. More than 45,000 sq. ft. of exhibit space now offer hundreds of activities for children from preschool age through middle school. Current exhibits include: "The Lab," math and physics experiments; "Challenges," living with disabilities; "The Times-Picayune Theatre"; "Body Works," physical fitness activities; "Kids' Cafe," pretend restaurant; "Water Works"; "Art Trek," an arts and crafts center; a working TV studio, supermarket, and more. In addition to the permanent exhibits, the museum hosts special scheduled programs, toddler activities, live performances and demonstrations, safety workshops and art workshops throughout the year.

Info in brief: A hands-on science museum for children. Now counted in the top 10 percent of children's museums according to square footage and attendance.

Location: Historic warehouse district, between Magazine and Tchoupitoulas streets and just four blocks from the Ernest N. Morial Convention Center and other riverfront attractions.

Hours: Tuesday–Saturday, 9:30 A.M. to 4:30 P.M.; Sunday, noon to 4:30 P.M.; Monday (summer only), 9:30 A.M. to 4:30 P.M. Closed major holidays.

Admissions: $7 for all visitors over 1 year old.

Other sites of interest nearby: The many tourist attractions in New Orleans.

For further information write to the Louisiana Children's Museum, 420 Julia St., New Orleans, Louisiana 70130, or call (504) 586-0725 or fax (504) 529-3666. *www.lcm.org*

SciPort

Shreveport

In 1986, the Exploratorium opened as a children's hands-on science and humanities museum. Many changes and innovations have been undertaken, including a name change in 1993 to "SciPort." The newest 92,000 sq. ft. children's museum, opened in 1998, offers more than 200 hands-on exhibits in halls themed as the Red River Gallery, Body Works, Physical Science, Technology, Children's Discovery, and the Traveling Exhibit Hall. An IMAX Dome Theater is also housed at this facility along with a laser SPACE DOME Planetarium, gift shop and café.

The Sci-Port Discovery Center in Shreveport.

The Sci-Port Discovery Center's world of water offers hands-on experiences.

Info in brief: A hands-on science and humanities museum for children and their caregivers.

Location: Downtown Shreveport Riverfront.

Hours: Monday–Friday, 10 A.M. to 5 P.M. (Memorial Day to Labor Day: 10 A.M. to 6 P.M.); Saturday, 10 A.M. to 6 P.M.; Sunday, 1 P.M. to 6 P.M.

Admissions: SciPort only: under 3, free; children (3–12), $9; adults, $12. IMAX only: under 3, free;

3–12, $7.50; adults, $8.50; COMBO Tickets: 3–12, $12; adults, $17. Memberships available. Member ASTC.

Other sites of interest nearby: Spring Street Museum, ARK–LA Antique & Classic Vehicle Museum, R.S. Barnwell Garden & Art Center, Sports Museum of Champions, and "Spirit of the Red" River Cruises.

For further information write to SciPort, 820 Clyde Fant Parkway, Shreveport, LA 71101, or call 1-877-SCIPORT or (318) 424-3466, or fax (318) 222-5592. *www.sciport.org* E-mail: *afumarolo@ sciport.org*

MAINE

Children's Discovery Museum
Augusta

Exhibit areas in the Children's Discovery Museum include: The Marine Room, Restaurant, Grocery Store, Bank, Reading Loft, Theater, Rainforest/Toddler Play Area, Kennebec River Room, Multi-Cultural Music Center, Tree House/Nature Center, and Engineering/Construction/Transportation.

Location: Historic downtown riverfront community, along the Kennebec River.

Hours: Tuesday, Wednesday and Thursday, 10 A.M.–4 P.M.; Friday and Saturday, 10 A.M.–5 P.M.; Sunday, 11 A.M.–4 P.M.

Admissions: Child, $5; adult, $4. Memberships available. Member ACM.

For further information write to the Children's Discovery Museum, 265 Water St, Augusta, Maine 04330 or call (207) 622-2209. *www.childrensdiscoverymuseum.org*

The Children's Museum of Maine
Portland

Having celebrated its 30th anniversary in 2007, the Children's Museum of Maine offers many hands-on exhibits for children of all ages, including farming, fishing, a fire engine, banking, shopping, a computer lab, a space shuttle experience, Camera Obscura and more. At least one major theme exhibit is offered each year, with special activities, events, workshops and speakers made available for visitors at various times throughout the exhibition period, along with the permanent displays. A calendar of events is available from the museum.

Info in brief: A hands-on participatory museum for children and their caregivers with new exhibits being offered on a regular basis.

Location: Arts district of Downtown Portland. Physical address: 142 Free Street.

Hours: Winter (Labor Day thru Memorial Day), Tuesday thru Sat., 10 A.M.–5 P.M.; Sunday noon–5 P.M. Summer (Memorial Day thru Labor Day), Monday thru Saturday, 10 A.M.–5 P.M.; Sunday, noon–5. Closed Thanksgiving, Christmas Eve & Day, New Year's Day, Easter, July 4th. Open Daily during Maine public school vacation weeks.

Admissions: Under 1, free; all others, $7. First Friday of each month, 5 P.M. to 8 P.M. is free to all. Parking garage 1½ blocks from museum — ticket validated at museum. Member ASTC.

For further information write to The Children's Museum of Maine, P.O. Box 4041, Portland, Maine 04101, or call (207) 828-1234 Ext. 001 or fax (207) 828-5726. *www.kitetails.com*

MARYLAND

Chesapeake Children's Museum
Annapolis

The mission of the Chesapeake Children's Museum is "to create an environment of discovery about oneself, the peoples, the technologies, and the ecology of the Chesapeake Bay area for all our children and for the children in us all." A number of both indoor and outdoor exhibit areas are featured currently, and the museum has plans for several additions to be made as funds become available.

Hours: 10 A.M.–4 P.M., except Wednesdays (Wednesday are reserved for groups of 10 or more.)

Admissions: $3 for ages 1 & up.

For further information write to Chesapeake Children's Museum, 25 Silopanna Rd., Annapolis MD 21403 or call (410) 990-1993. *www.theccm.org*

Discovery Station at Hagerstown
Hagerstown

The Discovery Station offers science, technology and history hands-on exhibits intended to stimulate a curiosity for discovery, exploration and further investigation by children and their caregivers to foster life-long learning. Special programs and special events are also offered occasionally (contact museum before visiting). Also on site is The Hagerstown Aviation Museum, which visitors may explore with museum admission.

The building that houses the museum is an attraction in itself. The historic Nicodemus Bank building originally housed the Federal Depository during the Civil War. The main vault, with leaded glass, was installed in 1913. The building's 3 floors contain 5 vaults. The exterior is white marble with soaring palladium windows.

Location: Beautiful, Civil-War–era Nicodemus Bank building across from the Washington County courthouse.

Hours: Tuesday thru Saturday, 10 A.M. — 4 P.M.; Sunday, 2 P.M.–5 P.M.; Closed major holidays.

Admissions: Under 2, free; ages 2–17, $6; adults, $7; seniors (55+) & military, $5. Limited on-site parking is available. Member ASTC.

For further information write to Discovery Station at Hagerstown, 101 West Washington St., Hagerstown, MD 21740 or call (301) 790-0076 or (877) 790-0076 or fax (301) 790-0045. *www.discovery station.org*

Maryland Science Center
Baltimore

The Maryland Science Center is a private, non-profit museum which features hundreds of hands-on activities, live demonstrations, and interactive displays, an IMAX Theater, and the Davis Planetarium in its three-story facility. The main exhibit galleries offer exhibits such as "Chesapeake Bay," "Experiment" (interactive activities for all ages), "Science Arcade" (more hands-on experiments), Van de Graaff Electrostatic Generator, "Energy," a Hubble Space Telescope, K.I.D.S. Room for 3–7 year olds, and more.

A large staff works along with several hundred volunteers to keep the exhibits up to date and relevant to children today. Various demonstrations and events are also offered throughout the year.

Info in brief: A large, hands-on, interactive museum for children and their caregivers.

Location: Southwest corner of Baltimore's Inner Harbor.

Hours: (April–May) Monday thru Thursday, 9:30 A.M.–5 P.M.; Friday and Sunday, 9 A.M.–5 P.M.; Saturday, 9 A.M.–6 P.M. (June–August) Monday thru Thursday 10 A.M.–6 P.M.; Friday and Saturday, 9 A.M.–8 P.M.; Sunday 9 A.M.–6 P.M.

Admissions: Under 3, free (Exhibit Hall & Planetarium) child (3–12), $10; adult, $14.50; senior (60+), $13.50. (Add one IMAX film) child (3–12), $14; adult, $18.50; senior, $17.50. U23D show: child, $10; adult, $12, senior, $11. IMAX only—evenings after 4 P.M., $8. Member ASTC.

Other sites of interest nearby: The many historic sites in Baltimore.

For further information write to the Maryland Science Center, 601 Light St., Baltimore, Maryland 21230-3812, or call (410) 685-5225 (24-hr. info line) or (410) 685-2370. *www.mdsci.org*

Port Discovery
Baltimore

Formerly known as The Baltimore Children's Museum and housed in The Cloisters in Lutherville, the museum was relocated to the historic Fish Market building in downtown Baltimore and re-opened as Port Discovery in 1998. Port Discovery offers exclusive interactive exhibits for children ages 2–10. Special programs and traveling exhibits are also featured. Three floors of exhibits include both permanent and visiting exhibits. Some of these exhibits include: Wonders of Waters, The Diner, Miss Perception's Mystery House, The Oasis, Sensation Station, Adventure Expeditions, The Soccer Field, and more. Walt Disney Imagineering designed several of the museum's permanent exhibits.

As Port Discovery, the museum has earned several awards: ranked among the Top 20 Children's Museum in the U.S. by *Grand* Magazine in 2007; named AOL Cityguide's "City's Best" Museum in 2004; Named top 16 Best Kids' Attractions in the World by British Airways' *High Life* In-flight magazine in 2002; ranked as the 12th top Children's Museums in the World by *The London Observer* in 2000; and, ranked 4th among the Top 10 Children's Museums in the U.S. by *Child Magazine* in February, 2002.

Info in brief: One of the top interactive hands-on children's museums in the U.S.

Location: Historic Fish Market building in downtown Baltimore.

Hours: (October–May): Tuesday thru Friday, 9:30–4:30 P.M.; Saturday, 10 A.M.–5 P.M.; Sunday, noon–5 P.M.; (Summer hours—Memorial Day–Labor Day): Monday thru Thursday, 10 A.M.–5 P.M.; Friday & Saturday, 10 A.M.–6 P.M.; Sunday, noon–5 P.M. (September): Labor Day, 10 A.M.–5 P.M.; Friday, 9:30 A.M.–4:30 P.M.; Saturday, 10 A.M.–5 P.M.

Admissions: Under 2, free; all others $10.75. There is a charge for parking.

Other sites of interest nearby: The many tourist attractions in Baltimore.

For further information write to Port Discovery, 35 Market Place, Baltimore, MD 21202 or call (410) 727-8120 or fax (410) 727-3042. *www.portdiscovery.org* E-mail: *info@portdiscovery.org*

Rose Hill Manor Children's Museum & Historic Park

Frederick

Built in the 1790s, Rose Hill Manor was the retirement home of Maryland's first elected governor, Thomas Johnson. Johnson had earlier nominated George Washington as commander-in-chief of the Continental Army. The manor was the center of social activity in the area for many years around the turn of the century.

Opened in 1972 as a 43-acre children's museum and park, costumed guides now conduct tours through exhibits which include the 200-year-old manor house; icehouse; smokehouse; herb, vegetable and rose garden; orchard; log cabin; blacksmith shop; and carriage collection. A Farm Museum tour is also available.

The manor is now divided into two sections. Downstairs is the Children's Museum, which offers more than 300 items for children to "explore." After an introduction by the tour guide, children are allowed to play and learn while taking stitches on a quilt, carding wool, playing with replica toys and costumes, and operating a beaten biscuit machine, food chopper, and cream separator. Upstairs, visitors can see historic furnishings in a study, master bedroom, children's bedroom and domestic quarters outfitted with furniture and accessories of that period.

Various activities and special events provide visitors of all ages with an educational hands-on and visual experience.

Info in brief: Hands-on experiences for children, along with village museum types of exhibits of interest to the entire family.

Location: Downtown Frederick, approximately 50 miles north of Washington, D.C.

Hours: Manor House (April–October) Monday–Saturday, 10 A.M. to 4 P.M.; Sunday, 1 P.M. to 4 P.M.; November — Saturday, 10 A.M.–9 P.M.; Sunday, 1–4 P.M. Park — Year-round, 8 A.M.–4:30 P.M.

Admissions: Under 3, free; children (3–17), $4; adults (18–54), $6; seniors (55+), $4.

Unique exhibitions: The combination of historical displays and hands-on exhibits offers a unique way for visitors to learn about and experience history in motion.

Other sites of interest nearby: Washington, D.C., attractions; Ceresville Mansion, four national battlefields (Monocacy, Antietam, Harpers Ferry, and Gettysburg National Military Park/National Cemetery), Catoctin Mountain Zoological Park, Lilypons Water Gardens, several historic churches, historic landmarks, and other historic sites. (Be sure to contact the Tourism Council of Frederick County, Inc., at 1-800-999-3613 or 301-663-8687 for tour map and information.)

For further information write to Children's Museum, Rose Hill Manor Park, 1611 N. Market Street, Frederick, Maryland 21701-4304, or call (301) 600-1650. *www.cofrederick.md.us*

MASSACHUSETTS

Amelia Park Children's Museum

Westfield

Amelia Park is a place where hands-on exhibits invite children to "experiment, create and play." The new 10,000 sq. ft. museum offers exhibits from their previous structure (Bicycle Tour of Westfield, Touch Tank, Doctor's Office, Lizard Habitat, Reading Treehouse and Bank) as well as new and larger exhibits.

Info in brief: Reopened in 2008 with a reduced number of exhibits until more money is raised.

Location: Downtown Westfield, next to the Boys & Girls Club, 29 S. Broad Street.

Hours: Monday, Wednesday, Thursday, Saturday, Sunday, 10 A.M. thru 4 P.M.; Tuesday, closed; Friday, 10 A.M. thru 7 P.M.

Admission: Adults, children 12 mos and older, $7; senior citizen, 60+, $3.50; military personnel, $3.50; children under age one, free.

For further information write to Amelia Park Children's Museum, P.O. Box 931, Westfield, MA 01086-0931 or call (413) 572-4014 or fax (413) 572-1206. *www.ameliaparkmuseum.org*

The Boston Children's Museum
Boston

Boston Children's Museum, one of the oldest children's museums in the U.S., has been in existence for more than 90 years, and has been a great influence on the development of children's museums for all those years. It is recognized internationally as a development and research center, and as a pacesetter for children's exhibitions, curriculum and educational programs. The "NEW Boston Children's Museum" opened in 2006. Again leading the way for children's museums across the country, The New Boston Children's Museum is committed to incorporating green strategies into the Children's Wharf activities as another standard for the youth museum industry. The museum team is proud to show off the "Dream Green" activities that are being put into place.

Exhibits at The Children's Museum in Boston target children from pre-school age to teens. Two popular exhibits are El Mercado del Barrio (a kid-size neighborhood market) and Teen Tokyo, where visitors can even try sumo wrestling.

Info in brief: A leading children's hand-on museum for infants thru teens and their families.

Location: Children's Wharf at 300 Congress St. in Boston. (Due to road construction in the area, as well as complicated driving conditions, it might be wise to use public transportation to visit the museum. If so, please note that children 11 and under ride free on MBTA Lines when accompanied by a paying adult.)

Hours: Open every day 10 A.M. to 5 P.M., with extended time on Fridays until 9 P.M. Closed Thanksgiving and Christmas.

Admissions: Under 1, free; 1 year-olds, $2; children (2–15), $8; seniors, (65+) $8; adults (16–64), $10. Memberships available.

Other sites of interest nearby: Other Children's Wharf activities, as well as the many historic and cultural sites of Boston.

For further information write to The Children's Museum, 300 Congress St., Boston, Massachusetts 02210, or call (617) 426-6500. *www.bostonchildrensmuseum.org* E-mail: *info@bostonchildrens museum.org*

Cape Cod Children's Museum
Mashpee

The Cape Cod Children's Museum's exhibits include a pirate ship, an indoor planetarium, a puppet theater, and a toddler play area. Permanent science exhibits include whisper dishes and Bernoulli exhibit. Math & problems-solving exhibits include geo-boards, brainteasers and optical illusions. Daily programs are also presented. New exhibits are being planned.

Hours: Tuesday–Thursday, 10 A.M.–3 P.M.; Friday & Saturday, 10 A.M.–5 P.M.; Sunday, noon–5 P.M. Summer hours (Memorial Day–Labor Day): Monday thru Saturday, 10 A.M.–5 P.M.; Sunday, noon–5 P.M. Open all Monday holidays and Mondays during local school vacation weeks. Closed most other major holidays.

Admissions: Under 1, free; kids (1–4), $5; seniors (60+), $5; adults (5–59), $6. Memberships available.

For further information write to Cape Cod Children's Museum, 577 Great Neck Road South, Mashpee, MA 02649 or call (508) 539-8788.

Children's Museum
Holyoke

At the time of this publication, the Children's Museum in Holyoke was undergoing major on-site construction, so contact the museum for updated information. Continuing exhibits include: Paperworks, where visitors make their own paper; Cityscape, a downtown city street role-play area; and TotLot, for preschoolers. New exhibits planned include: "Do Something Constructive," an interactive building site; "CMTV-40," television studio; "The Body Playground," a health and well-being center.

Info in brief: A hands-on museum for children and their caregivers. Undergoing major construction at time of publication, so contact the museum for current information about exhibits.

Hours: Wednesday–Saturday, 10 A.M. to 4 P.M.; Sunday, noon to 4 P.M. Open many school holidays. Check with museum for current hours.

Admissions: Under 1, free; $6 per visitor; seniors, $3. Memberships available.

For further information write to the Children's Museum, 444 Dwight St. at Heritage Park, Holyoke, Massachusetts 01040-5842, or call (413) 536-7048. *www.childrensmuseumholyoke.org*

The Children's Museum in Easton
North Easton

The Children's Museum in Easton is a small hands-on museum, with many different activities and exhibits to keep its visitors entertained and educated. Children can climb a fire pole and ring a bell, try on a new look at the face-painting center, or be a star on the stage in our Performance Center. They can also be a doctor in the Kidsclinic, or be a Lumberjack/Lumberjill in the new woodworking room. Changing themes and exhibits, special classes and workshops, and after-school programs are also offered throughout the year. Special events that help get the community and staff together, occur at different times during the year. Newest to the museum is the FETCH! Lab, which is a science education section of the museum based on the WGBH television show for children, *FETCH!* with Ruff Ruffman.

Info in brief: Small, hands-on, exploratory museum for young children and their caregivers.

Location: Historic North Easton Village in the Old Fire Station, 9 Sullivan Avenue.

Hours: Tuesday–Friday, 9 A.M. to 5 P.M.; Saturday & Sunday, noon to 5 P.M. Open some Monday holidays.

Admissions: Under 1, free; all others, $6.

For further information write to The Children's Museum in Easton, P.O. Box 417, North Easton, Massachusetts 02356, or call (508) 230-3789. *www.childrensmuseumineaston.org* Email: *info@child rensmuseumineaston.org*

Above: *The Children's Museum in Easton has a space for toddlers only.* Below: *The outdoor learning area at the Children's Museum in Easton.*

Children's Museum of Plymouth
Plymouth

The Children's Museum of Plymouth is both a hands-on children's museum with interactive exhibits and a whale watching boat.

Location (physical address): 46 Main St., Plymouth, MA in Cordage Park.

For further information write to the Children's Museum of Plymouth, P.O. Box 3030, Cordage Park, Plymouth, MA 02360.

Danforth Museum of Art
Framingham

The Danforth Museum of Art is a contemporary art museum which features six galleries of 19th- and 20th-century American prints, drawings, paintings, photographs and sculptures. Hands-on activities for children are offered on a regular basis. Be sure to contact the museum for current information.

Hours: Wednesday–Sunday, noon to 5 P.M.; Friday & Saturday, 10 A.M. to 5 P.M.

Admissions: Small admissions charge.

For further information write to the Danforth Museum of Art, 123 Union Ave., Framingham, Massachusetts, or call (508) 620-0060. *www.danforthmuseum.org*

Discover Westfield Children's Museum/Library
Westfield

Discover Westfield Children's Museum is a children's museum that offers interdisciplinary exhibits and a research library.

Location (physical address): 99 Elm Street, Westfield, MA 01085.

Hours: Monday, Thursday & Friday, 10 A.M.–4:30 P.M.; Saturday, 10 A.M.–1 P.M.; Sunday, 1 P.M.–4 P.M.

For further information write to Discover Westfield Children's Museum/Library, P.O. Box 931, Westfield, MA 01085 or call (413) 572-4014 or fax (413) 572-1206.

Discovery Days Children's Museum
DennisPort

Activities at Discovery Days teach about the environment, culture and more through the use of interactive exhibits.

For further information write to Discovery Days Children's Museum, 444 Main Street, Dennis-Port, MA 02639 or call (508) 396-1600.

The Discovery Museums
Acton

The Discovery Museums are actually two adjacent houses offering hands-on, interactive exhibits for children of all ages. The Children's Discovery Museum is housed in a 100-year-old

Victorian home, and offers ten hands-on exhibit areas specifically for toddlers and preschoolers and their caregivers. The Science Discovery Museum is in the second house and offers creative challenging interactive, hands-on experiences with basic science and math themes for older children.

The Children's Discovery Museum opened in 1981 in a three-story, 3,500 sq. ft. building, emphasizing "learning through play." The Science Discovery Museum opened in 1987 and is now an award-winning museum, with 8,500 sq. ft. of space dedicated to the sciences and math for older children (basically 6 years through the teens).

Info in brief: Two adjacent houses filled with hands-on, interactive exhibits; watch for "Bessie," the green dinosaur, out front.

Hours: Children's Museum: Tuesday thru Sunday, 9 A.M.–4:30 P.M. Science Museum: Tuesday, Thursday and Friday, 1 P.M.–4:30 P.M.; Wednesday 1 P.M.–6 P.M.; Saturday and Sunday, 9 A.M.–4:30 P.M. Both museums are open during some school holidays.

Admissions: Children's Museum: under 1, free; seniors, $8; all others, $9. Science Museum: under 1, free; under 3, $5; seniors, $8; all others, $9. Both Buildings same day: under 1, free; seniors, $12; all others, $13. Special days (Sunday mornings, 9 A.M.–noon): under 3, free; $6 for 1 building; $8 for both. Memberships available.

Other sites of interest nearby: Boston tourist attractions, including 34 museums.

For further information write to The Discovery Museums, 177 Main Street, Acton, Massachusetts 01720, or call (978) 264-4200. *www.discoverymuseums.org*

EcoTarium
Worcester

The primary target audience of the EcoTarium is families. It is an environmental museum whose aim is to use natural history collections, astronomy, living wildlife, cutting-edge technology and informations systems, and an extensive natural grounds area to encourage visitors to learn to live in and care for our natural environment. Events such as lectures, film series, and a jazz concert series are aimed at adults, but the museum does offer a "Discovery Room" for preschoolers and a special preschool day each month. A narrow-gauge railroad and the wildlife also attract young visitors.

The private non-profit organization that oversees EcoTarium was founded in 1825 as the Worcester Lyceum of Natural History. It was incorporated in 1884 as the Worcester Natural History Society, which is EcoTarium's legal identity. In 1998, the New England Science Center became EcoTarium, and refocused exhibits to feature more hands-on exploration and discovery for students in grades K–12. Along with the name change and refocus of exhibits, the building and grounds were greatly transformed.

EcoTarium now features three floors of exhibits that make creative use of the natural history collection and living wildlife already on site. Some of the exhibits include: Freshwater Ecosystems: Look, Touch, Explore; Water Planet; MicroDiner: African Communities; Thinking Globally, Abiding Locally; Minerals, DinoTracks, Secrets of the Forest, and Curator's Workshop. In addition, special programs and special events are offered throughout the year. Be sure to contact the museum for an events calendar. A Planetarium, Explorer Express Train and Tree Canopy Walkway (seasonal) are also on site.

Info in brief: An environmental education center with hands-on activities for students in grades K–12. Wildlife opportunities are also available.

Location: About 40 minutes east of Springfield and about 45 minutes west of Boston.

Hours: Tuesday–Saturday, 10 A.M. to 5 P.M.; Sunday, noon to 5 P.M. Closed some holidays.

Admissions: Under 3, free; children (3–18), $8; college students (with ID), $8; adults, $10; seniors,

$8. Planetarium shows, $5. Train rides, $2.50. Tree Canopy Walkway (seasonal), $9. Free parking is available. Member ASTC.

Unique features: The museum stems from one of the oldest natural history societies in America and has kept all of those collections.

Other sites of interest nearby: The Worcester Art Museum, Higgins Armory Museum, several Massachusetts Audubon Society sanctuaries, and many historic sites within the Blackstone River Valley National Heritage Corridor (birthplace of the American Industrial Revolution); Roger Williams Zoo (in Providence) and the Basketball Hall of Fame (in Springfield).

For further information write to EcoTarium, 222 Harrington Way, Worcester, Massachusetts 01604, or call (508) 929-2700 or fax (508) 929-2701. TDD (508) 929-2702. E-mail: *info@ecotarium.org*

Hull Lifesaving Museum
Hull

Although primarily a special-interest collections museum, the Hull Lifesaving Museum offers hands-on learning activities for children. An 1889 U.S. Life Saving Station has been furnished and equipped as a living museum about Boston harbor shipwreck rescues.

Most hands-on exhibits are housed in "The Children's Navigation Loft," a special play attic for kids, with dress-up trunks, games, puzzles, maritime activities, and a climb-in sailing ship. Besides the hands-on exhibits, visitors can see the surfboat "Nantasket," a watchtower, a lighthouse display and can participate in rowing programs.

Info in brief: A collections museum with some hands-on activities for children.

Location: Physical location —1117 Nantasket Avenue.

Hours: Open year-round. Contact museum for seasonal hours.

Admissions: Adults, $5; seniors, $3; 18 & under, free.

Other sites of interest nearby: The many tourist attractions of nearby Boston.

For further information write to the Hull Lifesaving Museum, P.O. Box 221, Hull, Massachusetts 02045, or call (781) 925-LIFE (5433) or fax (781) 925-0992. E-mail: *lifesavingmuseum@comcast.net*

MIT Museum
Cambridge

The MIT Museum offers visitors of all ages the chance to explore fascinating new technologies. Among other exhibits, visitors can create intricate mathematical structures and experiment to see how art and science are related.

Info in brief: A technical science museum with some hands-on exhibits for children.

Hours: Daily, 10 A.M. to 5 P.M. Closed major holidays.

Other sites of interest nearby: Sports Museum of New England, USS *Constitution* Museum, Paul Revere House, New England Aquarium, Museum of Our National Heritage, Museum of Science (Boston), Children's Museum (Boston), Computer Museum, Danforth Museum of Art, Discovery Museums (Acton), and many more tourist attractions in Boston and the surrounding areas.

For further information write to MIT Museum, 265 Massachusetts Ave., Cambridge, Massachusetts, or call (617) 253-4444. *http://web.mit.edu/museum*

Museum of Our National Heritage
Lexington

The Museum of Our National Heritage is an American History museum which features changing exhibits, including decorative arts, folk art, toys, famous Americans, and more. Although no permanent hands-on exhibits are on display, hands-on activities are offered by the museum frequently.

Hours: Monday–Saturday, 10 A.M. to 5 P.M. Sunday, noon–5 P.M.

Admissions: Free. Free parking.

For further information write to the Museum of Our National Heritage, 33 Marrett Road, Lexington, Massachusetts 02173, or call (781) 861-6559 or (781) 861-9846. *www.nationalheritagemuseum.org*

Museum of Science
Boston

The Museum of Science in Boston is a hands-on, exploratory museum for children with over 700 interactive exhibits on display, New England's only 180° IMAX Dome Theater, the Charles Hayden Planetarium, the Theater of Electricity, the Butterfly Garden, the 3-D Digital Cinema, and much more.

Location: Science Park in Boston.

Hours: (Labor Day–July 4) Saturday–Thursday, 9 A.M. to 7 P.M.; Friday, 9 A.M. to 9 P.M.; (July 5–Labor Day) Saturday–Thursday, 9 A.M. to 5 P.M.; Friday, 9 A.M. to 9 P.M.

Admissions: Member ASTC, AZA.

Other sites of interest nearby: Children's Museum on Congress St., Sports Museum of New England, USS *Constitution* Museum, Charles River Museum of Industry, Computer Museum on Museum Wharf, Discovery Museum on Main Street and more.

For further information write to the Museum of Science, Science Park, Boston, Massachusetts 02114-1099, or call (617) 723-2500. *www.mos.org*

New England Science Center *see* EcoTarium

Our World, Children's Global Discovery Museum
Cohasset

Our World Children's Global Discovery Museum was formally incorporated in 2001. Fundraising activities have been on-going, with plans to use the funds to renovate the original space into a state-of-the-art 10,000 sq. ft. children's cultural museum. Currently, the museum is located in a wing of the Cohasset Paul Pratt Memorial Public Library, and is accessible through the children's reading room.

In the fall of 2004, the first floor of the museum opened offering the Brooks Thomsen Singer Performance Center, the Culture Café and "Small World" (a toddler play space). The main exhibit hall opened in the Fall of 2005 with an exhibit called "Biodiversity 911: Saving Life on Earth," which was created by the World Wildlife Fund. This interactive exhibit showcases the world from an environmental perspective, helping visitors learn about our planet's precious resources. Global awareness, including cultural appreciation, is the focus for future exhibits as well.

Info in brief: A cultural awareness children's museum, with a goal of teaching a sense of global citizenship on both environmental and human levels.

Location: Attached to the Cohasset Paul Pratt Memorial Public Library, 100 Sohier Street.

Hours: Wednesday thru Friday, 10 A.M.–5 P.M.

Admissions: $5 per person. Memberships available.

For further information write to Our World, Children's Global Discovery Museum, P.O. Box 422, Cohasset, MA 02025 or call (781) 383-3198. *www.ourworld3.homestead.com*

The Sports Museum
Boston

"As A Boston taxi driver once remarked, 'A sports museum in Boston is like an art museum in Paris,' Indeed, nowhere else in the country is the passion for sports so intense, the tradition as deep, or the shared experience as broad." (Rusty Sullivan, Exec. Dir.) The Boston Sports Museum honors our leading athletes and citizens by preserving and showcasing the distinctly rich sports heritage of New England through an unparalleled collection (reportedly covering a space of more than a half-mile) of artifacts, multimedia, works of art, and interactive exhibits. Film, videos, photographs and research materials are also one of the finest of its kind in North America.

Founded in 1977, the mission of the museum is to use sports to teach the values of leadership, respect, and cooperation to our youth. Some of the programs/exhibits offered to enhance this mission include: "Stand Strong" (standing against drugs and violence), "Sports Figures," "Careers in Sports," and "The Will McDonough Writing Contest."

Location: Levels 5 and 6 of the TD Banknorth Garden.

Hours: Monday–Sunday, 11:00 A.M. to 5 P.M. (Admission is limited to 11 A.M., 12 P.M., 1 P.M., 2 P.M. and 3 P.M.) Hours subject to change due to TD Banknorth Garden events—call ahead for current hours.

Admissions: Under 6, free; ages 6–17 & seniors (60+), $4; adults, $6. Memberships available. (Visitors may purchase tickets at the TD Banknorth Garden Box Office, located on the West Side of the North Station Platform, next to the Pro Shop. The Museum's entrance is located at the Premium Club's Private Entrance also located on the West Side.) Be sure to inquire about parking before visiting.

Other sites of interest nearby: Children's Museum on Congress St., Sports Museum of New England, USS *Constitution* Museum, Charles River Museum of Industry, Computer Museum on Museum Wharf, Discovery Museum on Main Street and more.

For further information write to The Sports Museum, 100 Legends Way, Boston, Massachusetts 02114, or call (617) 624-1237. *www.tdbanknorthgarden.com/sportsmuseum/*

MICHIGAN

Alfred P. Sloan Museum
Flint

The Sloan Museum chronicles Flint's dramatic history as the birthplace of General Motors. Basically a historical museum, the Sloan Museum also offers a hands-on children's discovery center, offering permanent exhibits, changing exhibitions and special events in three historic sites throughout the year.

Info in brief: A historical, collections-type museum with one special center designated as a hands-on "Discovery Center" for children.

Hours: Monday–Friday, 10 A.M. to 5 P.M.; Saturday and Sunday, noon to 5 P.M. Closed New Year's Eve & Day, Easter, Memorial Day, July 4th, Labor Day, Thanksgiving Day, and Christmas Eve & Day.

Admissions: (Includes Sloan Museum — main building, Buick Gallery & Research Center) under 2, free; child (3–11), $4; adult, $6; senior, $5. Member ASTC.

Unique exhibits: The history of General Motors is extensive.

Other sites of interest nearby: Crossroads Village & Huckleberry Railroad, The (Flint) Children's Museum, Flint Institute of Arts, Junction Valley Railroad, and many other tourist attractions in Flint and the surrounding areas.

For further information write to Alfred P. Sloan Museum, 1221 E. Kearsley St., Flint, Michigan 48503, or call (810) 237-3450. E-mail: *sloan@sloanlongway.org*

The Ann Arbor Hands-On Museum
Ann Arbor

The Ann Arbor Hands-On Museum was conceived in 1978. It took four years to renovate the city's historic landmark firehouse and convert it into a museum that officially opened in October of 1982 with only 25 exhibits. The facility has grown into an outstanding science center with over 250 participatory exhibits that teach about science, art and history. Over 500 volunteers work with the full-time staff members to offer programs that have won the museum several awards. Current plans call for even more expansions in the near future.

Currently, the 40,000 sq. ft. museum offers four floors of exhibits, including: First floor — "The Subject is You," where visitors learn about our bodies; second floor — "The World Around You" and "The Discovery Room," where visitors learn about physics, structures, waves, energy, other cultures and nature; third floor — "Crane's Roost," where visitors can explore light and optics; and the fourth floor — "How Things Work," where visitors play with simple machines, computers, math games and puzzles. Traveling exhibitions, classes and workshops, weekend demonstrations and other special programs are also offered throughout the year.

In 2003, the museum was named, "Best Museum" by the Detroit Free Press. In 2006, it was named the winner of "Best Museum" and "Best Kids' Activity" by Ann Arbor New Readers. It has also received national recognition from the National Science Foundation, the Institute of Museum and Library Services and the Association of Science and Technology Centers.

Info in brief: A hands-on, exploratory museum for children through middle-school ages and their families.

Location: Ann Arbor's Historic Landmark Firehouse and adjoining buildings.

Hours: Monday thru Saturday, 10 A.M. to 5 P.M.; Sunday, noon to 5 P.M. Closed most major holidays.

Admissions: Under 2, free; ages 2 & up, $7. Memberships available. Member ASTC.

For further information write to The Ann Arbor Hands-On Museum, 220 East Ann Street, Ann Arbor, Michigan 48104, or call (734) 995-5439. *www.aahom.org*

Curious Kids' Museum
St. Joseph

Over 100 hands-on-exhibits and activities in Science, history, culture and technology await families and children from ages 1 to 100. Some exhibits are: "The Global Child" (A day in the

Above: *Pretending is fun at the Curious Kids' Museum in Michigan.* Below: *The volcano slide is popular at the Curious Kids' Museum.*

life of a child from around the world, including language, costumes, music, family kitchen, school and outdoor activities), "Awesome Apple Orchard," "The RainForest," "Media Mania," "Curious Kids in Outer Space," "Earthquakes and Volcanoes," "Dino-riffic," "and more. Other activities include new programs each week, birthday parties, scout badge Quest programs and overnighters, traveling exhibits, and summer day camps. Plans are also underway for a new "Curiosity Zone" facility and a "Silver Beach Carousel Society" to open in 2009.

Info in brief: Hands-on discovery exhibits and programs in science, history, culture and technology.

Location: Downtown St. Joseph on the bluff overlooking Lake Michigan.

Hours: (Mid-September to Memorial Day) Wednesday–Saturday, 10 A.M. to 5 P.M.; Sunday, noon to 5 P.M. (June–Labor Day). Monday–Thursday and Saturday, 10 A.M. to 5 P.M. Fridays, 10 A.M. to 7 P.M. Sundays, noon to 5 P.M. Closed during major holidays and Labor Day to mid–September.

Admissions: Under 1, free; ages 1 & up $4.

Other sites of interest nearby: The beaches of Lake Michigan, Krasl Art Center, Bluff Trail with sculptures, lighthouses, and downtown St. Joseph shops and restaurants.

For further information write to Curious Kids' Museum, 415 Lake Boulevard, St. Joseph, Michigan 49085, or call (616) 983-CKID (2543). *www.curiouskidsmuseum.org* E-mail: *ckm@curiouskids museum.org*

The Detroit Science Center
Detroit

The Detroit Science Center offers live science demonstrations, hands-on exhibit galleries, and family programs, as well as Michigan's only IMAX Dome Theatre and a Dassaut Systemes Planetarium. The Dassault Systemes Planetarium's Digistar technology provides computer-generated images that have the ability to move in vibrant ways with more than 40 different special effects projectors, unlike traditional planetariums that have a "fixed" star field.

The 3,500 sq. ft. space features eight major exhibit areas— Dinosaurs, The Boundary Experience, Scapes, The Garden, Make and Take, The Family Area, Dramatic Play, and How Does Your Garden Grow. Various programs are offered monthly, and include classroom experiences and discussions, experiments, and hands-on activities to take home.

Info in brief: A hands-on and more museum for visitors of all ages.

Location: Corner of Warren Avenue and John R Street in the University Cultural Center.

Hours & Admissions: Visit the museums website for current information.

Other sites of interest nearby: The Charles H. Wright Museum of African American History, Detroit Institute of Arts, Detroit Historical Museum and Detroit Public Library.

For further information write to The Detroit Science Center, 5020 John R Street, Detroit, MI 48202. *www.detroitsciencecenter.org*

The Flint Children's Museum
Flint

Opened in 1986, the Flint Children's Museum is a "please touch" museum that offers hands-on experiences and programs for children 10 years and younger. More than 40 exhibits are offered, encouraging children to learn more about their world through the act of play. Main exhibit areas include: " "How Things Work," "Performing Stage and Dress-Up," "The Coach," "Smart Mart grocery store," "Fractions Pizza Parlor," "Sam's House," "Aerobic Sounds," "Recycled Rhythms," "Climbing Wall," and more. The *Tot Spot* is an area dedicated to museum visitors who are 3 and under.

Special programs are also offered, and children get to meet "Stuffee," a life-size stuffed doll that helps visitors learn about the human body.

Info in brief: A hands-on arts and humanities museum for children 10 years and younger.

Hours: Tuesday–Friday, 9 A.M. to 5 P.M.; Saturday, 10 A.M. to 5 P.M.; Closed Sundays, Mondays and major holidays.

Admissions: Under 1, free; all others, $4; groups of 20+. $3 per person. Memberships available. Member ASTC.

Other sites of interest nearby: Crossroads Village & Huckleberry Railroad, Alfred P. Sloan Museum, Flint Institute of Arts, Junction Valley Railroad, and many other tourist attractions in Flint and the surrounding areas.

For further information write to The Children's Museum, 1602 W. Third Ave., Flint, Michigan 45804, or call (810) 767-KIDS (5437). *www.flintchildrensmuseum.org*

Grand Rapids Children's Museum

Grand Rapids

The Grand Rapids Children's Museum is designed in such a way as to help children enjoy learning, by providing an interactive, hands-on environment that encourages self-directed exploration and learning. The target audience is children ages 2–10, and the exhibits reinforce cooperation, problems solving and life-long learning.

Every visit is a new experience, as exhibits are continually moved around the museum and major exhibits are rotated. Permanent exhibits include: Bubbles, Bubbles, Bubbles; Amigo Amphitheater; Mirror Magic; Funstruction; and Wee Discover (specifically for ages 5 and under).

Info in brief: A multi-disciplinary hands-on children's museum.

Hours: Tuesday thru Saturday, 9:30 A.M.–5 P.M.; Sunday, noon–5 P.M. Every Thursday from 5–8 P.M. is Family Night —$1 admission. Summer hours. (June thru August) include Monday, 9:30 A.M–5 P.M.

Admissions: Under 2, free; Seniors, $4.25; AAA discount $4.50; U.S. Military (with ID), half price; all others, $5. Paid parking is available.

For further information write to Grand Rapids Children's Museum, 11 Sheldon NE, Grand Rapids, MI 49503 or call (616) 235-GRCM (4726) or fax (616) 235-4728. *www.grcm.org*

Impression 5 Science Museum

Lansing

Impression 5 is a hands-on, participatory learning environment with a goal of challenging its visitors to experience, discover, and explore the world in which they live. Many exhibits have interpretive labels to help visitors explore specific concepts, while others are unlabeled, encouraging visitors to "learn by doing." Outreach programs are also offered.

Info in brief: Hands-on learning museum for children and their families.

Hours: Sunday, 12 P.M.–5 P.M.; Monday–Thursday, 10 A.M.–5 P.M.; Friday & Saturday, 10 A.M.– 7 P.M.

Admissions: Under 2, free; students (ages 3 to college, with ID), $4; seniors, $4; adults, $5. Member ASTC and ACM. 10% AAA Discount available.

For further information write to Impression 5 Science Center, 200 Museum Drive, Lansing, MI 48933 or call (517) 485-8116 or fax (517) 485-8125. *www.impression5.org*

Mid-Michigan Children's Museum

Saginaw

Scheduled to open in the Spring of 2008, the Mid-Michigan Children's Museum will be mid–Michigan's only hands-on museum offering exhibits for children 12 and under, with over

16,000 sq. ft. of gallery space, that is creatively designed to accommodate 11 continuing exhibit galleries. Rotating traveling exhibits and workshops will also be provided. The museum's exhibits and programs will work in conjunction with the school curriculum.

Info in brief: Hands-on museum specifically for children 12 and under.

Hours & Admissions: Costs have not yet been established at time of publication.

For further information write to the Mid-Michigan Children's Museum, 315 W. Genesee, Saginaw, MI 48602 or call (989) 399-6626. *www.midmicm.org*

The Old Deerfield Children's Museum at Indian House Memorial Hall
Deerfield

The new Children's Museum at Indian House Memorial Hall in Old Deerfield features age-appropriate hands-on experiences of history for children. Memorial Hall displays exhibits as they would have looked 100 years ago. The first floor offers hands-on experiences. (The door is kept locked, so visitors must ring the bell for admission.) Some of these experiences allow children and their caregivers to dress in 18th century clothing, try out a straw mattress, card and spin wool, write with a quill pen, play with old fashioned toys, read from a hornbook, make a tavern game, carry buckets with a yoke on your shoulders, and see what a 1700's kitchen and dinner looked like.

Info in brief: A hands-on history museum for children.

Location: Corner of Memorial Street and Rts. 5 & 10 in Deerfield.

Hours: Daily, May 1 to October 31, 11 A.M.–5 P.M.

Admissions: Memorial Hall Museum: under 6, free; youth/students (6–21), $3; adults, $6. "All of Deerfield Ticket" (includes Memorial Hall and the 14 historic houses in Historic Deerfield): under 6, free; youth/students, $5; adults, $14. (This ticket is valid for two consecutive days.) Memberships available.

For further information write to Memorial Hall Museum, 8 Memorial St., Deerfield, MA 01342 or call (413) 774-3768. E-mail: *pvmaoffice@deerfield.history.museum*

MINNESOTA

Duluth Children's Museum
Duluth

The Duluth Children's Museum, founded in 1930, is the fifth oldest children's museum in the country, and is one of the very few collection-based children's museums in the world. It is still an interactive, hands-on museum for children and their families. Major exhibits areas include: *Go Figure!* an interactive mathematics-based exhibit using giant storybook adventures; *Little Builders,* where children create and play as they learn construction, motion and simple machines concepts; *The Campsite,* where visitors can go on an outdoor camping adventure without even going outside; and *The Collection,* where visitors explore objects from around the world through game play and displays.

Info in brief: Both a hands-on and a collections-based museum.

Location: Historic Union Depot.

Hours: Labor Day to Memorial Day: Tuesday thru Saturday, 10 A.M.–5 P.M.; Sunday, 1 P.M.–5 P.M. Memorial Day to Labor Day: Monday thru Sunday, 9:30 A.M.–6 P.M.

Admissions: 2 & under, free; children 3–13, $5.50; adults, $10. These tickets also give access to the Duluth Art Institute, Lake Superior Railroad Museum, Veteran's Memorial, and the St. Louis County Historical Society exhibits. Memberships available. Member ACM and ASTC.

Other sites of interest nearby: Duluth Art Institute, Lake Superior Railroad Museum, Veteran's Memorial, and the St. Louis County Historical Society exhibits.

For further information write to the Duluth Children's Museum, 506 W. Michigan St., Duluth, MN 55802 or call (218) 733-7543 or fax (218) 733-7547. *www.duluthchildrensmuseum.org* E-mail: *explore@duluthchildrensmuseum.org*

Headwaters Environmental Learning Center
Bemidji

The Headwaters Environmental Learning Center opened in March of 1994 and is a science- and nature-oriented museum located in downtown Bemidji. Some of the 50 exhibits offered include: "Frozen Shadows," a darkroom with a strobe light; "Pitching Cage," which measures the velocity of a pitched ball; "Bubble Race"; a Bernouli Ball; "Symmetrigraph," a large apparatus that creates spirograph-type pictures; "Whisper Dishes"; "Laser Spirograph"; a small Hot Air Balloon; "Mirror Kaleidoscope"; and more. Several programs and demonstrations are also offered throughout the week.

Info in brief: A hands-on, interactive science museum for all members of the family, but of special interest to children.

Location: Downtown Bemidji, one block from Lake Bemidji.

Hours: Monday–Saturday, 9:30 A.M. to 5:30 P.M.; Sunday, 1 P.M. to 5 P.M.

Admissions: (Exhibit Floor) under 12, $3; adults & children 12 & older, $4; $20 max per family. (Demonstrations) $2. Hands-on activities, $3 per person. Memberships available. Member ASTC.

For further information write to Headwaters Science Center, 413 Beltrami Ave., Bemidji, Minnesota 56601, or call (218) 444-4472 or fax 444-4473. *www.hscbemidji.org*

Laura Ingalls Wilder Museum
Walnut Grove

Although not strictly a hands-on interactive area for children, this museum is included in this book because of its special appeal to children. For several generations children (and adults) have been fascinated by the "Little House on the Prairie" books and TV series. Memorabilia from Wilder's life and from the TV series are seen here.

Included in the exhibits are a quilt made by Laura and her daughter, a Bible from the Ingalls' church, scale models of the Ingalls' farm and TV series homes, historic documents, memorabilia of visits by "Little House" TV stars, the Kelton Doll Collection and much more. Seven buildings encompass the Museum displays with a life size Dugout, Early Settlers Home and small One-Room Schoolhouse. Hands-on activities are located throughout the complex.

The Wilder Pageant, an outdoor drama based on the life of Laura Ingalls Wilder in Walnut Grove, is presented regularly, and has been selected as one of the Top Annual Group Tour Festivals and Events for several years.

The Walnut Grove Family Festival is held in the City Park on Saturdays of the Laura Ingalls Wilder Pageant. Many special activities are being presented during that month, including historic bus tours, visiting dignitaries, and many other quality activities in City Park every Saturday.

Info in brief: A type of village museum of interest to all ages, but with special interest to children.

Hours: Memorial Day–Labor Day, 10 A.M. to 7 P.M.; May and September, 10 A.M. to 5 P.M.; April and October, 10 A.M. to 3 P.M.; appointments available.

Admissions: $2 per person.

Other sites of interest nearby: Mankato & N. Mankato (Minnesota's other Twin Cities), Minneopa State Park, New Ulm (an old German city), the town of Sleepy Eye, Petroglyphs, Lower Sioux Agency, Pipestone Monument and more.

For further information write to the Laura Ingalls Wilder Museum, 330 Eighth Street, Walnut Grove, Minnesota 56180, or call 1-866-305-2872 *www.walnutgrove.org*

Minnesota Children's Museum
St. Paul

Opened in 1995, the Minnesota Children's Museum is an interactive museum which encourages families to come and explore their world together through the arts, sciences and humanities. Children ages six months to 10 years are targeted in the hands-on exhibits and various programs. The six main galleries are called "One World," "World Works," "Habitot," "Earth World," "Changing World," and "World of Wonder." In the galleries, children are encouraged to crawl through a giant anthill, operate a crane, clamber up a musical sculpture, and more.

The Minnesota Children's Museum is in St. Paul.

Changing exhibits are also offered periodically. A daily reading time, special Bedtime Thursday Night reading time and book swaps are part of the program the museum has initiated to encourage reading in the community.

Info in brief: Hands-on, interactive museum for children 10 years and younger and their families.

Location: Downtown St. Paul at the corner of 7th Street and Wabasha.

Hours: The museum is typically open Tuesday through Sunday 9A.M.–5 P.M. and Fridays, 9 A.M.–8 P.M.

Admissions: Under 1, free; ages 1–101, $7.95. Memberships available.

Other sites of interest nearby: World Trade Center, Science Museum of Minnesota, Rice Park/Cultural District, Union Depot Place, Town Square entertainment complex, State Capitol buildings, and the Valleyfair Amusement Park located in Shakopee (about 20 minutes away).

For further information write to Minnesota Children's Museum, 10 W. 7th St., St. Paul, Minnesota 55102, or call (651) 225-6001. *www.MCM.org*

Runestone Museum
Alexandria

The Runestone Museum is named for the Kensington Runestone, a large stone with Runic writing carved on it, dating back to 1362. It was carved and left by Viking explorers who came from a settlement called Vinland in Nova Scotia. Vinland was the area of North America discovered by Leif Eriksson around a.d. 1000.

Other display areas include the Alexandria Room, featuring items from the 1800s specifically used in the area, a small theater showing a video about the Vikings and the Runestone, a Minnesota Wildlife area and an outside area called Fort Alexandria. This area enables visitors to see an actual fort built in 1863 due to the unrest between the Sioux Indians and the area settlers. In the fort are an authentic local area one-room schoolhouse with original artifacts, an old log cabin, a general store, a one-room church, and an agricultural building which features antique farm machinery, a rare old snowmobile, a doctor's office and other artifacts.

Although the museum is not an official children's museum, the managers say that the exhibits are displayed "with the intent of as much hands-on orientation as possible."

Info in brief: A small tourist attraction–type museum with opportunities for hands-on experiences.

Hours: Monday–Friday, 10 A.M. to 5 P.M.; Saturday, 10 A.M. to 4 P.M. (Summer) Monday–Friday, 9 A.M. to 5 P.M.; Saturday, 9 A.M. to 4 P.M.; Sunday, 11 A.M. to 4 P.M.

Admissions: Under 5, free; students (ages 5–17), $3; adults, $6; seniors, $5; family, $15.

Other sites of interest nearby: The Budd Car/North Shore Scenic Railroad in Duluth, Duluth-Lakefront Tour in Duluth, Lake Superior & Mississippi Railroad in Duluth, Lake Superior Museum of Transportation in Duluth, Minnesota Transportation Museum in Stillwater, North Star Rail in Bloomington, Paul Bunyan Center in Brainerd, and the Valleyfair Amusement Park in Shakopee. The Canadian border is also nearby.

For further information write to Runestone Museum, 206 Broadway, Alexandria, Minnesota 56308, or call (320) 763-3160 or fax (320) 763-9705. *www. runestonemuseum.org* E-mail: *bigole@rea-alp.com*

Science Museum of Minnesota
Minneapolis

The Science Museum of Minnesota features both natural history and technology. It has been a national leader in developing hands-on exhibits, Omnitheater films, school outreach and youth science programs, and more. Current exhibits include: "Dinosaurs and Fossils"; "Green Street," with exhibits about energy use and conservation; "Anthropology Hall," exploring the world's cultures; and "Experiment Gallery" with hands-on experiments galore. Other features of the museum include the Youth Computer Center (one of the first nationwide), Warner Nature Center (a 600-acre nature preserve), and the Omnitheater (second one built in the country).

The museum entered the new millennium, with a new, five-level Science Museum. This 350,000 sq. ft. facility features the latest Omnifilm technology, educational entertainment, outdoor activities at the Mississippi River, expanded and interconnected science halls indoors and out, a multi-acre nature center; discovery programs; hundreds of hands-on experiments, and a Youth Science Center for teens.

Info in brief: A hands-on (and more) science museum for children of all ages and their caregivers.

Location: Off I-94 and I-35E on the corners of Exchange and Wabasha in downtown St. Paul, 15 minutes from the Mall of America or downtown Minneapolis.

Hours: (Museum) Monday–Wednesday, 9:30 A.M. to 5 P.M.; Sunday, 11 A.M. to 5 P.M. Thursday to Saturday, 9:30 A.M. to 9 P.M.; Omnitheater show times. And Science Live Theater Performances, Contact the museum for times.

Admissions: Under 4, free. (Omnitheater/exhibits) children (4–15), $13; adults, $16; seniors (65+), $13. (Omnitheater only) children, $6.50; adults, $7.50; seniors, $6.50. (Exhibits only) children, $8.50; adults, $11; seniors, $8.50. (Omnifest) purchase a combination Omnitheater and exhibit hall ticket to see one film. Member ASTC.

Other sites of interest nearby: Paul Bunyan Center (Brainerd), Valleyfair Amusement Park (Shakopee), and the Ramsey & Dakota County Historical Tours (railroad).

For further information write to the Science Museum of Minnesota, 120 W. Kellogg Blvd., St. Paul, Minnesota 55102, or call (651) 221-9444 (TDD 221-4585) or fax (651) 221-4777. *www.smm.org* E-mail: *info@smm.org*

MISSISSIPPI

Mississippi Children's Museum
Jackson

The Mississippi Children's Museum is currently in the construction phase, with an expected opening date in 2009 or 2010. The new space will be a 43,000 sq. ft. structure with 20,000 sq. ft. of exhibit space. Five main themes based on Mississippi heritage will be: health & nutrition, literacy, cultural arts, and science & technology.

Location: Old National Guard Armory on the Mississippi State Fairgrounds.

For further information write to Mississippi Children's Museum, 2260 Ridgewood Rd., Ste. 500, Jackson, MS 39216 or P.O. Box 55409, Jackson, MS 39296-5409 or call (601) 981-5469.

MISSOURI

American Royal Museum, American Royal Association
Kansas City

The American Royal Association is sponsor of the American Royal Livestock, Horse Show and Rodeo. The American Royal Museum is another facet of the Association, offering three main exhibit areas: "History," "The American Royal" (a livestock horse show/rodeo), and "Hands-On" (exploratory museum for children).

In the hands-on area, children can judge livestock and compare their scores with professional judges, weigh themselves on a real Fairbanks livestock scale, grind wheat, learn about milling, use microscopes (to inspect hides, hooves, bones, and more), dress up in Western and English riding attire, sit on saddles and see themselves in the ring, play with puppets in the barn area, visit a mini theater showing rodeo and horseshow vignettes, see movies about the American Royal and agriculture, and play computer games such as The Oregon Trail and Ag Ease. Docents are available if needed, or visitors can explore the museum and some of its facilities on their own.

Info in brief: A hands-on museum for children, with other areas more of interest to adults. Targeted audience would be families especially interested in livestock, horses and other agricultural pursuits, as well as families with an interest in the American West and history.

Location: Historic River Bottoms District.

Hours: Tuesday–Friday, 10 A.M. to 4 P.M.; Saturday and Sunday, by appointment only. Open some weekends for special events. Be sure to contact the Association for current information.

Admissions: In the process of changing at time of publication.

Unique exhibits: Unique theme of livestock, and agriculture, chronicling the history of Kansas City and America's move West.

Other sites of interest nearby: Oceans of Fun Water Park, Worlds of Fun Amusement Park, and other Kansas City tourist attractions.

For further information write to the American Royal Association & Visitors Center, 1701 American Royal Court, Kansas City, Missouri 64102, or call (816) 221-9800 or fax (816) 221-8189. *www.americanroyal.com*

Bootheel Youth Museum
Malden

The Bootheel Youth Museum offers children and their caregivers a number of interactive, hands-on exhibits with multidisciplinary focuses on math, science, human relations, natural resources and the arts. Besides the 22,000 sq. ft. exhibit hall, a 180-seat theater is on site. Their traveling museum is often taken to schools within a 100-mile radius. *This Island Mars* features more than 20 interactive exhibits and an innovative visit to the Red Planet. Other exhibits include the construction zone, and Mother Nature's earthquake exhibit.

Info in brief: A 22,000 sq. ft. hands-on children's museum.

Location: Southeastern Missouri. Physical address: 700A N. Douglas, Malden.

Hours: Tuesday thru Saturday, 10 A.M.— 4 P.M.; Sunday, 1 P.M.–4 P.M.; Mondays are by appointment only.

Admissions: Under 3, free; children 3–17, $5; all others, $3.

For further information write to Bootheel Youth Museum, P.O. Box 182, Malden, MO 63863 or call (573) 276-3600. *www.bootheelyouthmuseum.org*

Discovery Center of Springfield, Inc.
Springfield

Incorporated in 1991, the Discovery Center first purchased and renovated the building site in downtown Springfield in 1998. In 2006, the facility was expanded and exhibits were permanently installed. Between 1992 and 1998 more renovations and improvements were made, until, in 1998, the DCS opened its doors with one programming area, a small summer workshop program and a handful of exhibits. In 2007, another renovation and a 30,000 sq. ft. expansion doubled exhibit space and created the first "Green" building in southwest Missouri.

The Discovery Center currently houses 60,000 square feet of interactive exhibit space offering a broad array of exhibits in hard sciences, technology, math, health, the environment, culture, art and communication. Specific traveling exhibits are brought in two or three times a year.

Info in brief: A 60,000 sq. ft. children's museum with a variety of exhibits.

Location: Downtown Springfield.

Hours: Tuesday thru Thursday, 9 A.M.–5 P.M.; Friday, 9 A.M.–8 P.M.; Saturday, 10 A.M.–5 P.M.; Sunday, 1 P.M.–5 P.M. Closed New Year's Day, Easter, Thanksgiving and Christmas Day.

Admissions: Under 3, free; children ages 3–12, $5; seniors (65+), $6; adults, $7. Special Experience Tickets: Highwire Bike Ride, $3 and Immersion Cinema, $3. Memberships available. Member ASTC.

For further information write to the Discovery Center of Springfield, Inc., 438 E. St. Louis St., Springfield, MO 65806. Or call (417) 862-9910 or fax (417) 862-6898. *www.discoverycenter.org*

Hallmark Visitor's Center
Kansas City

Located in the same facility as Kaleidoscope, the Hallmark Visitor's Center offers visitors an opportunity to watch Hallmark artists at work. Both facilities are part of the Crown Center complex which is a three-level area offering shopping and dining, two luxury hotels, exquisite office building, a residential community and several entertainment attractions (including the Visitor's Center and Kaleidoscope).

Visitors get a close-up look at Hallmark's creative staff; watch a 15-minute media presentation (*Coming From the Heart*), and experience the fun of Hallmark's interactive exhibits. Some of the exhibits offered include a virtual visit with Hoops & YoYo, Astroid Andy, and other colorful Hallmark characters; experiences with new computer kiosks where visitors learn about Hallmark; make a bow; and visit with on-site craftspeople.

Info in brief: An interactive way to learn about Hallmark Cards, artists, etc.

Location: Crown Center Complex, Hallmark Square.

Hours: Tuesday thru Friday, 9 A.M.–5 P.M.; Saturday, 9:30 A.M.–4 P.M.

Admissions: Free; parking is also free with a three-hour validation in the Crown Center parking garage, 2450 Grand Blvd.

Other sites of interest nearby: Kaleidoscope, American Royal Museum, Oceans of Fun Water Park, Worlds of Fun Amusement Park, and other Kansas City tourist attractions.

For further information write to Hallmark Visitor's Center, 2405 Grand Blvd, Ste. 200, Kansas City, MO 64108 or call (816) 274-3613 www.hallmarkvisitorscenter.com or www.visitorscenter@hallmark. com

Kaleidoscope
Kansas City

Kaleidoscope is a creative art experience, where children and their families can be creative, have fun, and feel good about their own special ideas. At Kaleidoscope, children use their imagination to make art with paper, ribbon, melted crayons, and tons of bright, shiny, wiggly, sparkly, fluffy, puffy stuff. Kaleidoscope offers two different session types: Independent Art sessions for school-aged children to enjoy the studio all on their own (while the adults get a chance to do some shopping), or Family Art sessions for children of all ages to enjoy the experience with their adults.

Info in brief: A hands-on participatory creative art program

Location: Crown Center, outside of the third level of Halls, at Crown Center, an 80-acre campus in Kansas City that includes hotels, great shopping and dining and the worldwide headquarters of Hallmark Cards, Inc.

Hours: Session types and times vary. Reservations may be needed depending on the size of the group and the type of session selected. Call (816) 274-8300 or visit the website below.

Admissions: Free. Kaleidoscope is a public service of Hallmark Cards, Inc.

Other sites of interest nearby: The Toy and Miniature Museum of Kansas City, Kansas Cosmosphere & Space Center, Kansas City Museum, Jesse James historic sites, Kansas City Zoo, NCAA Hall of Champions, Nelson-Atkins Museum of Art, Auto Museum, American Royal Museum & Visitors Center, and other Kansas City tourist attractions.

For further information write to Kaleidoscope, Hallmark Square at Crown Center, P.O. Box 419580, Kansas City, Missouri 64141-6580, or call (816) 274-8300 or 8301. www.hallmarkkaleidoscope.com

Kansas City Museum/Science City
Kansas City

The Kansas City Museum/Science City is housed in Union Station, along with other museum offering historic exhibits and displays. Science City is the children's hands-on museum offering more than 50 exhibit areas.

Info in brief: A family museum with hands-on activities for children.

Location: Kansas City's historic Union Station.

Hours: Tuesday–Friday, 9:30 A.M. to 5:30 P.M.; Sunday, noon to 5 P.M. Contact museum for up-to-date schedules for Regnier Extreme Screen, and H&R Block City State showtimes. Closed most major holidays.

Admissions: Under 3, free; children (3–17), $2; adults, $2.50; seniors, $2. Member ASTC. Parking—first 3 hours are free, then $1 per half hour thereafter, with $10 maximum.

Other sites of interest nearby: Kaleidoscope, Toy and Miniature Museum, Jesse James historic sites, Kansas City Zoo, NCAA Hall of Champions, American Royal Museum & Visitors Center, Kansas Cosmosphere & Space Center, and other Kansas City attractions.

For further information write to the Kansas City Museum/Science City, 30 W. Pershing Rd, Kansas City, Missouri 64108, or call (816) 460-2020. www.sciencecity.com or www.unionstation.org

Science City at Union Station is in Kansas City, Missouri.

The Magic House, St. Louis Children's Museum

St. Louis

According to their research, The Magic House in Kirkwood in St. Louis is the third most popular children's museum in the United States. This hands-on museum is partially housed in a Victorian mansion built in 1901 as a private home for the George Lane Edwards family. After serious renovations, The Magic House opened to the public in October of 1979 operating solely on admissions fees. In 1985, a 2,000 sq. ft. exhibition area for children ages 1–7 was added, with

Artist's rendering of The Magic House, soon to be opened in St. Louis.

exhibits encouraging the enhancement of gross motor skills, self-concept and self-esteem. In 1987, "The Gallery" opened with a collection that explores the relationship between art and modern technology. Today, after more renovations and improvement, four floors are packed with more than 100 hands-on exhibits for children of all ages. Special events, outreach programs and workshops are also offered. At the time of this writing, the museum had plans for an expansion program that would double the size of the museum.

Info in brief: Large participatory museum for children of all ages.

Location: One mile north of I-44 on Lindbergh Blvd.

Hours: (School year) Tuesday–Thursday, 12 P.M. to 5:30 P.M.; Friday, 12 P.M. to 9 P.M.; Saturday, 9:30 A.M. to 5:30 P.M.; Sunday, 11:00 A.M. to 5:30 P.M. (Summer) Monday, Wednesday, Thursday and Saturday, 9:30 A.M. to 5:30 P.M.; Tuesday & Friday, 9:30 A.M. to 9 P.M.; Sunday, 11:30 A.M. to 5:30 P.M.

Admissions: Under 1, free; adults & children, $7.50. Member of AYM. Free parking is available.

Other sites of interest nearby: St. Louis Gateway Arch, the St. Louis Zoo, Six Flags Over Mid-America and other St. Louis tourist attractions.

For further information write to The Magic House, St. Louis Children's Museum, 516 S. Kirkwood Rd. (Lindbergh Blvd.), St. Louis, Missouri 63122, or call (314) 822-8900. *www.themagichouse.org*

St. Louis Science Center
St. Louis

The St. Louis Science Center is a complex of three buildings which feature more than 650 exhibits on ecology and environment, aviation, technology, human adventure and space sciences. Exhibits include life-size, animated dinosaurs, an underground tunnel, and 24 outdoor playground-type exhibits. An Omnimax Theater shows films on a four-story domed screen and a planetarium features high-tech star shows and laser shows. Traveling exhibitions are also offered twice each year.

Info in brief: A hands-on, interactive and exploratory museum for children and their caregivers.

Location: West of Kings Highway, off I-64.

Hours: Monday–Thursday, 9:30 A.M. to 4:30 P.M.; Friday, 9:30 A.M. to 9:30 P.M.; Saturday, 9:30 A.M. to 4:30 P.M.; Sunday, 11:30 A.M. to 4:30 P.M.

Admissions: Free. Discovery Room, $3. Lego MINDSTORMS, $3. OMNIMAX — students (wID), $8; child & senior, $9; adults, $10. Planetarium —child & senior, $9; adult, $5. Monster Exhibit — child & senior, $7; adult, $8. Segway Courses, $5–35. Science Café— students, $10; adult, $20. All-day parking, $8. Member ASTC.

Other sites of interest nearby: The many tourist attractions in St. Louis.

For further information write to the St. Louis Science Center, 5050 Oakland Ave., St. Louis, Missouri 63110, or call 1-800-456-SLSC or (314) 289-4400 or fax (314) 533-8687. Website: *www.slsc.org* E-mail: *bpharms@slsc.org*

Science City at Union Station *see* Kansas City Museum/Science City

The Toy and Miniature Museum of Kansas City
Kansas City

Although The Toy and Miniature Museum is not a hands-on museum, the content of the collections is of much interest to children. It is the only museum of its kind in the Midwest and is considered to be one of the best in the world. At the museum, visitors find miniatures, toys, dolls and doll houses dating from the 19th century to the present day. All miniatures have been reduced to an exact scale and represent an historically correct replica of the original — most of which actually work. The Toys and Dolls exhibits help teach children about past generations and their surroundings. The doll houses in this collection range in date from the early 1800s to the mid–20th century.

Besides the regular exhibits, puppet shows and other special events for children are offered throughout the year. Holiday events are especially festive. Contact the museum for an updated schedule.

After opening several years ago in an elegant and historic Kansas City mansion, a renovation plan and addition were finally completed in 1989, bringing the total exhibit space up to over 21,000 sq. ft. The mansion/museum actually sits on the University of Missouri–Kansas City campus.

Info in brief: A collections-type museum whose content is of special interest to children.

Location: University of Missouri–Kansas City campus.

Hours: Wednesday–Saturday, 10 A.M. to 4 P.M.; Sunday, 1 P.M. to 4 P.M. Closed Monday and Tuesday, major holidays and annually the first two weeks in September.

Admissions: Under 5, free; children (5–12), $4: seniors/students, $5; adults, 6.

Other sites of interest nearby: Kaleidoscope, Jesse James historic sites, Kansas City Zoo, NCAA Hall of Champions, American Royal Museum & Visitors Center, Kansas Cosmosphere & Space Center, and other Kansas City attractions.

For further information write to The Toy & Miniature Museum of Kansas City, 5235 Oak St., Kansas City, Missouri 64112, or call (816) 333-9328. *www.umkc.edu* E-mail: *tmm@umkc.edu*

YouZeum/Health Adventure Center
Columbia

Opening in the Spring of 2008, the YouZeum will offer a multitude of interactive exhibits, programs and activities about how your body works and about what you should do to keep it healthy. Exhibits let visitors ride through the Cycle Challenge, "test your reflexes" in virtual reality games, experience a 3D adventure through the body, visit an All Foods Diner, visit "Snackster"—a talking vending machine and more.

Info in brief: An interactive science center dedicated to health topics.

Hours & Admissions: Not available at time of publication.

For further information write to YouZeum, 608 Cherry St., Columbia, MO 65201 or call (573) 886-2006 or fax (573) 874-1566. *www.youzeum.org* E-mail: *info@youzeum.org*

MONTANA

Children's Museum of Bozeman
Bozeman

The Children's Museum of Bozeman opened in 2003. Exhibits include permanent exhibits like *Our Big Sky Home, Bubble Wall, Magnetic Canvas Toddler Area, Visit the Old West, Bobcat*

Court, Doctor's Office, Reading Corner, Puppet Theater and Pinball Machine. Traveling exhibits are also offered periodically. The museum also has a Mobile Experiment Laboratory (MEL).

Info in brief: A hands-on museum for children.

Location: Downtown Bozeman.

Hours: Monday thru Thursday, 10 A.M.–5 P.M.; Friday, 10 A.M.–8 P.M.; Saturday, 10 A.M.–5 P.M.; Sunday, noon–5 P.M. "Free Friday Nights" from 5–8 P.M.

Admissions: $3 per person. Memberships available.

For further information write to the Children's Museum of Bozeman, 234 E. Babcock St., Bozeman, MT 59715 or call (406) 522-9087. E-mail: *info@cmbozeman.org*

Children's Museum Missoula
Missoula

The Children's Museum opened with a pilot project located in a donated retail space at Southgate Mall. They relocated in 2003 and again in 2006 into a larger facility. Exhibits include opportunities for face painting, playing with bubbles, exploring a child-sized fort, beating a drum, donning a costume, digging for dinosaur fossils and more.

Info in brief: A hands-on museum for young children.

Location: Downtown Missoula.

Hours: Open Daily. Monday thru Saturday, 10 A.M.–5 P.M.; Sunday, noon–5 P.M. Closed Memorial Day, July 4th, Labor Day, Thanksgiving and Christmas. Also closed for Annual Maintenance — March 9th–13th, 2008.

Admissions: $3.50 per person; under 1, free.

Other sites of interest nearby: spectrUM Discovery Area.

For further information write to the Children's Museum Missoula, 225 W. Front St, Missoula, MT 59802 or call 541-7529. E-mail: *info@learnplayimagine.org*

Explorationworks
Helena

Opened on November 1, 2007, Explorationworks is a science and culture museum for children of all ages. Permanent and changing exhibits are currently offered, as well as one permanent exhibit area for children ages 5 and under, "Little Sky Country." As Montana's largest children's museum, this author would predict that this museum will continue to grow, offering more and more exhibits as time goes by.

Info in brief: A hands-on children's museum with an emphasis on science and culture.

Location: North end of the Great Northern Town Center.

Hours: Tuesday thru Saturday, 10 A.M.–6 P.M.; Wednesday evening, 10 A.M.–8 P.M.; Sunday, noon to 5 P.M.; Closed Mondays except for Helena Public School holiday Mondays. Closed major holidays.

Admissions: Under 2, free: under 18, $5.50; seniors (65+) & students (with ID), $6.50; adults, $8. Free parking available. Memberships available.

Other sites of interest nearby: The Children's Museum of Missoula.

For further information write to Explorationworks, 905 Carousel Way, Helena, MT 59601 or call (406) 457-1800. *www.explorationworks.org* E-mail: *info@explorationworks.org*

spectrUM Discovery Area
Missoula

Opened in October, 2007, spectrUM Discovery Area is a new, interactive science museum with hands-on exhibits, special programs. Community outreach programs continue the museum's goal of inspiring a culture of learning and discovery for people of all ages.

Info in brief: Hands-on science museum.

Location: Skaggs Building on The University of Montana campus.

Hours: Academic school year — Thursday, 3:30–7 P.M.; Saturday & Sunday, 11 A.M.–4:30 P.M. Check with the museum for spring and summer hours.

Admissions: 3 & under, free; all others, $3.50. Free passes are available for families in need (check with the Missoula Public Library). Memberships available.

For further information write to spectrUM Discovery Area, Davidson Honors College, Lower Level, the University of Montana, Missoula, MT 59812-1049 or call (406) 243–4828 or fax (406) 243–5461. *www.umt.edu/spectrUM/contact.htm.* E-mail: *Holly.Truitt@umontana.edu*

NEBRASKA

Children's Museum of Central Nebraska
Hastings

The Children's Museum of Central Nebraska is a place "where children play to learn, and grown-ups learn to play!" Hands-on educational exhibits explore themes of growing, living, working and creating. Some of these exhibits are: Fire & Child Safety Area, Construction Zone, Stage & Dress Up, Puppet Theatre, Creative Art Station, Grocery Store, Greenhouse, Pizza Shop, Doctor/Veterinary Clinic, Infant/Toddler-Barnyard, Chicka Chicka Boom Literacy Area, Train Table Exhibit, Giant PVC Pipe Organ, Magnetic Gear Wall, and more. Traveling Exhibits are also offered regularly. The museum has been open since December 9, 2003.

Info in brief: A hands-on, interactive multi-disciplinary children's museum.

Location: Imperial Mall at 12th St. and Marian Rd. in Hastings.

Hours: Tuesday thru Saturday, 10 A.M.–6 P.M.; Sunday, 1 P.M.–5 P.M.

Admissions: Under 2, free; all others, $5. Memberships available.

For further information write to the Children's Museum of Central Nebraska, Imperial Mall, 12th & Marian Rd, Hastings, NE 68901 or call (402) 463-3300. *www.cmocn.org*

Edgerton Explorit Center
Aurora

The mission of the Edgerton Explorit Center is to feature and expand on the work of Dr. Harold Edgerton of MIT, who is probably most famous for his stop-action photography and the invention of the strobe light. The museum hopes to nurture in people Dr. Edgerton's joy of learning by creating hands-on learning experiences for people of all ages and backgrounds. The 12,000 sq. ft. building includes a rotunda, classroom, theater/lecture hall, main exhibit hall, offices and shop area. The Plainsman Museum is adjoining, connected by "strobe alley," a duplication of the area outside Edgerton's MIT office. Eighteen major exhibit areas are offered in the exhibit galleries, while in-house education programs, traveling exhibits and programs, historical preservation, special events, and educational products and exhibit development are also emphasized.

Info in brief: A hands-on science museum for children and their caregivers.

Location: 1 hour west of Lincoln, Nebraska on I-80 and 3 miles north of the I-80 Aurora exit. The Plainsman Museum is adjoining.

Hours: Monday–Saturday, 9 A.M. to 5 P.M.; Closed holidays.

Admissions: Under 5, free; others, $5. Member ASTC.

Other sites of interest nearby: The Plainsman Museum, Courthouse Square (historic downtown area), and several historic homes open for viewing.

For further information write to Edgerton Explorit Center, 208 16th St., Aurora, Nebraska 68818 or call (402) 694-4032. *www.edgerton.org*

Kearney Area Children's Museum
Kearney

The Kearney children's museum opened in 1989 with a 7,000 sq. ft. facility, but increased its size in 2005. Plans are currently in the works for another expansion (scheduled for 2008) which will increase the facility to 13,000 sq. ft. In the 13,000 sq. ft. facility, exhibit areas will include 12 "Primary Zones": Agricultural Zone, Automotive Zone, Bank Zone, Captured Shadows Zone, Construction Zone, Grocery Zone, Hospital Zone, Restaurant Zone, Science Zone, Toddler Zone, Theatre/Music Zone, and Water Zone. Plans also call for a Program Room and a real Soda Fountain.

Hours: Wednesday, Thursday, Friday and Saturday, 10 A.M.–5 P.M.

Admissions: 24 months & under, free; all others, $3.

For further information write to the Kearney Area Children's Museum, 2005 1st Ave, Kearney, NE 68847 or call (308) 698-2228 or fax (308) 698-2229. E-mail: *kearneychildrensmuseum@alltel.net*

Lincoln Children's Museum
Lincoln

The Lincoln Children's Museum first opened in 1989, moving to its current location in the fall of 1991. The five full-time and 11 part-time staff, along with several hundred volunteers, encourage children, youth and adults to explore and discover their environment in this 15,524 sq. ft. space. The four main exhibit areas are: "Science/Technology Discovery Area," "History/Culture Area," "Toddler Area," and "Fine Arts Area." Other exhibits include the "Little Husker Stadium," "Bubbles," "Experiencing Agriculture," "Lunar Lander," "Recollections," "KIDS Radio station," "LCM Bank," "Super Market," "Celebrate Abilities" and more.

Info in brief: A growing, hands-on museum especially for children.

Location: Historic building in the heart of downtown Lincoln.

Hours: Tuesday–Saturday, 9:30 A.M. to 5 P.M.; Sunday, 1 P.M. to 5 P.M.; closed Monday and most major holidays.

Admissions: Under 2, free; 2 & over, $6; seniors (62+), $5.50. Memberships available.

Unique exhibits: Celebrate Abilities— designed to create awareness of the basic needs of all humans, and to encourage a positive attitude toward people with disabilities.

Other sites of interest nearby: Nebraska State Capital, Sheldon Art Gallery, Lied Center for Performing Arts, Museum of Nebraska History, Morrill Hall Museum of Natural History, Kennard House and the entertainment and restaurant district of downtown Lincoln.

For further information write to Lincoln Children's Museum, 1420 P St., Lincoln, Nebraska 68508, or call (402) 477-0128 or 477-4000. *www.lincolnchildrensmuseum.org*

Omaha Children's Museum
Omaha

The Omaha Children's Museum celebrated its 30th anniversary in October 2006. Beginning as a portable "traveling" museum which basically operated out of the trunk of a car, the goal of the museum has always been to offer educational exhibits and activities of specific interest to children. Now housed in a permanent 60,000 sq. ft. building, the primary goal is still to educate and benefit children in the metropolitan community. Their stated purpose is to "provide high quality participatory and educational experiences, oriented to the interests of children, in the areas of the arts, humanities, and natural and applied sciences." More than 100,000 people participated in these experiences in 1995.

The layout of the museum offers 11 main areas of exploration, along with offices and restroom facilities. The areas include: Model of Omaha, Toddler Space, Legos/Giant Blocks, Face Paints, Temporary Exhibitions, Charlie Campbell Science & Technology Center, Creativity Center, Performance Area, Activity Rooms, Birthday Room and the OCM Museum Store.

Info in brief: Hands-on, participatory exhibits are emphasized. (All children must be accompanied and supervised by an adult.)

Location: 500 South 20th Street, Omaha, Nebraska.

Hours: Tuesday–Saturday, 10 A.M. to 5 P.M., and Thursday until 8 P.M.; Sunday, 1 P.M. to 5 P.M. (Closed Monday and major holidays.)

Admissions: Age 2–adult, $7; seniors (60+), $6; children under 2, free. Memberships are offered. Member ASTC.

Unique exhibits or exhibitions: Toddler Space (for those under 6 years of age).

Other sites of interest nearby: Joslyn Art Museum, Henry Doorly Zoo, Brandeis Building, Old Market, Western Heritage Museum, Omaha Theater Company for Young People, Great Plains Black Museum, Boys Town, Burlington Building, Central High School.

For further information write to the Omaha Children's Museum, 500 South 20th St., Omaha, Nebraska 68102, or call (402) 342-6164 or fax (402) 342-6165. *www.ocm.org* or E-mail: *discover@ocm.org*

NEVADA

Guinness World of Records Museum
Las Vegas

Although the Guinness World of Records Museum is not strictly a children's museum, the items on display are of definite interest to children (and their caregivers) around the world.

With over 5,200 sq. ft. of exhibits, the museum brings "amazing feats" and "astonishing facts" to life in its three-dimensional displays. Visitors find exhibits, displays, rare videos, artifacts, computerized data banks, life-size replicas of famous people and much more.

Main theme areas are "The Human World," "The Animal World," "The World of Sports," "Space," "The Arts & Entertainment," "The World of Cinema," "The Natural World," and "The World of Las Vegas."

Ripley's Haunted Adventure and Tomb Rider 3D adventures are at the same location, and combination admission tickets are available.

Info in brief: A visual museum with items of interest to most children, while the other adjacent "adventures" do offer some interactivity.

Location: On the Strip one block north of the Circus Circus Hotel.

Hours & Admissions: Contact museum for current information.

Other sites of interest nearby: The many tourist attractions in Las Vegas.

For further information write to the Guinness World of Records Museum, 2780 Las Vegas Blvd. S., 89109.

Lied Discovery Children's Museum
Las Vegas

The Lied Discovery Children's Museum was founded in 1984 as a private, nonprofit educational institution. Several temporary exhibits were set up at different locations around the

The Lied Discovery Children's Museum.

Las Vegas Valley in order to promote the idea of building a proper museum. A permanent home was finally opened for visitation in 1990, but ongoing plans call for continued growth and improvements.

The 22,000 sq. ft. (exhibit area) museum currently features over 100 hands-on exhibits in the arts, sciences and humanities. Special demonstrations, activities, and workshops are also offered throughout the year. Some of the permanent exhibits include "Toddler Towers" (crawl and slide), "Performing Arts Stage," a space shuttle, a gyrochair, color computers complete with printers, "Musical Pathway," a giant bubble machine, KKID radio and more.

Info in brief: A hands-on arts, sciences and humanities museum mainly for children ages 6–12 and their caregivers.

Location: Adjoining the Las Vegas Library in Downtown Las Vegas' Cultural Corridor.

Hours: (General hours) Tuesday–Friday, 9 A.M.–4 P.M.; Saturday 10 A.M.–5 P.M.; Sunday, Noon–5 P.M.; Closed Mondays except most school holidays. Closed New Year's Day, Easter, Thanksgiving Day, Christmas Eve and Christmas Day.

Admissions: Under 1, free; children (1–17) & seniors & military, $7; adults, $8. Memberships available. Member ASTC.

Other sites of interest nearby: The many tourist attractions in Las Vegas. (Food and motel rates are especially low.)

For further information write to Lied Discovery Children's Museum, 833 Las Vegas Blvd. North, Las Vegas, Nevada 89101, or call (702) 382-KIDS(5437) or fax (702) 382-0592. *www.ldcm.org*

The Wilbur D. May Center
Reno

The Wilbur D. May Center has three distinct areas—The Wilbur D. May Museum, The Great Basin Adventure and the May Arboretum. The museum is a collection of artifacts and trophies from around the world. It also hosts a variety of traveling exhibits throughout the year, including Dinamation, a science carnival, rain forest exhibit, computer exhibit and more. Visitors are given "treasure hunt" sheets upon entry, and are awarded a prize at the end of their visit if they find all the "treasures" while visiting the museum exhibits.

The May Arboretum is open to the public all day and offers special children's tours and family tours upon request.

While all three areas are family oriented, the Great Basin Adventure is of special interest to children. Included in this small theme park are pony rides, a log flume ride, a dinosaur playground, gold panning, a petting zoo, a discovery room and a concession stand.

Info in brief: Small participatory theme park for children, as well as an arboretum and historical museum.

Location: A few miles from downtown Reno.

Hours: Vary according to the season. Contact museum for specific dates and times. Arboretum is open different hours. Contact the center before visiting.

Admissions: Fees vary with exhibits. Contact museum for current exhibit.

Other sites of interest nearby: Reno, Nevada, attractions.

For further information write to The Wilbur D. May Center, Rancho San Rafael Park, 1595 N. Sierra, Reno, Nevada 89503-1713, or call (775) 785-5961. *www.maycenter.com*

NEW HAMPSHIRE

The Children's "Met"amorphosis
Derry

This two-story museum is a total hands-on museum for children between the ages of 1 and 8. Exploration areas include: "The Sticky Room," with magnets, a sticky mural, and snap blocks; "Emergency Room," where children can be patient or doctor; "The Waterplay Area"; "The Construction Site"; "The Rainbow Room," where children learn about color and light; "Dinosaur Times"; "Grammy's Attic"; "Puppet Theatre"; "Post Office"; "Nature Center"; "World Culture" and "Toddler Play." There is also a train and picnic area outside.

Group tours are available along with birthday parties, overnight programs and special events.

Info in brief: Hands-on, participatory children's museum.

Location: Rear of 6 West Broadway in downtown Derry, on Abbott Court.

Hours: Tuesday–Thursday & Saturday, 9:30 A.M. to 5 P.M.; Sunday, 1 P.M. to 5 P.M.; Friday, 9:30 A.M. to 8 P.M. Also open Mondays of school vacations and July and August. Closed major holidays.

Admissions: Ages 1 through adult, $6. Friday evenings, $10 per family, after 5 P.M. (Children must always be accompanied by an adult.) Memberships are offered.

Other sites of interest nearby: The Stonyfield Farm Yogurt Works tours and Mack's Apples, a National Bicentennial Farm U-Pick and farm market.

For further information write to The Met Children's Museum, 6 West Broadway, #24, Derry, New Hampshire 03038, or call (603) 425-2560. *www.childrensmet.org*

The Children's Museum of New Hampshire
Dover

The Children's Museum of Portsmouth opened in 1983 after two years of planning. Since that time, expansions and new innovations have taken place so that the museum now features more than 20 hands-on theme exhibits to explore, along with special events, programs, workshops, etc. The museum is now in a new location on the Cocheco River in Dover, with three times the space, and has a new name: The Children's Museum of New Hampshire. Ongoing exhibits will include "Earthquakes Are Natural," "Different Lands, Different Masks," "Magicam," "Body Bits," "Lobstering," "Yellow Submarine" (a two-story play structure), "Siss Boom Bang" (music room), "Primary Place & Resource Center," "Forms of Expression," "Space Shuttle," and more. A project area and mini-exhibits are also on display.

The new museum is housed in a former armory building on the banks of the Cocheco River. The building is leased from the City of Dover for $1 a year, and the interior was completely transformed following a $3.3 million capital campaign.

Info in brief: A hands-on and interactive museum for children and their caregivers.

Location: Henry Law Park, which has a playground, picnic tables, benches and an outdoor amphitheater.

Hours: Open year-round with expanded hours in the summer. Closed some holidays.

Admissions: Not yet set at time of publication. Be sure to contact the museum before visiting.

For further information write to The Children's Museum of New Hampshire, 6 Washington St., Dover, New Hampshire 03820, or call (603) 436-3853 or fax (603) 436-7706. *www.childrens-museum.org* E-mail: *questions@childrens-museum.org*

New Hampshire Farm Museum
Milton

The mission of The New Hampshire Farm Museum is to preserve, interpret and carry forward New Hampshire's agricultural heritage. The Museum complex consists of two adjoining properties on 50 acres on Plummer's Ridge in Milton. The historic Jones Farm and the Plummer Homestead were occupied by the same families for more than two centuries and are now listed on the National Register of Historic Places. The site offers a working farm, an historic farmhouse, barns and outbuildings. Museum exhibits are housed in the barns and outbuildings.

Visitors can tour the historic Jones farm and learn about three centuries of farm life in New Hampshire. Children love the Big Yellow Barn Hunt in the three-story, 104-ft. long Great Barn filled with a vast collection of agricultural machinery, farm tools, carts, sleighs and more. Visitors can pump water, feed chickens and meet other farm animals. A blacksmith shop, shoe shop and special events are also offered.

The Museum Store features handmade items by New Hampshire's traditional artisans as well as books, toys, games and New Hampshire made ice cream and cheeses.

Info in brief: Living history museum which is open to the general public from May through October and for special programs and events throughout the year.

Location: Route 125, Plummer's Ridge, in Milton (Exit 18 off the Spaulding Turnpike).

Hours: 10 A.M. to 4 P.M.—(Mid-May through the last Saturday in October) Wednesday through Sunday.

Admissions: Under 3, free; children (3–17), $3; adults, $6; family rate, $16. Concerts and some special events require additional charges. Memberships available.

Other sites of interest nearby: The White Mountains, The New Hampshire Lakes Region, and the Atlantic Ocean. Many bed and breakfasts and resorts are in the area.

For further information write to the New Hampshire Farm Museum, P.O. Box 644, Milton, New Hampshire 03851, or call (603) 652-7840. *www.farmmuseum.org*

SEE Science Center
Manchester

The SEE Science Center is a hands-on discovery center whose aim is to promote the understanding, enjoyment and achievements of science for visitors 4 years of age and older. More than 65 hands-on exhibits are offered along with workshops, seminars, overnighters, and outreach programs.

Major exhibits emphasize electricity, momentum and light. Visitors weighing less than 80 pounds can even experience moon-like conditions in the Moonwalk Exhibit. The LEGO Millyard project is a permanent exhibit at SEE and is available for viewing whenever SEE is open.

Info in brief: Hands-on, participatory museum for children and their caregivers.

Hours: Monday–Friday, 10 A.M. to 4 P.M.; Saturday & Sunday, 10 A.M. to 5 P.M.

Admissions: Under 1, free; all others, $5. Memberships available. Member ASTC.

Unique exhibits: Moonwalk Exhibit for visitors weighing less than 80 pounds.

Other sites of interest nearby: Anheuser Busch, Amoskeag Fishways, Christa McAuliffe Planetarium, and the Boston Museum of Science.

For further information write to SEE Science Center, 200 Bedford St., Manchester, New Hampshire 03101, or call (603) 669-0400 or fax (603) 669-0400. *www.see-sciencecenter.org*

NEW JERSEY

Bergen Museum of Art and Science
Paramus

The Bergen Museum is a large, two-story, family-oriented arts and sciences museum which offers exhibitions for all age ranges. A hands-on science area especially for children is one of the exhibits. The Mastodon skeleton collection, the Lenape Indian exhibit and the Nature Room are also of special interest for children, but are not hands-on. Other permanent collections include artwork by important artists of Northern New Jersey and Metropolitan New York, the Science in Art Collection, and an Ethnic Heritage Collection.

Many classes, workshops, concerts and special events for children are sponsored by the museum year round. A variety of visiting exhibits is also offered throughout the year, making it an ever-changing museum.

Info in brief: Arts and sciences museum with some areas specifically for children.

Location: Ridgewood and Fairview avenues in Paramus.

Hours: Tuesday–Thursday, 10 A.M. to 5 P.M.; Sunday, 1 P.M. to 5 P.M. Closed Monday.

Admissions: Fees vary according to tour chosen. Generally $3 to $5.

Unique exhibits: Mastodon collection and Lenape Indian exhibit.

Other sites of interest nearby: Clementon Lake Park (Clementon), Six Flags Great Adventure (Jackson).

For further information write to the Bergen Museum of Art and Science, 327 E. Ridgewood Ave., Paramus, New Jersey 07652-4832, or call (201) 291-8848. *www.thebergenmuseum.com* E-mail: *nicklus@thebergemuseum.com*

Children's Museum at Rockingham, Rockingham Historic Site
Princeton

As part of the Rockingham Historic Site, the Children's Museum makes history come alive for children by surrounding them with an environment typical of 18th-century life. Hands-on activities are offered in the museum (a one-room colonial building) and in the kitchen of the Rockingham mansion. Activities include calligraphy, carding wool, a colonial clothes closet, designing a papyrotamia picture, "Fox and Geese" games, sewing a sampler, experiencing a colonial kitchen, and stuffing a pallet with hay.

Built in the early 1700s by John Harrison, Rockingham was General George Washington's last wartime headquarters. It was here, in 1783, where he wrote his farewell address to the troops. The exhibits and displays in the mansion, the museum, and the kitchen help children to become aware of the rich cultural history and beginnings of the United States. The grounds and exhibits are now under the supervision of the New Jersey Department of Environmental Protection.

Besides the hands-on exploratory displays, the museum also offers annual events on special holidays.

Info in brief: A village museum of interest to all ages, with specific activities in a small children's museum on campus.

Hours: Admission to historic house is by guided tour only. Wednesday–Saturday, 10 A.M. and 11

A.M. and 1, 2, & 3 P.M.; Sunday, 1, 2, & 3 P.M. Closed Monday & Tuesday, all State and Federal holidays and on Wednesday after a Monday or Tuesday holiday.

Admissions: Free, but donations to The Rockingham Association are always appreciated. Due to the small number of staff, it is suggested that you call ahead to be sure the site is open.

Unique exhibits: A specific history hands-on children's museum as one exhibit on a larger campus.

Other sites of interest nearby: The many tourist attractions in New Jersey, including Allaire State Park, Grover Cleveland Birthplace, the Hermitage, Six Flags Great Adventure amusement park, Clementon Lake Park amusement park, Black River & Western Railroad, New Jersey Museum of Transportation and much more.

For further information write to the Rockingham Historic Site, 108 CR 518, RD #4, Princeton, New Jersey 08540, or call (609) 921-8835. *www.rockingham.net*

Children's Museum of EHT, The Jersey Shore Children's Museum
Egg Harbor Township

The Jersey Shore Children's Museum is a small hands-on museum for children ages 1 through 10 and their families. Exhibits are based on workplace themes with authentic props and clothing to allow creative role-play. Exhibits include: *The Pediatric ER, Construction Zone, TV/Weather Newsroom, Center Court (be an NBA player), Dental Office, Puppet Corner,* and *Car Factory.* Also on site are a music wall, a dinosaur table and a tot area.

Location: Shore Mall.

Hours: Open daily. Monday thru Saturday, 10 A.M.–5 P.M.; Sunday, noon–5 P.M. Closed Thanksgiving Day, Christmas Day, and Easter Sunday.

Admissions: Contact museum for current price.

Other sites of interest nearby: Atlantic City sites nearby.

For further information write to The Jersey Shore Children's Museum, 3112 Fire Rd., Egg Harbor Township, NJ 08234 or call (609) 645-7741. *www.eht.com/childrensmuseum/*

Community Children's Museum
Dover

The Community Children's Museum is a hands-on museum for children ages 6 months to 10 years old. Children can be an astronaut in John Glenn's space capsule, visit Nancy's Lake House (especially for children 6 months to 5 years old), sit on Vincent Van Gogh's bed, sculpt a portrait and explore electricity.

Hours: Thursday thru Saturday, 10 A.M.–5 P.M.; Sunday, noon to 5 P.M.

Admissions: Under 6 months, free; Seniors, $4; all others, $5. Free parking available.

For further information write to Community Children's Museum, 77 E. Blackwell St., Dover, NJ 07801 or call (973) 366-9060. *www.communitychildrensmuseum.org*

Discovery House
East Brunswick

Discovery House is a hands-on learning museum for children ages two and up and their families. The museum is dedicated to "stimulating the natural creativity and curiosity in all of us." Over 100 hands-on activities are offered to inspire and delight all visitors. Experimenting, imagining, playing, and pretending are encouraged here.

Hours: Tuesday thru Sunday, 10 A.M.–5 P.M.

Admissions: Under 18 months, free; all others, $7.50.

For further information write to Discovery House, 152 Tices Lane, East Brunswick, NJ 08816 or call (732) 254-3770. *www.Discovery-house.com*

Garden State Discovery Museum
Cherry Hill

Named one of the top 20 children's museum in the country by *Child Magazine*, the Garden State Discovery Museum offers 15 exhibit areas for children up to 10 years old and their caregivers.

Hours: Year-round. Monday thru Sunday, 9:30 A.M.–5:30 P.M.; Saturdays (Oct.–April), open until 8:30 P.M. Closed Thanksgiving & Christmas.

Admissions: 1 & under, free; seniors, $8.95; all others, $9.95.

For further information write to the Garden State Discovery Museum, 2040 Springdale Rd., Suite 1000, Cherry Hill, NJ 08003 or call (856) 424-1233. *www.discoverymuseum.com*

Imagine That! Discovery Museum for Children
Florham Park

This museum for 3 to 10-year-olds features 40 interactive exhibits in a 16,000 sq. ft. area covering 8 major themes: *Creative Expression, Science, Art Studio, Around the World, Computers, Community (911 Emergency Area and Grocery Store), TV Newsroom,* and *Automobiles* (offering the cockpit of a real Piper airplane, the cab of a truck, a real VW Bug, a firetruck and more).

Other services provided include birthday parties, a new "drop off" service, puppet shows, storytelling and other supervised activities. A café and gift shop are also on-site.

Info in brief: A large hands-on multi-disciplinary children's museum.

Hours: Open daily, 10 A.M.–5:30 P.M.

Admissions: Under 1, free; children, $7.99; adults, $4.99.

Other sites of interest nearby: Holmdel Arboretum, Monmouth Museum, U.S. Army Communications & Electronics Museum, Twin Lights Historic Site, Fort Hancock and Brookdale Ocean Institute.

For further information write to Imagine That! 4 Vreeland Rd., Florham Park, NJ 07932 or call (973) 966-8000. *www.imaginethatmuseum.com*

The Jersey Explorer Children's Museum
East Orange

The Jersey Explorer Children's Museum is one of the first non-profit children's museum in the country to display true-to-life, interactive exhibits that are the work of at-risk youth. The Youth Corps members who work at the museum receive on-the-job-training and interpersonal and developmental skills in preparation for their high school equivalency diplomas. Permanent exhibits developed so far include: *Time Traveler, Tomb of Ancient Kings, Stargazer,*

Main St. Village, Arts & Crafts, and *WJEX-TV.* Changing exhibits are also featured regularly. Other presentations include: *Off the Page Theater, Magic Carpet* and *Scienceworks.*

Info in brief: A hands-on, interactive children's museum.

Hours: Open to the public, Saturdays, 10 A.M.–3 P.M. only. Tuesday thru Friday, open to groups by reservation only. Walk-in Wednesdays: call for availability.

Admissions: 2 & under, free; all others, $6. Last Saturday of each month is free with a valid East Orange Public Library Card. Memberships available.

For further information write to The Jersey Explorer Children's Museum, 192 Dodd St., East Orange, NJ 07017 or call (973) 673-6900 or fax (973) 673-8660. *www.jerseyexplorerchildrensmuseum*

Liberty Science Center
Jersey City

The mission of the Liberty Science Center is to offer informal hands-on and exploratory science and technology experiences in order to "inspire, explain, entertain, engage, involve, challenge, motivate and empower" young minds. Conceived in 1977, the actual building was not begun until 1989. The museum now has a staff of 200 and has had more than one million guests.

The distinctive building offers hundreds of exhibits along with the nation's largest IMAX Dome theater. The exhibits are displayed on three theme floors, with interactive demonstrations, discovery room dialogues and multimedia theater presentations available. "The Invention Floor" features structures, energy and light, images, action and effects. "The Health Floor" encourages self-awareness with exhibits on perception, bodies in motion and making lifestyle choices. "The Environment Floor" emphasizes the atmosphere, marine life, a bug zoo and geology.

Besides its own permanent and rotating displays, the center hosts several national touring exhibitions, offers teacher training, and provides special programs and workshops throughout the year.

Info in brief: Large hands-on science museum for children and their caregivers.

Location: Liberty State Park, Jersey City, a few minutes from New York City. Liberty State Park houses the Statue of Liberty and Ellis Island.

Hours: Exhibits— Tuesday–Friday, 9:30 A.M. to 5:00 P.M. Weekends & holidays, 9 A.M.–6 P.M. Open some Monday holidays. Closed Thanksgiving and Christmas. Kodak OMNI Theater (IMAX)—10 A.M. to 5 P.M., on the hour.

Admissions: Exhibits only — adults, $15.75 students/seniors, $8.50; children (2–12), $11.50. IMAX Theater — adults, $9; students/seniors, $7; children (2–12), $5. Theater —$2. Combo tickets: adults, $24.50; seniors, $18.50; children, $18.50. Community days, $5. Memberships are available. Member of ASTC.

Unique exhibits: LSC's signature exhibit is a 700-pound unfolding geodesic aluminum sphere designed by Chuck Hoberman and on "display" in the four-story atrium.

Other sites of interest nearby: Statue of Liberty, Ellis Island Museum, World Trade Center, Six Flags Great Adventure (Jackson), Coney Island's Astroland (Brooklyn) and the many tourist attractions of both New York and New Jersey.

For further information write to the Liberty Science Center, Liberty State Park 222 Jersey City, Blvd., Jersey City, NJ 07305-4699, or call (201) 200-1000. *www.lsc.org*

The New Jersey Children's Museum
Paramus

The New Jersey Children's Museum, opened in 1992, is a hands-on museum especially for children under 8 years of age. More than 40 permanent exhibits are housed in the 15,000 sq. ft.

Boys play on a real backhoe at the New Jersey Children's Museum.

Firefighters-in-training at the New Jersey Children's Museum.

converted warehouse. Each exhibit area is designed for specific age groups, from the "Baby Nook" to "Science and Technology" for 1st and 2nd graders.

Daily and weekly activities are regularly scheduled along with special events. The permanent exhibits include a working fire engine, an authentic helicopter, a kids-sized grocery, pizzeria, giant waterplay area, a huge interactive kaleidoscope, a castle, costumes, puppets, frogs, magnets, electricity and more.

Info in brief: A hands-on museum for young children (8 years or younger).

Location: Winters Ave. between the Fashion Center Mall and Paramus Park Mall.

Hours: The Museum is open 7 days a week, from 10 A.M. to 6 P.M. on weekdays; 10 A.M. to 5 P.M. on summer weekends; 10 A.M. to 6 P.M. on winter weekends.

Admissions: Under 1, free; others, $10.

For further information write to The New Jersey Children's Museum, 599 Valley Health Plaza, Paramus, New Jersey 07652, or call (201) 262-5151. *www.njcm.com*

NEW MEXICO

Explora! Science Center
Albuquerque

Explora is part science center, part children's museum, part free-choice school, part grandma's attic, part grandpa's garage, part laboratory, part neighborhood fun of interesting

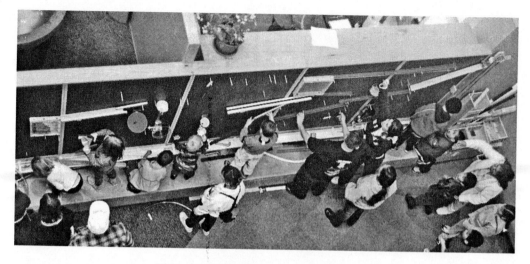

Visitors to Explora learn that physics is fun.

people, and part of many people's lives. Her exhibits engage people of all ages with small-scale materials and equipment in personal spaces where they can communicate comfortably with others, manipulate a wide range of materials and develop their own thinking about what they are experiencing.

Hours: Monday–Saturday 10 A.M. to 6 P.M.; Sunday, 12 P.M.–6 P.M.

Admissions: Under 1, free; children (1–11), $3; seniors (65+), $5; adults (12–64), $7. Member ASTC.

For further information contact: Explora!, 1701 Mountain Road, NW, Albuquerque, New Mexico 87104, or phone: (505) 224-8300. E-mail: *ckaser@explora.us*

Farmington Museum
Farmington

The City of Farmington oversees the management of the Farmington Museum, one main section of which, the Children's Gallery, is a hands-on museum for children. In the Children's Gallery visitors will find the Shadow Room, the Orchard Street Theater, Mirror Games, The Artist's Nook, a small puppet theater, the Frozen Bubble Box, the Ecosurvival video game STUFFEE, and more. Various temporary and traveling exhibits are also on display throughout the year.

Besides the Children's Gallery, the village-type museum houses historic exhibits from pioneering days, a Natural History gallery and traveling shows. Special classes, workshops and events are also offered.

The historic displays include a replica of a 1930s trading post which includes the Bull Pen, an Office and the Pawn Room, along with a corral area outside.

Info in brief: A village museum with one gallery devoted to hands-on activities for children and their caregivers.

Hours: Tuesday–Saturday, noon to 5 P.M.; Saturday, 10 A.M. to 5 P.M.

Admissions: No admissions fee, but donations are appreciated.

Other sites of interest nearby: Aztec Ruins National Monument and Aztec Museum. Within 100 miles are Mesa Verde National Park (116 miles), Anasazi Heritage Center, Salmon Ruins, Chaco Culture National Historical Park and Durgano, Colorado.

For further information write to the Farmington Museum, 302 N. Orchard, Farmington, New Mexico 87401-6227, or call (505) 599-1174. *www.farmingtonmuseum.org*

Santa Fe Children's Museum

Santa Fe

Founded in 1985 by four local educators, the Santa Fe Children's Museum opened in its present location in 1989. It is governed by a 21-member Board of Trustees and maintains a staff of 16 paid employees and 100 volunteers. The building and grounds are leased from the State of New Mexico. The building itself was constructed in the 1930s as a national guard armory. The grounds now house a half-acre horticulture garden.

The 5,000 sq. ft. exhibit area houses both temporary and permanent interactive, hands-on displays for children and their caregivers. Permanent exhibits include a Life Science Area, Technical Climbing Wall and a Toddler Area. Movable or rotating exhibits include "Water-works," "Bubbles," "Make and Take," "Architectural Building Blocks," "Magnet Table," "Maxi-Rollways," "Zeotropes," "Pin Screen," "Sound Dishes," "Pulley Power," "A Thousand Faces," and more.

Special workshops and events are also offered throughout the year. Some special events have included a monthly "Very Special Arts" day, Museum on Wheels (taken to Children's Hospital of New Mexico), Artists in the Museum, Sunday Science, outreach programs and much more. Contact the museum to find out more about these events.

Info in brief: Interactive, hands-on displays with special programs offered throughout the year.

Location: South of the Capitol Building and the Plaza.

Hours: Winter/Spring/Fall — Wednesday–Saturday, 10 A.M. to 5 P.M. and Sunday noon to 5 P.M.; Summer: Tuesday–Saturday, 10 A.M. to 5 P.M. and Sunday, noon to 5 P.M.

Admissions: $8 for out-of-state visitors; $4 for in-state-visitors, and on Sundays, New Mexico residents pay $1. Member Association of Youth Museums.

For further information write to the Santa Fe Children's Museum at 1050 Old Pecos Trail, Santa Fe, New Mexico 87501, or call (505) 989-8359. *www.santafechildrensmuseum.org* E-mail: *jpadilla@santafechildrensmmuseum.org*

Nothing's bugging this youngster at the Santa Fe Children's Museum.

A young visitor makes it to the top of the climbing wall at the Santa Fe Children's Museum.

NEW YORK

Brooklyn Children's Museum

Brooklyn

The Brooklyn Children's Museum was the first museum created specifically for children. The mission of the Brooklyn Children's Museum was and is to actively engage children in educational and entertaining experiences through innovation and excellence in its exhibitions, programs and collections usage. The primary target age group is school children. It is the oldest museum in the United States designed specifically for children, founded by the Brooklyn Institute of Arts and Sciences in 1899 as an alternative to existing museums, whose exhibits, it was felt, were too sophisticated for children.

The first facility was located in the Adams Building, a Victorian mansion located in Bedford Park (later renamed Brower Park) in Crown Heights. In 1929, the museum moved to the Smith Mansion. After a couple of other moves, the permanent facility was built on the site of the Smith Mansion in Brower Park, and opened in 1977. This 35,000 sq. ft. unique underground structure, designed by the architectural firm of Hardy Holzman Pfeiffer Associates, cost $3.5 million with most of the funds provided by the City of New York.

An expanded facility, opened in 2008, increases the facility to over 102,000 sq. ft. Nine permanent innovative galleries and a traveling exhibition space are on site.

Info in brief: A mainly hands-on science and humanities museum for children and their caregivers.

Location: Corner of Brooklyn and St. Mark's avenues.

Hours: (Winter) Wednesday–Friday, 2 P.M. to 5 P.M.; Saturday and Sunday, noon to 5 P.M.; open noon to 5 P.M. most school holidays. Call the museum hotline number for summer hours.

Admissions: $7.50 per person; free for Museum members and children under 1 year of age. Member ASTC and AAM.

Unique features: The oldest children's museum in the United States.

Other sites of interest nearby: Children's Museum of the Arts, Children's Museum of Manhattan, Staten Island Children's Museum, Brooklyn Botanic Garden and the many other historic sites in New York.

For further information write to the Brooklyn Children's Museum, 145 Brooklyn Ave., Brooklyn, New York 11213, or call the museum hotline—(718) 735-4400 or Fax (718) 604-7442. *www.brooklynkids.org*

Cayuga County Agricultural Museum

Auburn

The Cayuga County Agricultural Museum is owned and maintained by Cayuga County and is run strictly by volunteer workers.

This village-type museum displays many farm implements dating from 1830 to 1930, along with antique tractors, sleighs and buggies, a 1900s farm kitchen and herb garden, a village square, general store, blacksmith shop, wood & wheelwright shop, creamery, veterinarian's office, a live colony of honey bees (in summer), and more. Although it is not strictly a children's museum, many of the items on display and the set-up of the museum itself is of interest to children.

Of special interest to all ages are the special events held throughout the year: an antique tractor show (August), "Old Ways" Day in June, and an old-fashioned Christmas with carolers, barbershop quartets, hot cider, Christmas cookies and horse-drawn sleigh rides, horse show and threads show (exhibiting anything made of cloth).

Info in brief: Village museum.

Location: North tip of Owasco Lake, Auburn, New York.

Hours: Memorial Day–Labor Day. June, Saturday and Sunday, 1 P.M. to 5 P.M.; July and August, Wednesday–Sunday, 1 P.M. to 5 P.M.

Admissions: Free.

Unique exhibits or exhibitions: Large collection of farm implements, many of which were patented out of Cayuga County.

Other sites of interest nearby: The William Seward home (Secretary of State under Abraham Lincoln, famous for his part in the purchase of Alaska), listed on the National Registry of Historic Places.

For further information write to Cayuga County Agricultural Museum, c/o Norman Riley, RD 6, Box 263, Auburn, New York 13021-9806, or call (315) 252-5009 or (315) 253-5611.

Center for Science Technology & Learning
Rockville Centre

The Center for Science Technology & Learning (CSTL) is an international organization whose mission is to encourage science literacy and create lifelong learners. They provide programs for schools, corporations and community groups. Their Tanglewood facility campus has buildings, ponds, streams and nature trails. Kids conduct guided investigations, draw conclusions and communicate their results.

Info in brief: Rockville Center offers guided scientific investigations for kids.

Location: Tanglewood Preserve.

Admissions: $5 per person; minimum group size of 15.

For further information write to CSTL, 1 Tanglewood Rd., Rockville Centre, NY 11570, or call (516) 764-0045. E-mail: *HelpDesk@cstl.org*

The Children's Museum at Saratoga
Saratoga Springs

The Children's Museum at Saratoga is designed to be developmentally appropriate for children age 7 and under. Interactive exhibits encourage exploration into science, history, community living and the arts. (Be sure to call the museum for these activities before visiting.) Older children may enjoy the museum, especially if visiting with younger children, and some special programs are designed to include them. The museum is also committed to fostering active parent involvement, serving as a resource for schools in the area, and ensuring that all children have access to its programs.

The museum was founded in 1990 and first occupied donated space in the Downstreet Marketplace building. In 1994, space was rented at 36 Phila Street. Finally, in 2001, the museum moved to its present location, renovating the building space and adding several exhibits. The two floors of exhibit space feature the following exhibits: Congress Park, Harvey & Company,

Lillian Andrew's Attic, Saratoga Trolley, Spa Little Theatre, Adirondack Trust Bank, Central market Grocery Store and Post Office, Construction Zone, Fire Truck and Fire House, Happy's Diner, and School House.

Info in brief: An interactive, hands-on museum for young children ages 7 and under.

Location: Downtown Saratoga Springs.

Hours: Summer hours (July 1 thru Labor Day): Monday thru Saturday 9:30 A.M.–4:30 P.M.; closed Sunday. Winter hours (Labor Day thru June): Tuesday Thru Saturday, 9:30 A.M.–4:30 P.M. Sunday, noon–4:30 P.M.; Closed Mondays. Closed most major holidays.

Admissions: Under 1, free; all others, $5. Free parking is available.

For further information write to The Children's Museum at Saratoga, 69 Caroline St., Saratoga Springs, NY 12866. Or call (518) 584-5540. *www.cmssny.org* E-mail: *info@cmssny.org*

Children's Museum of Manhattan
New York

The Children's Museum of Manhattan was founded in 1973 with an aim to engage children and their families in a partnership of learning through the arts, literacy, media and communications, science and the environment, and family learning activities. The targeted audience is families with children from birth to 12 years of age.

The original site was a basement storefront serving Harlem and the Upper West Side residential neighborhoods of Manhattan, and was called G.A.M.E. (Growth Through Art and Museum Experience). By 1984, the museum took its present name, the staff had grown to 20 full-time and 20 part-time members, and many improvements had been made. Currently, the five floors of hands-on exhibits are enhanced with daily family workshops, performances and

Curiosity abounds at the Children's Museum of Manhattan (photograph by Gaetano Salvador).

The Children's Museum of Manhattan features Alphie's Letter Garden (photograph by Gaetano Salvador).

special events throughout the year. In 2006, the third floor was completely gutted and turned into a 4,000 sq. ft. permanent state-of-the-art play and learning space called *Playworks* for children from birth to four-year-olds.

Info in brief: A hands-on museum for children and their families.

Location: The Tisch Building between Broadway & Amsterdam.

Hours: Tuesday–Sunday and public school holidays, 10 A.M. to 5 P.M. (Tuesdays CMOM is closed for educational and community outreach programming.) Special hours are offered throughout the year. Contact the museum for a current schedule.

Admissions: Under 1, free; children & adults, $9; seniors, $6. Memberships available. Member ADM.

Other sites of interest nearby: Coney Island's Astroland (Brooklyn), Broadway theaters and many other New York attractions.

For further information write to the Children's Museum of Manhattan, The Tisch Building, 212 W. 83rd St., New York, New York 10024, or call (212) 721-1223. *www.CMOM.org*

Children's Museum of the Arts
New York

In the heart of SoHo, New York's artist community, the Children's Museum of the Arts is dedicated to helping children develop their full artistic potential through teaching, collecting, creating and exhibiting children's art. Founded in October of 1988, the Children's Museum of the Arts is one of the oldest children's art museums in the world.

The museum employs an artist-in-residence format, where teaching artists work directly with children and their families. Interactive arts programs and exhibitions for children ages 18 months through 10 years are offered.

Info in brief: An arts museum with an emphasis on the arts for children.

Location: The SoHo district.

Hours: Wednesday, 10:45 A.M.–noon, Early Childhood Drop-in; noon–5 P.M., General Programs; Thursday, 10:45 A.M.–noon, Early Childhood Drop-in; noon–6 P.M. General Programs; Friday, 10:45 A.M.–noon, Early Childhood Drop-in; noon–5 P.M., General Programs; Saturday & Sunday, noon–5 P.M., General Programs.

Admissions: $9 per person (1–65 yrs); Thursday, 4–6 P.M., "Pay as you wish"; Wee Arts, $20 per family.

Unique feature: A museum dedicated strictly to the arts for children.

Other sites of interest nearby: The Brooklyn Children's Museum, the Children's Museum of Manhattan, Staten Island Children's Museum, and other New York City tourist attractions.

For further information write to the Children's Museum of the Arts, 182 Lafayette St., New York, New York 10013, or call (212) 274-0986 or fax (212) 274-1776. *www.cmany.org*

Children's Museum of History, Natural History, Science, and Technology
Utica

The only children's museum adopted by NASA and the Office of Science, and declared a NYS and Federal Historic Building, this 4-story educational museum offers hundreds of hands-on exhibits for children of all ages. Some of the exhibits include historical dioramas, International Hall of Fame, Iroquois Longhouse, PlaySpace, and much, much more. Visitors need to plan to spend several hours in order to tour the entire museum.

Info in brief: A large hands-on multi-disciplinary children's museum for all ages.

Location: Main Street in Utica.

Hours: Monday, Tuesday, Thursday, Friday and Saturday, 9:45 A.M.–3:45 P.M. Closed New Year's Eve & Day, Easter, July 4th, Labor Day, Thanksgiving, Christmas Eve & Day.

Admissions: Under 1, free; all others, $9.

For further information write to The Children's Museum of History, Living History, Science & Technology, 311 Main St., Utica, NY 13501 or call (315) 724-6129. *www.museum4kids.net*

The Children's Museum of Science and Technology (CMOST)
Troy

CMOST is the only science center in the Tech Valley that is designed especially as a catalyst for children and their parents to "explore, discover and imagine the world of science together." Exhibits are titled: Hudson River; Animal Nursery; Weather Front; Go Power; Light, Optics & Vision. The Lally Digital Dome Planetarium and a PlayMotion exhibit are also on site.

Location: Rensselaer Technology Park.

Hours: September thru June: Thursday–Sunday, 10 A.M.–5 P.M.

Admissions: Under 2, free; all others, $5; Dome Shows, $1.

For further information write to CMOST, 250 Jordan Rd., Troy, NY 12180 or call (518) 235-2120 or fax (518) 235-6836. *www.cmost.org*

Children's Museum of the East End
Bridgehampton/Sag Harbor

A "fantasyland" for young children, the Children's Museum of the East End is a 10,000 sq. ft. museum which offers hands-on exhibits, like serving (fake) ice cream and potato chips and sailing a pirate ship. An art studio and infant area are also on site. Everything can be played with and explored. Other exhibits allow children to walk along a raised wooden boardwalk, crawl through a hollow log, crawl out of a mouse hole and into a fantasy tree house bedroom, visit a Crawler Garden with cuddly bugs and fruits and vegetables, and more. Both indoor and outdoor exhibit spaces are on site. Traveling exhibits are also offered periodically.

Location: 376 Bridgehampton/Sag Harbor Turnpike, Bridgehampton.

Hours: Monday, Wednesday, Thursday and Saturday, 9 A.M.–5:30 P.M.; Friday, 9 A.M.–6:30 P.M.; Sunday, 10 A.M.–5:30 P.M. Closed Tuesdays.

Admissions: Under 1, free; 12 & under, $5; seniors, 5; all others, $7.

For further information write to Children's Museum of the East End, P.O. Box 316, Bridgehampton, NY 11932 or call (631) 537-8250 or fax (631) 537-2413. *www.cmee.org*

The Discovery Center of the Southern Tier
Binghamton

Opening in The Discovery Center is just that—an opportunity for children to discover things about themselves and their environment. Many of the interactive displays are permanent exhibits, while rotating exhibits are also offered throughout the year. A hands-on policy is enforced.

Some of the exhibits offered include "Giant Market," "EJ Factory," "Retail Store," "Ecology," "Geology," "The Cody Gallery," "Archaeology," "The Plum Dragon," and more. Special workshops, classes and programs are also offered.

Info in brief: A hands-on children's museum especially for children and their caregivers.

Hours: Tuesday thru Friday, 10 A.M.–4 P.M.; Saturday, 10 A.M. to 5 P.M.; Sunday, noon to 5 P.M.; Open special holiday Mondays.

Admissions: Under 1 year, free; ages 1–16, $6; adults 17 & over, $5.

For further information write to The Discovery Center of the Southern Tier, 60 Morgan Rd., Binghamton, New York 13903, or call (607) 773-8661 or fax (607) 773-8019. *www.thediscoverycenter.org* E-mail: *help@thediscoverycenter.org*

Goudreau Museum of Mathematics in Art and Science
New Hyde Park

The Goudreau Museum "seeks to promote and encourage interest in mathematics for everyone, regardless of age or mathematical background." The museum features programs specially designed for children and their families, many of which involve hands-on projects that participants can take home. Program topics include: Videospheres, Tangrams, Origami, Math in Navigation, Math in Architecture, Egg Decorating, Calendars, Paper Airplanes, Music and Math, and more.

Location: Herricks Community Center, a former school building, with the number "999" over the center doors in the front of the building. The museum does not have a sign outside.

Hours & Admissions: Please call ahead to confirm times, as they are not open to the public when they have a group visiting.

For further information write to the Goudreau Museum of Mathematics in Art and Science, Herricks Community Center, 999 Herricks Rd., Room 202, New Hyde Park, NY 11040-1353 or call (516) 747-0777. E-mail: *info@mathmuseum.org*

Hagadorn House Museum
Almond

The Hagadorn House was built around 1837 and has been restored to display furnishings and artifacts from that time period. Of special interest to children is the Children's Room with antique dolls, toys, and more. The "Little Gallery" holds changing exhibits which are often of interest to children — old uniforms, old greeting cards, clothing, and more.

The museum is run on an all-volunteer basis. Besides the museum itself, research materials about the area and family genealogy information is available in the Archives Room on Friday afternoons from 2 to 4 and by appointment.

Info in brief: An historic museum more of interest to adults, but with exhibits of interest to children.

Location: Main Street in Almond, New York, at Exit 33 on Rte. 17.

Hours: Friday, 2 P.M. to 4 P.M. or by appointment.

Admissions: Donations accepted.

Other sites of interest nearby: Alfred University, Letchworth State Park, Strong Museum, Niagara Falls and other tourist attractions in Buffalo and Rochester.

For further information write to the Hagadorn House Museum, Almond Historical Society, 7 N. Main Street, Almond, New York 14804, or call (607) 276-6324 or (607) 276-6760. *www.rootsweb. com/~nyahs/*

Hudson Valley Children's Museum
Nyack

This small museum offers 5,000 sq. ft. of exhibits encouraging learning about subjects from physics to geography, including an Early Childhood area.

Hours: Tuesday thru Friday, 10 A.M.–4 P.M.; Saturday, 10 A.M.–5 P.M.; Sunday, noon–5 P.M.

Admissions: $4.

For further information write to Hudson Valley Children's Museum, 21 Burd St., Nyack, NY 10960 or call (845) 358-2191.

Iroquois Indian Museum
Howes Cave

The Iroquois Indian Museum consists of the adult museum, the Nature Park and the Children's Iroquois Museum. The adult museum emphasizes regional archaeology — combining anthropological research with contemporary interests. The building itself is designed to resemble the longhouse and the powerful symbols of Iroquois culture. Exhibits include the largest collection of contemporary Iroquois art and craftwork, major archaeological collections, a performing arts amphitheater, dancers (outside in the summer), festivals, storytelling, an Iroquois log cabin and garden, and more. Various outreach programs, demonstrations, and programs are offered throughout the year.

The Nature Park is a 45-acre site with an emphasis on the Iroquois view of nature. Interpreters are available and guidelines are provided.

The Children's Iroquois Museum interprets the adult museum and also offers children the opportunities to learn to dance in native traditions, fashion clay into a pot, bead a necklace, make a cornhusk doll, use a spear thrower or use a lacrosse stick. Iroquois educators are available at all times. Special events and Family Days are held at various times. Contact the museum to see what special activities are taking place before your visit.

Info in brief: An educational, interpretive three-part museum with one part specially designated for children's exhibits and activities.

Location: Exit 22 off I-88, follow signs, approximately 2 miles.

Hours: Closed January thru March. (April–June) Tuesday thru Saturday, 10 A.M.–5 P.M.; Sunday, noon–5 P.M.; Closed Easter. (July & August) Monday thru Saturday, 10 A.M.–5 P.M.; Sunday, noon–5 P.M.; (September thru December) Tuesday thru Saturday, 10 A.M.–5 P.M.; Sunday, noon–5 P.M.; Closed Thanksgiving, Christmas Eve & Day.

Admissions: Under 5, free; children (5–12), $5; students (12–17), $4; adults, $6.50; seniors, $6.50.

Unique exhibits: Entire museum dedicated to Iroquois history, traditions and culture.

Other sites of interest nearby: Howe Caverns, Secret Caverns and the old Grist Mill.

For further information write to Iroquois Indian Museum, P.O. Box 7, Caverns Road, Howes Cave, New York 12092, or call (518) 296-8949 or fax (518) 296-8955. *www.iroquoismuseum.org*; E-mail: *info@iroquoismuseum.org*

Jewish Children's Museum
Brooklyn

Opened in 2005, this 50,000 sq. ft. children's museum is divided into three main sections, each featuring dioramas, video presentation, and various activities. "Exploring Jewish Life" offers explanations of the shabbath, holidays, keeping kosher and other Jewish traditions/ceremonies. "A Voyage Through Jewish History" offers exhibits tracing Jewish history from biblical times to the present day. The third section is more interactive featuring a Noah's Ark playroom for toddlers, a miniature golf course that takes children on a journey through the milestones of Jewish life, and a game show studio which pits visitors against each other to answer questions about Jewish life through a Jeopardy or Wheel of Fortune format. More than 80 exhibits are offered, along with a lending library, a screening room, an arts and crafts studio, a banquet hall and more.

Info in brief: A children's museum geared specifically to teaching about Jewish life.

Location: Kingston Avenue in Crown Heights, Brooklyn, New York.

Hours: Sunday thru Thursday, 10 A.M.–6 P.M.; closed on all Jewish holidays.

Admissions: Under 2, free; all others $10. Be prepared to park on the streets, or take the subway (take 3 to Kingston Avenue) or the bus (B43).

Other sites of interest nearby include the many Brooklyn sites, Manhattan sites and New York City sites including Ground Zero, Statue of Liberty, Ellis Island, Broadway shows, and much, much more.

For further information write to the Jewish Children's Museum, 792 Eastern Parkway, Brooklyn, NY 11213 or call (718) 467-0600. *www.jcm.museum.org*

The Junior Museum *see* Children's Museum of Science and Technology

Long Island Children's Museum
Garden City

Since its opening in November 1993, the Long Island Children's Museum has emphasized expansion and change. Currently located in space donated by LILCO, the staff and support group hope to eventually become self-supportive and have a permanent location. A new, larger facility opened in 2002, offering 14 hands-on interactive galleries, a 145-seat state-of-the-art theater and three classroom-size learning studios. Indoor and outdoor gallery spaces are also available.

The Children's Museum is one of the founding members of the Long Island Nature Collaborative for Kids. This collaboration enabled Long Island to become designated to a national demonstration site for outdoor education for young children. LICM was awarded a Museums for America grant from the Institute of Museum and Library Services in 2007, which the museum will use to work with children and families served by Nassau County social service agencies. LICM is also Long Island's most well-attended museum.

Info in brief: All exhibits at LICM are interactive, and "hands-on" is the key term used here. All children must be accompanied by an adult. Adults without children must check in at the office.

Hours: July–August: Daily, 10 A.M. to 5 P.M.; September–June: Tuesday–Sunday 10 A.M. to 5 P.M. Call ahead during holiday times. Closed most major holidays.

Admissions: Under 2, free; general admission, 9; over 65, $8, Memberships are available.

Unique exhibits or exhibitions: "stART" emphasizes cooperative learning.

Other sites of interest nearby: Long Island has many tourist attractions, including Old Westbury Gardens, the Cradle of Aviation, the Roosevelt Field shopping mall and miles of beautiful East Coast beaches.

For further information write to the Long Island Children's Museum, 11 Davis Avenue, Garden City, New York 11530, or call (516) 224-5800. *www.licm.org*

Long Island Culture History Lab & Museum
Stony Brook

Although more than 10,000 children visit the Long Island Culture History Lab & Museum, it is only open to the public for group tours. Two main programs are offered: Colonial Life & Technology and Long Island Native Life & Archaeology.

Info in brief: A hands-on children's archaeological discovery experience. Open only to groups.

For further information write to the Long Island Culture History Lab & Museum, P.O. Box 1542, Stony Brook, New York 11790, or call (631) 929-8725.

The Marble School House
Eastchester

The Marble School House was built in 1835 and is now open to the public by appointment only. The Eastchester Historical Society provides a "teacher" who will take visitors through a day's activities similar to what students would have experienced at that time.

Info in brief: Historical site which offers a typical 1835s day of schooling experiences.

Hours and Admissions: Open by appointment only. Children, $1; adults, $1.50. Be sure to contact the museum before visiting.

For further information write to The Marble School House, c/o Eastchester Historical Society, P.O. Box 37, Eastchester, New York 10709, or contact Mr. Mike Fix at (914) 395-3247.

Mid-Hudson Children's Museum
Poughkeepsie

Two floors of exhibit space, with over 50 exhibits are featured for children and adults to explore together. After a 5-year search for a permanent location, MHCM finally moved to Poughkeepsie's historic waterfront. Some of the exhibits include the Hudson River Tides Water Play Table, WKID Disney Radio Station, River Town Exhibit, Little Sprouts Farm, The Power Bike, Brain Games, "The Battle for Liberty," The Heart Play Space, The Hudson River Dive Bell and more.

Info in brief: A hands-on children's museum with an emphasis on science and technology.

Location: Poughkeepsie's historic waterfront.

Hours: Tuesday thru Sunday, 11 A.M.–5 P.M.; Infant/Toddler Area opens at 9:30 A.M. on Thursdays. December 24th & 31st, 10 A.M.–3 P.M. Closed Mondays except for selected school holidays and special summer hours. Closed New Year's Day, Memorial Day, Fourth of July, Labor Day, Thanksgiving Day, and Christmas Day.

Admissions: Under 1, free; all others, $6.50. Memberships available.

For further information write to the Mid-Hudson Children's Museum, 75 N. Water St., Poughkeepsie, NY 12601 or call (845) 471-0589 or fax (845) 471-0415. *www.mhcm.org*

Milton J. Rubenstein Museum of Science & Technology (aka: The Discovery Center)
Syracuse

Three main exhibit areas offer fun for all ages. The Earth Science Discovery Cave offers hands-on archaeology experiences. The Science Playhouse offers 5 floors of activities in a giant climbing maze, including levers, pulleys, bridges and more. A Telecommunications Laboratory features three visual exhibit areas of its own: "Morse Code & Telegraphy," "Amateur Radio Station," and "Computers." An IMAX Theater (The Bristol Omnitheater) and Science Store are also on the premises.

Info in brief: A children's museum for all ages.

Hours: Wednesday thru Sunday, 11 A.M.–5 P.M.

Admissions: Exhibit Hall only: under 2, free; children (2–11), $4; seniors (65+), $4; adults, $5. IMAX only children & seniors, $7; adults, $9. Combo Ticket: children & seniors, $9; adults, $11. Motion Simulator or Planetarium: $2, with museum admissions.

For further information write to the Milton J. Rubenstein Museum of Science & Technology, 500 S. Franklin St., Syracuse, NY 13202 or call (315) 425-9068. *www.most.org*

The New York Hall of Science
New York City

The New York Hall of Science is a children's science and technology center featuring more than 400 hands-on exhibits, with an emphasis on biology, chemistry and physics. Exhibits include: *Connections — The Nature of Networks, Feedback, Hidden Kingdoms — The World of Microbes, Marvelous Molecules — The Secret of Life, Mathematica — a World of Numbers, Preschool Place, Realms of the Atom, Rocket Park, Science Playground, Science Technology Library, The Search for Life Beyond Earth, Seeing the Light, Sound Sensation — The Inside Story of Audio, The Sports Challenge* and *Technology Gallery*.

A Science Playground is also open to children of all ages (with adult supervision), weather permitting, March through December.

Info in brief: A large science and technology children's museum.

Locations: In Flushing Meadows Corona Park.

Hours: September–March: Tuesday thru Thursday, 9:30 A.M.–2 P.M.; Friday, 9:30 A.M.–5 P.M. (free 2–5 P.M.); Saturday & Sunday, 10 A.M.–6 P.M. (free Sunday, 10–11 A.M.) Winter Holiday hours: December 24, 9:30 A.M.–2 P.M.; December 25, closed; December 26–28, 9:30 A.M.–5 P.M.; December 29 & 30, 10 A.M.–6 P.M.; December 31 & January 1, 9:30 A.M.–5 P.M. April–June: Monday thru Thursday, 9:30 A.M.–2 P.M.; Friday, 9:30 A.M.–5 P.M. (free 2–5 P.M.); Saturday & Sunday, 10 A.M.–6 P.M. (free Sunday 10–11 A.M.) July & August: Monday thru Friday, 9:30 A.M.–5 P.M.; Saturday & Sunday, 10 A.M.–6 P.M. HOLIDAY WEEKS: Monday thru Friday, 9:30 A.M.–5 P.M.; Saturday & Sunday, 10 A.M.–6 P.M. Closed Labor Day, Thanksgiving Day and Christmas Day.

Admissions: Under 2, free; children (2–17), $8; college students (w/ID), $8; seniors (62+), $8; adults (18+), $11. Science Playground fee: $4 per person, $3 for groups. Free admission is available September through June, on Fridays from 2–5 P.M. and Sundays from 10–11 A.M. Memberships available. Member ASTC.

Other sites of interest nearby: All the New York City sites.

For further information write to The New York Hall of Science, 47-01 111th St., Queens, NY 11368, or call (718) 699-0005. *www.nyscience.org*

Sci-Tech Center of New York
Watertown

Advertised as "a playground for the mind," the Sci-Tech Center is an interactive science museum with over 40 hands-on exhibits. Also offered are special workshops throughout the year, school tours, after school classes, and special annual events sponsored by the museum.

Many of the exhibits at the museum center around electricity, biology, and light. Other exhibits include a sand pendulum, binary numbers display, magnets, pulleys, dinosaurs and more.

Location: Downtown Watertown within walking distance of other attractions.

Hours: Tuesday–Thursday, 10 A.M.–2 P.M.; Friday and Saturday, 10 A.M.–4 P.M.

Admissions: Adults, $4; under 18, $3; under 2, free; family, $14. Memberships available.

Other sites of interest nearby: Jefferson County Historical Museum, historic Downtown Watertown shopping district, two whitewater rafting groups, Thompson Park Zoo, Salmon Run Mall, and the Thousand Islands vacation region. Call the Greater Watertown Chamber of Commerce (315) 788-4400 or Thousand Islands International Council 1-800-8-island (847-5263).

For further information write to Sci-Tech Center, 154 Stone St., Watertown, New York 13601, or call (315) 788-1340. *www.scitechcenter.org*

Science and Discovery Center
Horseheads

Interactive museum with exhibits that include fiber optics lab and kinetic ball machine.

Admissions: Member ASTC.

Other sites of interest nearby: Mark Twain State Park and several other museums in the area.

For further information contact: Science and Discovery Center, 3300 Chambers Rd., Horseheads, New York 14845, phone: (607) 739-5297.

The Science Discovery Center of Oneonta
Oneonta

The Science Discovery Center of Oneonta has concentrated on creating as many novel, original exhibits as possible, although several of the 80 plus exhibits could be considered "classics." Some of the exhibit areas include *Forces, Motion, Mechanisms; Fluids at Rest and In Motion; Sound and Vibration, Wave; Electricity and Magnetism; Optics and Light,* and more. About one hour is a good length of time to allow for grades 3 to 7 to visit.

Info in brief: A specially designed children's museum for children of all ages.

Location: Physical Science Building of State University College in Oneonta.

Hours: July & August: Monday–Saturday, noon to 4 P.M.; September–June: Thursday thru Saturday, noon–4 P.M.

Admissions: Free admission, donations welcome.

Other sites of interest nearby: National Soccer Hall of Fame, Yager Museums, Fine Arts Gallery, National Baseball Hall of Fame (in nearby Cooperstown) and Farmer's Museum and Fenimore House (also in Cooperstown).

For further information write to The Science Discovery Center of Oneonta, Physical Science Bldg, State University College, Oneonta, NY 13820 or call (607) 436-2011 or fax (607) 436-2654. E-mail: *scdisc@oneonta.edu*

Sciencenter
Ithaca

Supported by such notables as the late Carl Sagan and Ann Druyan, the mission of the Sciencenter is to offer people of all ages the opportunity "to experience the excitement of scientific exploration and discovery ... through interactive exhibits and programs." The museum started as a hands-on science program at a local elementary school, but became a museum in 1984. After occupying several temporary homes, the museum moved into Phase I of its permanent quarters in 1993. Phase II opened in 1996, and Phase III (a 10,000 sq. ft. addition) was scheduled to begin in 1999.

Several full-time and four part-time employees run the museum along with over 250 volunteers. The staff oversees more than 80 hands-on educational exhibits in the museum proper, which includes an outdoor science park. Also on the premises is a Tide Pool Touch Tank and Galaxy Golf. Programs for at-risk youth, school visits, after-school outreach programs and public events are also offered.

The Sciencenter is the only community-built science museum in the world. Other unique features: It is the only outdoor science park in upstate New York, it is the world's only public connection to the National Lightning Detection Network, and it made the world's first Internet connection via local cable TV network.

Info in brief: Over 80 hands-on exhibits especially of interest to children, but appealing to all ages; large museum with innovative exhibits and programs.

Location: Corner of First and Franklin streets in upstate Ithaca, New York.

Hours: Tuesday–Saturday, 10 A.M. to 5 P.M.; Sunday, noon to 5 P.M. Open only these Monday holidays—M.L. King, Jr., President's Day, Memorial Day, Labor Day, and Columbus Day. 3rd Thursdays—open to 8 P.M. Tide Pool Touch Tank hours—Saturday & Sunday, noon–4 P.M.; Tuesday & Thursday, 2–4 P.M. Galaxy Golf is closed in winter months—contact museum for summer hours.

Admissions: Under 3, free; child (ages 3–17), $4; adults (18+), $6; seniors (65+), $5; Galaxy Golf, $4. Memberships available. Member ASTC.

Unique exhibits: 17-foot-tall ball machine, Emerson Science Park, and more.

For further information write to Sciencenter, 601 First Street, Ithaca, New York 14850-3507, or call (607) 272-0600 or fax (607) 277-7469. Website: *http://www.sciencenter.org* E-mail: *scictr@sciencen ter.org, info@sciencenter.org*

Scotia-Glenville Traveling Children's Museum
Scotia

After fifteen years, the Scotia-Glenville Children's Museum remains a unique traveling museum. The basic mission is to "stimulate curiosity and interest in learning; enrich the school curriculum, and serve children, families, and the general public of all ages." Now chartered by the New York State Board of Regents, the museum services all educational institutions within a 50-mile radius of Scotia, New York, including fairs and festivals, scout troops, libraries, hospitals, nursing homes and retirement centers, and more. Funding comes from various sources— from the Town of Glenville and Village of Scotia, grants and contributions from various foundations, corporations and individuals, as well as from fees for the programs themselves.

Twenty-five part-time museum teachers operate the programs while offices and storage are now located at a permanent site.

Info in brief: Hands-on programs geared to specific groups, but limited to the area in and around Scotia—approximately a 10-county area.

For further information write to Scotia-Glenville Children's Museum, 303 Mohawk Ave. Scotia, New York 12302-1815, or call (518) 346-1764 or fax (518) 377-6593. E-mail: *dbennett@the traveling-museum.org*

Sony Wonder Technology Lab
New York

Children of all ages can explore the latest technology on a simplified scale in this four-story, interactive technology and entertainment museum. The goal of the museum is to inspire creativity in a high-quality, engaging, and family-friendly learning environment. Using permanent exhibits and innovative programs, along with Sci-Tech workshops, ongoing screenings and association/affiliations, "SWTL aims to educate and cultivate the next generation of visionaries who will help shape the future of media, entertainment, science, technology, and the arts."

Info in brief: An interactive, participatory technology museum for children and their caregivers.

Location: Mid-town Manhattan in the Sony Plaza Public Arcade at 56th St. and Madison Ave. in New York City.

Hours: Tuesday and Friday, 10 A.M. to 9 P.M.; Wednesday, Thursday and Saturday, 10 A.M. to 6 P.M.; Sunday, noon to 6 P.M. Closed Sundays and major holidays.

Admissions: Free. Paid parking is available at several private parking garages nearby.

For further information call the Sony Wonder Technology Lab at (212) 833-8100. *www.sonywon dertechlab.com*

Staten Island Children's Museum
Staten Island

Founded in 1974, the Staten Island Children's Museum is now housed in a three-story building provided by the City of New York. The museum is committed to introducing children to experiences that enrich their knowledge of themselves and the world around them and is continuing to do so by providing award-winning interactive exhibitions in art, science and the humanities.

Exhibits on display in 1996–97 included "Adventures in Three Dimensions" (art and technology), "Wonder Water," "Bugs & Other Insects," "Block Harbor," "WKID" (cameras and the media), "Walk-In! Workshop" (visual arts), "Portia's Playhouse" (theater) and more.

Info in brief: Interactive and hands-on exhibits especially for children and their caregivers.

Location: Snug Harbor Cultural Center.

Hours: Tuesday–Sunday noon to 5 P.M. when schools are open; 10 A.M.–5 P.M. when schools are closed (including week-ends). Closed Mondays, except for most school holidays.

Admissions: Under age 1, free; others, $5. Grandparents are free on Wednesday.

Unique exhibits: Ten-foot-tall "Praying Mantis" sculpture by the artist Robert Ressler stands at the entrance where children are invited to climb on its wood and steel exoskeleton.

Other sites of interest nearby: The Alice Austen House, Clove Lakes Park, College of Staten Island, Center for the Arts, The Conference House, The Garibaldi-Meucci Museum, Historic Richmond Town, Jacques Marchais Center of Tibetan Art, National Lighthouse, Museum Richmond County Court House, Snug Harbor Cultural Center, St. George Historic District, Staten Island Borough Hall, Staten Island Botanical Garden, Staten Island Ferry, Staten Island Mall, Staten Island Museum of the Staten Island Institute of Arts and Sciences, Staten Island Yankees at Richmond County Bank Ballpark, Staten Island Zoo, and the many other New York tourist attractions.

For further information write to the Staten Island Children's Museum, 1000 Richmond Terr., Staten Island, New York 10301-9910, or call (718) 273-2060 (Ext. 147) or fax (718) 273-2836. *www.statenislandkids.org* E-mail: *info@statenislandkids.org*

Strong National Museum of Play
Rochester

"Strong is the only museum in the world devoted to play." The museum explores play because it is critical to learning and human development and offers a unique look into American culture. High interactivity and extensive collections offer visitors of all ages the opportunity to explore the past and imagine the future through play.

Location: Downtown Rochester.

Hours: Monday thru Thursday and Saturday, 10 A.M.–5 P.M. (Butterfly Garden, 11 A.M.–5 P.M., Friday until 6 P.M.) Sunday, noon to 5 P.M.

Admissions: Under 2, free; children (2–17), $7.50; seniors, $8.50; adults, $9.50. Matinees are shorter and cost less. Military discounts are available. Memberships available.

For further information write to the Strong National Museum of Play, One Manhattan Square, Rochester, NY 14607 or call (585) 263-2700. *www.strongmuseum.org*

NORTH CAROLINA

Catawba Science Center
Hickory

The Catawba Science Center's permanent exhibit areas explore the physical and natural sciences. These exhibits include *Sharks & Stingrays, Coastal North Carolina, Catawba River, Energy Avenue, Inventor's workshop, VR Xtreme, EarthWatch Center, the Science Courtyard, Naturalist Center, Explore It!, RaceWays, and Carpenter Hall.* Traveling exhibits are also offered regularly throughout the year. Educational programs, and the Science Emporium gift shop are also on site.

Info in brief: A hands-on museum for children of all ages and their caregivers.

Location: 243 Third Ave., NE.

Hours: Tuesday thru Friday, 10 A.M.–5 P.M.; Saturday, 10 A.M.–4 P.M.; Sunday 1 P.M.–4 P.M.

Admissions: Under 3, free; youth (3–18), $3; seniors (62+), $3; adults, $5. Memberships available. Member ASTC, NC Grassroots Science Museums Collaborative, and North Carolina Museums Council.

For further information write to Catawba Science Center, P.O. Box 2431, Hickory, NC 28603 or call (828) 322-8169 or fax: (828) 322-1585. *www.catawbascience.org* E-mail: *info@catawbascience.org*

Charlotte at Play
Charlotte

Charlotte at Play is "a museum where little hands touch, little minds grow, and imaginations come alive." Exhibits for little ones include: The Smile Center, Pirate Adventure, Dino Dig, Transportation Station, Art Smart, Wilderness Campground, Queen City Mark and Diner, Construction Zone, Fairy Tale Castle, Performance Place, Toddler Park (under 2) and Busy Bee Baby Center. Special programs are also offered regularly for babies and their moms.

Info in brief: A hands-on museum especially for young children and their families.

Hours: Monday thru Saturday, 9 A.M.–5 P.M.; Sunday, 1–5 P.M.

Admissions: Under 1, free; all others, $6. Memberships available.

For further information write to Charlotte at Play, 10504 McMullen Creek Parkway, Charlotte, NC 28226 or call (704) 542-0877. *www.charlotteatplay.com* E-mail: *info@charlotteatplay.com*

Charlotte Nature Museum
Charlotte

Touching, encountering and discovering nature has been the main emphasis at the Charlotte Nature Museum since it opened in 1946. Programs on wildlife, hands-on exhibits, a puppet theatre, live creatures and a scenic nature trail make this a top educational resource both to school groups and the general public. A new addition is "Grandpa Tree," star of the new "Creatures of the Night" exhibit. Grandpa is an animated storytelling tree who helps visitors learn about nature and science.

Info in brief: A hands-on nature center where children are encouraged to touch and participate.

Hours, Admissions, and Other Sites of Interest see Discovery Place Science & Technology Museum

Unique exhibits: Grandpa Tree.

For further information write to Charlotte Nature Museum, 1658 Sterling Road, Charlotte, North Carolina 28209, or call (704) 337-6261 or 337-2660. *www.discoveryplace.org*

The Children's Museum & Science Center
Rocky Mount

The mission of the Children's Museum is to raise the visitors' awareness of our global connectedness and our "unique place in space by encouraging participation in mathematics, science and technology activities."

The Children's Museum is a division of the City of Rocky Mount Parks and Recreation Department. It is a hands-on museum with exhibits on science, technology and history. Main exhibit areas include: "The News Zone," a multimedia recreation of a television broadcast news experience; "Kidspace," an interactive play area for children 6 years and younger; "The Civitan Planetarium"; "The Living Marsh," a 600-gallon saltwater touch pool; "Animal Gallery"; "The Edison Effect," an historical exhibit chronicling Thomas Alva Edison's life; and "Indians of the Tar River," an historical diorama of the culture of the Tuscarora Indians. Various temporary exhibits are also offered about three times each year.

Location: Imperial Centre.

Info in brief: A hands-on museum for young children and their caregivers.

Hours: Monday (Closed); Tuesday–Saturday, 10 A.M. to 5 P.M.; Sunday, 1 P.M. to 5 P.M. (Closed Thanksgiving Day and Christmas Day.)

Admissions: 2 & under, free; children (3–16), $3; adults, $4; seniors (60+), $3. Wonderful Wednesday offers free admission from 2 P.M. to 5 P.M. Planetarium (all ages), $3.50. Memberships available. Member ASTC.

Other sites of interest nearby: Ten other children's museums located in North Carolina: National Railroad Museum in Hamlet, Great Smoky Mountains Railway in Dillsboro, North Carolina Transportation Museum in Spencer, Wilmington Railroad Museum in Wilmington, Ghost Town in the Sky in Maggie Valley, Paramount's Carowinds amusement park in Charlotte, Santa's Land in Cherokee, and Tweetsie Railroad amusement park in Blowing Rock.

For further information write to The Children's Museum & Science Center, 270 Gay Street, Rocky Mount, North Carolina 27804, or call (919) 972-1167 or fax (919) 972-1232. *www.rockymount.gov/museum/*

The Children's Museum of Wilmington
Wilmington

The Children's Museum of Wilmington first opened its doors in 1997 on Market Street with a 3,000 sq. ft. facility. In 2004, the museum purchased a new site at the corner of 2nd and Orange Streets in downtown Wilmington in the former St. John's Museum of Art facility. In 2005, a groundbreaking ceremony marked the beginning of new construction on an atrium to join the three existing structures. The doors for the new 17,000 sq. ft. facility opened on April 23, 2006 with seven all new state-of-the-art hands-on exhibits, an outdoor courtyard, a secret garden and a gift store. Exhibits include: *Ahoy Wilmington, Imagination Circus, Grocery Store, Traveler's Stories, Animal Adventures, Toddler Room* and *International Diner.*

Info in brief: A hands-on multidisciplinary museum for children ages 0–11 and their caregivers.

Location: Downtown Wilmington.

Hours: Monday–Saturday, 10 A.M.–5 P.M.; Sunday, 1 P.M.–5 P.M.

Admissions: 1 year & under, free; all others, $8.

Other sites of interest nearby: (in New Hanover) Cape Fear Museum, Poplar Grove Historic Plantation, St. John's Museum of Art, and the USS *North Carolina* Battleship Memorial.

For further information write to The Children's Museum of Wilmington, 116 Orange St., Wilmington, NC 28401-4326 or call (901) 254-3534. *www.wilmingtonchildrensmuseum.org*

Children's Museum of Winston-Salem
Winston-Salem

Opening in 2004 with the backing and support of the Junior League, the Children's Museum of Winston-Salem has a vision to nurture "children's imaginations, creativity and love of reading by bringing stories to life." The museum focuses on literature, storytelling and the arts. The 26,000 sq. ft. facility holds exhibit space, museum offices, Junior League offices, and the Whistlestop Toy Station.

Regular daily and weekly programs are offered. Special programs and special events are also offered, with a goal of offering families opportunities to learn together.

Info in brief: A children's museum with an emphasis on the arts.

Hours: Tuesday thru Saturday, 9:30 A.M.–5 P.M.; Sunday 1–5 P.M. Mondays, 9:30 A.M.–5 P.M. between Memorial Day and Labor Day, and on public school holiday Mondays.

Admissions: Under 1, free; all others, $7. Some discount Friday nights (4–8 P.M.), $3. Some Wonderful Wednesdays (2–5 P.M.), $3. Be sure to contact the museum about special admissions nights.

Other Sites of Interest Nearby: SciWorks Children's Museum.

For further information write to the Children's Museum of Winston-Salem, 390 Liberty St., Winston-Salem, NC 27101, or call (336) 723-9111. *www.childrensmuseumofws.org*

Discovery Place Science & Technology Museum
Charlotte

The Discovery Place is a large science and technology museum for children and their families. Besides the many hands-on exhibits available, visitors can experience a planetarium show, "Challenger Center," a Rainforest, a Science Circus, Aquarium, Life Center, IMAX Theater, collection displays, and much more. A new contemporary food court featuring several nationally recognized chain restaurants is now also on campus.

Opened in 1981, Discovery Place has become a major tourist attraction with over 140,000 sq. ft. of major exhibit areas. Many displays are permanent, but there are also rotating and changing exhibits on display throughout the year. Special workshops, educational programs, campouts and other activities are also offered.

Note: The museum is being renovated one section at a time, with a completion date of 2010. Be sure to contact museum before visiting to determine what sections will be open.

Info in brief: One of the largest children's museums in the country, emphasizing hands-on displays.

Location: Uptown Charlotte between 6th and 7th streets. Easily accessible from I-77 and I-85. (Suggested parking off the corner of 6th Street and Church Street—$3.)

Hours: Monday thru Friday, 9 A.M.–5 P.M., Saturday, 9 A.M.–6 P.M.; Sunday, noon–6 P.M.

Admissions: Discovery Hall: child (ages 2–13), $8; adult (14–59), $10; seniors (60+), $8. Various combination tickets are available. Contact museums website for exact details of the option you choose. Memberships with special options are available. Member ASTC.

Other sites of interest nearby: Nature Museum, Paramount's Carowinds amusement park, Santa's Land amusement park, and Tweetsie Railroad (Blowing Rock).

For further information write to Discovery Place, 301 N. Tyron St., Charlotte, North Carolina 28202, or call (704) 372-6261 or 1-800-935-0553. *www.discoveryplace.org*

Fascinate-U
Fayetteville

Fascinate-U is an interactive, hands-on museum for young children. Exhibits are located in a kid-sized city design that allows kids to shop at the Gro-Right Grocery, be a judge with a robe and gavel, explore the 911 center, forecast the weather at the WNUZ center, and more. A series of interactive special programs are also offered throughout the year.

Info in brief: An interactive, hands-on museum for young children.

Location: Next to the Market House in Historic Downtown Fayetteville.

Hours: Tuesday, Thursday & Friday, 9 A.M.–5 P.M.; Wednesday, 9 A.M.–7 P.M.; Saturday, 10 A.M.–5 P.M.; Sunday, noon–5 P.M.

Admissions: $3 per child; $1 per adult.

For further information write to Fascinate-U, 116 Green St., Fayetteville, NC or call (910) 829-9171 or fax (910) 433-1639. *www.fascinate-u.com* or E-mail: *webmail@fascinate-u.com*

Greensboro Children's Museum
Greensboro

The Greensboro Children's Museum is a hands-on, interactive museum for children ages 10 and under. The vision of the museum is to "inspire learning through play in a fun, energetic and safe environment." More than 20 permanent exhibit areas are offered in the 37,000 sq. ft. facility. The exhibit hall is designed as an "Our Town–Main Street" where the large exhibit areas are placed along "main street." Exhibits include *The Market, Nonie's House, Pizza Pan, The Theater, Our Town Bank, Tot Spot/Play Lot, Our Town Doctor's/Dentist's Office, Construction Zone, Creation Station, Media Room, Get Out and Play, Big Bubble Springs, Transportation Gallery, Lighthouse and Sandbox, Trains* and *Learning Garden.*

Info in brief: An interactive, hands-on museum for children ages 10 and under. Picnic facilities are available.

Hours: Monday, 9 A.M.–noon (for members only); Tuesday–Saturday, 9 A.M.–5 P.M.; Sunday, 1–5 P.M.; Family Friday Nights, 5–8 P.M. Open on Guilford County teacher workdays, most holidays, and Mondays on Guilford County Monday holidays. Closed July 4, Thanksgiving Day, Christmas Eve & Day, New Year's Eve & Day, and Easter Sunday.

Admissions: Under 1, free; children, $6; seniors, $5; adults, $6. On special Fridays and Sundays, $3. Free parking is available at the museum and across the street in the Church Street Parking Garage.

For further information write to the Greensboro Children's Museum, 220 N. Church St., Greensboro, NC 27401 or call (336) 574-2898 or fax (336) 574-3810. *www.gcmuseum.com*

The Health Adventure
Asheville

The Health Adventure was founded in 1968 as a family health and science attraction. The museum's first location was a small storage room at Memorial Mission Hospital, and its focus then was to reduce children's fear of hospitals. The facility has moved several times since that initial placement — to an abandoned gymnasium, a log cabin, the Mountain Area Health Education Center (where the first paid director was hired), and finally into the Park Place Education, Arts and Science Center in 1992. This site provides more than 12,000 sq. ft. of exhibit space for visitors of all ages to enjoy.

Two levels and eleven galleries of hands-on exhibits offer visitors of all ages opportunities to learn about health awareness, promote wellness lifestyles, and increase science literacy. Children's exhibits explore such topics as peer pressure, substance abuse, mathematics, physics, human sexuality, AIDS, nutrition, exercise, bones, senses, DNA, lasers, biology and more. Adult program topics include cholesterol, arthritis, allergies, humor and memory.

Traveling exhibits are also featured four times a year. School programs are also offered.

At time of publication, The Health Adventure is celebrating its 40th Anniversary, and is making plans for a new "future": Momentum Science and Health Adventure Park. Be sure to contact the museum for further information.

Info in brief: A hands-on museum focusing on family health and science.

Location: Park Place Education, Arts and Science Center on Park Square in downtown Asheville.

Hours: Tuesday thru Saturday, 10 A.M.–5 P.M.; Sunday, 1–5 P.M.

Admissions: Under 2, free; children (2–15), students & seniors, $5; adults, $7. Free parking is available. Member AAM, ASTC, NC Museums Council, and the Southeastern Museums Conference.

Other sites of interest nearby: The Fine Arts Theatre, University of North Carolina–Asheville, and other sites in historic Asheville.

For further information write to The Health Adventure, 2 S. Park Square, Asheville, NC 28801 or call (828) 254-6373. *www.thehealthadventure.org*

Imagination Station
Sanford

Imagination Station is a small (3,800 sq. ft.) hands-on, interactive children's science museum for children ages 1–10 years old. The 3,800 sq. ft. facility allows children to explore and imagine, in a simulated "grown-up" world. A variety of play stations allow children to experience such activities as being the head conductor of a 22-foot train, or be the manager of a grocery store. Children are given a 50-minute session to explore these stations, and each "session" starts at the top of each hour. Children can then move freely from station to station during their 50-minute play session.

Hours: Tuesday thru Saturday, 10 A.M.–6 P.M. (Closed daily from 1–2 P.M.); Sunday, private parties only.

Admissions: $5 per session for each child ages 1–10 years old.

For further information write to Imagination Station, 529 Wicker St., Sanford, NC 27330 or call (919) 708-5900. *www.imaginationstation.org*

Imagination Station
Wilson

Imagination Station is a small hands-on, interactive children's science museum for children ages 1–10 years old. Science comes alive in such activities as "Race the Wild" and other Fun Factory exhibits. Daily Science and outreach programs, as well as workshops and birthday parties are also available. The average visit lasts 1 to 2 hours.

Location: Downtown Wilson.

Hours: Monday–Saturday, 9 A.M. to 5 P.M.; Closed Thanksgiving, Christmas Eve, Christmas Day and New Years Day.

Admissions: Under 3, free; children (4–17), $3; seniors (62+), $3; adults, $4. AAA discount available. Member ASTC. Special group offerings are also available, $5 per person.

For further information contact: Imagination Station, 224 E. Nash Street, Wilson, North Carolina 27894, phone: (252) 291-5113. *www.imaginescience.org/programs*

Iredell Museums, Children's Museum & Play Space
Statesville

The Iredell Museums are a complex of museums including the Court Street Gallery, the Heritage Farmstead & Learning Center and the Children's Museum & Play Space. Information about the Children's Museum is provided here.

In the Children's Museum, children are allowed to touch, explore and play. Hands-on exhibits are offered in the arts, culture and sciences. Besides exhibits, programs, classes and performances are featured. Families are encouraged to actively participate in the interactive exhibit area, where visitors can experience a child-sized grocery store and café, costumes and puppet theatre, art and music, a sand table and architectural blocks, and more. Special classes and workshops are offered in the visual arts, science and language and culture.

Info in Brief: A hands-on, interactive, multidisciplinary museum for children and their families.

Location: Signal Hill Mall.

Hours: Monday thru Friday, 10 A.M.–5 P.M.; Saturday, 10 A.M.–3 P.M.; Closed on New Year's Day, Memorial Day, Labor Day, Thanksgiving and Christmas Day.

Admissions: Under 12, free; all others, $2.

Other sites of interest nearby: The other Iredell Museums: Court Street Gallery (art museum), Heritage Farmstead & Learning Center.

For further information write to the Children's Museum & Play Space, Signal Hill Mall, 1613 E. Broad St., Statesville, NC or call (704) 872-7508. *www.iredellmuseums.org*

KidSenses Children's InterACTIVE Museum
Rutherfordton

KidSenses is a hands-on, interactive museum for children and their families. Exhibits and special workshops are intended to "stimulate the imagination and educate the mind."

Hours: Tuesday thru Saturday, 9 A.M.–5 P.M.; Sunday, 1–5 P.M.

Admissions: All guests, $5. Special discount for Seniors. Memberships available.

For further information write to KidSenses Children's InterACTIVE Museum, 172 N. Main St., Rutherfordton, NC 28139 or call (828) 286-2120.

Kidzu Children's Museum
Chapel Hill

The Kidzu Children's Museum is an interactive museum especially for young children ages 0–8 years and their families. Hands-on exhibits, weekly programs and nationally recognized traveling exhibits are featured.

Founded in 2006, the museum is currently located in a 2,700 sq. ft. former storefront, with plans for expanding to a larger, permanent facility in the next few years.

Location: Historic Franklin Street just across from the University of North Carolina.

Hours: Tuesday thru Saturday, 10 A.M.–5 P.M.; Sunday 1–5 P.M. Closed December 24–26 and December 31–January 1.

Admissions: 2 years & under, free; all others, $4. Free parking is available.

For further information write to the Kidzu Children's Museum, 105 E. Franklin St., Chapel Hill, NC 27514 or call (919) 933-1455. *www.kidzuchildrensmuseum.org* E-mail: *info@kidzuchildrens museum.org*

Marbles Kids Museum
Raleigh

Marbles Kids Museum is a hands-on, interactive museum featuring exhibits designed to build imagination through self-led exploration of new ideas and interactions. The museum features five main galleries of hands-on exhibits, four of which hold permanent exhibits and the fifth is for special traveling exhibits. The four permanent galleries are titled: *Around Town!, Splash!, 2-B-Me!, and IdeaWorks*. Also on site is the Wachovia IMAX Theatre.

The museum also offers two outdoor adventure areas, and a courtyard that links the museum and the IMAX theatre, so they suggest visitors wear appropriate clothing to be able to experience these activities. The Corner Store at Marbles Kids Museum offers a variety of gifts, including a gift registry. A Starbucks Coffee Bar is also on site.

Info in brief: A hands-on children's museum which also features an IMAX experience.

Hours: Museum: Tuesday thru Saturday, 9 A.M.–5 P.M.; Sunday, noon–5 P.M.; Closed most Mondays (be sure to check with museum). Wachovia IMAX Theatre: call the theatre or check their website for exact times.

Admissions: Museum: under 1, free; youth (1–12), $5; senior, $5; adult, $5. IMAX Documentary: youth, $6.50; senior, $7.95; adult, $8.95. IMAX Feature: youth, $9.50; senior, $10.95; adult, $11.95. Combo Pass: youth, $9.50; senior, $11.95; adult, $12.95. Double Feature, Documentary films only: youth, $10; senior, $12; adult, $14. Group discounts are available.

Unique features: Starbucks Coffee Bar.

For further information write to Marbles Kids Museums, 200 E. Hargett St., Raleigh, NC 27601 or call (919) 834-4040. IMAX (919) 882-IMAX. *www.marbleskidsmuseum.org*

The Museum of Life and Science
Durham

The Museum of Life and Science began in 1946 as a small children's nature trail center and has developed into a leading destination for families. The museum is located on 70 beautiful acres with 90,000 sq. ft. of indoor exhibit space and several acres of outdoor exhibit areas, including a farmyard, playground and wild animal exhibits. The state-of-the-art interactive indoor exhibits allow visitors to sit in a real Mercury Capsule, watch a baby alligator eat, touch a 13-foot tornado, explore a full-scale Lunar Lander, investigate global communications in "Data Earth," visit more than 75 animal species on display or forecast the weather.

The Magic Wings Butterfly House combines a dramatic three-story Conservatory with the Bayer Crop Science Insectariums and Lepidoptera Learning Lab. Visitors can also take a ride on the Ellerbee Creek Railway through the Museum Nature Park where red wolves and black bears reside. A stop at the Museum gift shops or the Caterpillar Café can round out a full-day's visit.

Besides the permanent exhibits, 25 unique hands-on science programs are available to classrooms. Summer Science Camps and classes for young children are also offered. "Small Science" is one of the museum's most popular exhibits and is dedicated to children seven and younger and their caregivers. Visitors can explore chain reactions, bubbles and color. Another popular exhibit the "Scientifica Discovery Room" where visitors can take apart computers, VCR's and other objects to see how they work or experiment with magnets, tops, balls and flying machines.

Info in brief: A children's science and life science museum.

Hours: Monday thru Saturday, 10 A.M.–5 P.M.; Sunday, noon–5 P.M. Closed Thanksgiving, Christmas Day and New Year's Day.

Admissions: 2 & under, free; children (3–12). $7.50; seniors (65+) & military, $8.50; adults, $9.50; Free admission for Durham County residents every Wednesday from 1–5 P.M. Group rates available.

Other sites of interest nearby: North Carolina Transportation Museum, NC Museum of Art, Battleship North Carolina, Ackland Art Museum, NC National Parks, historic Durham sites.

For further information write to the Museum of Life and Science, 433 W. Murray Ave., Durham, NC 27704 or call (919) 220-5429. E-mail: *contactus@ncmis.org*

Natural Science Center of Greensboro
Greensboro

The first phase of a 10-year, $15 million uplift of the Natural Science Center of Greensboro is nearing completion. The first phase is creating a new Animal Discovery center/zoo, with more than 90 species of animals on site.

Further phases call for renovations to the current 60,000 sq. ft. building, which will include an updated dinosaur exhibit, an exhibit on the human body, several other new interactive, multimedia exhibits, a room for traveling exhibits and an omnisphere theater in the planetarium. The final phase will be the creation of a separate building to house an aquarium and exhibits on the science of water.

Hours: Monday–Saturday, 10 A.M.–4 P.M.; Sunday, 12:30–4 P.M.

Admissions: 2 & under, free; 3–13, $7; adults, $8; seniors (65+), $7.

For further information write to the Natural Science Center of Greensboro, 4301 Lawndale Dr., Greensboro, NC 27455 or call (336) 288-3769. *www.natsci.org*

Old Salem Children's Museum, Old Salem Museums and Gardens
Winston-Salem

Old Salem Children's Museum is one of the Old Salem Museums and Gardens complex. The other museums are the Historic Town of Salem, MESDA (Museum of Early Southern Decorative Arts), and the Toy Museum. For the purposes of this book, the following information refers to the children's museum.

The Old Salem Children's Museum is designed as a place for children ages 4 through 9 to learn about 18th century concepts through play. Visitors can roll marbles through a marble run, weave ropes on an old-fashioned loom, draw one's pre-camera portrait, build a brick wall, keep house in a child-sized Miksch house, use a balance scale, climb a structure, crawl through a maze or read under the reading tree.

Info in brief: An interactive history/play-museum for young children, ages 4 through 9.

Location: Historical Winston-Salem, North Carolina.

Hours: January and February: Tuesday thru Saturday, 9:30 A.M.–4:30 P.M.; Sunday 1–5 P.M. March to December: Monday thru Saturday, 9:30 A.M.–4:30 P.M.; Sunday, 1–5 P.M.

Admissions: Several types of tickets are available: All-in-one Ticket, Two-Stop Ticket, or Children's Museum & Toy Museum Ticket. The Children's Museum & Toy Museum Ticket is $6. Discounts are offered for AAA and AARP members. Member AAM.

For further information write to Old Salem Museum & Gardens, P.O. Box F Salem Station, Winston-Salem, NC 27108 or call 1-888-653-7253 or (336) 721-7300 or fax (336) 721-7335. *www.old salem.org*

Playspace Children's Museum
Raleigh

Playspace is geared toward children from birth to seven years of age. Interactive "play stations" include a bank, art room, castle, grocery store, kitchen, medical services, acting, a fire engine, an ambulance, water play, computer lab and more.

Admissions: $5 per person.

For further information write to Playspace Children's Museum, 410 Glenwood Ave., Ste. 150, Raleigh, NC 27603 or call (919) 832-1212.

SciWorks
Winston-Salem

SciWorks offers visitors more than 45,000 sq. ft. of hands-on exhibits, along with a 15-acre environmental park, a 120-seat state-of-the-art planetarium, demonstrations, special programs and special events. All exhibits and programs are based on science and the environment.

SciWorks first opened in 1965 as the Nature Science Center, with an emphasis on the environment. Expansions and improvements have added the hands-on science experiments and the planetarium to the list of opportunities for visitors to explore.

Info in brief: A hands-on museum and nature center especially for children and their caregivers, but of interest to all age groups.

Location: Off U.S. Hwy. 52 or University Parkway on Hanes Mill Road.

Hours: Monday–Friday, 10 A.M. to 4 P.M.; Saturday, 11 A.M. to 5 P.M. Closed Sunday Extended hours and free admission on 2nd Friday of each month (to 8 P.M.). Park facilities close ½ hour before the building each day.

Admissions: Under 2 free; children (2–5), $5; youth (6–19) & seniors, $7; adults, $10. No extra charge for park or planetarium. Member ASTC.

For further information write to SciWorks, 400 Hanes Mill Road, Winston-Salem, North Carolina 27105, or call (336) 714-7109 or fax (336) 661-1777. *www.sciworks.org*

NORTH DAKOTA

The Children's Museum at Yunker Farm
Fargo

Yunker Farm Park is owned and maintained by the Fargo Park Board. The Children's Museum, started in 1985, is housed in a historic building leased from the Park Board. The original part of the building was built in 1876 as a farmhouse. Additions have increased the floorspace to 4,000 sq. ft., enabling the museum to house over 50 hands-on educational exhibits. The Children's Museum at Yunker Farm has been ranked in the Top 25 of Children's Museums in the U.S. by *Child Magazine.*

Outside, visitors can ride a train and a carousel. A playground and picnic area are also available. Special programs offered include outreach classes for local schools, Yunkie Club for preschoolers and "Think Thursday."

Info in brief: A hands-on museum for children 12 and under and their families.

Hours: School year — Tuesday, Wednesday, Friday, and Saturday, 10 A.M. to 5 P.M.; Thursday, 1 P.M. to 8 P.M.; Sunday, 1 P.M. to 5 P.M. Closed Mondays except during school holidays. Summer — Add Mondays, 10 A.M.–5 P.M.

Admissions: Under 1, free; others, $3; Thursday — Dollar Day. Train and carousel tickets are extra. All children must be accompanied by an adult. Member of Association of Youth Museums.

Unique exhibits: Train and carousel outside.

For further information write to The Children's Museum at Yunker Farm, 1201 28th Ave. N., Fargo, North Dakota 58102, or call (701) 232-6102. *www.childrensmuseum-yunker.org*

Gateway to Science Center
Bismarck

Gateway to Science is North Dakota's only hands-on *science* center and is located in the Frances Leach High Prairie Arts & Science Complex in Bismark. In November, 1994, Gateway opened its doors with a goal of offering a variety of informal science learning/experimenting opportunities, which include interactive exhibits as well as special programs and special events. (Girl Scout patch opportunities are available.)

Location: Frances Leach High Prairie Arts and Science Complex.

Hours: Monday–Thursday, Noon–7 P.M.; Friday–Saturday, Noon–5 P.M.; Closed Sunday.

Admissions: Under 4, free; children (4–12), $2; adults, $5. Member ASTC.

For further information write to the Gateway to Science Center, 1810 Schafer St., Bismarck, North Dakota 58501-1218, or call (701) 258-1975. *www.gscience.org* E-mail: *gscience@gscience.org*

OHIO

The Boonshoft Museum of Discovery
Dayton

The Boonshoft Museum of Discovery is a science and technology museum for children, with an accredited zoo, a Planetarium and an observatory. Besides the more than 60 animals at the zoo, the museum features several permanent exhibits, including the Bernoulli Blower, Explorers Crossing, the Water Table, the Color Wall, and a pioneer cabin. Other permanent exhibits include the "Hall of Universe," "Oscar Boonshoft Science Central," "Mead Tree House," "African Room" (home of Neshur the Mummy), and much more.

Info in brief: Combination children's science and technology museum, zoo, planetarium and observatory.

Hours: Monday thru Friday, 9 A.M.–5 P.M.; Saturday, 11 A.M.–5 P.M.; Sunday, noon–5 P.M. Closed New Year's Eve and Day, Thanksgiving, Christmas Eve & Day, and Easter.

Admissions: Under 2, free; children (2–12), $7; seniors, $7; adults, $8.50.

For further information write to Boonshoft Museum of Discovery, 2600 DeWeese Parkway, Dayton, OH 45414 or call (937) 275-7431 or fax (937) 275-5811. *www.boonshoftmuseum.org*

Cincinnati Fire Museum
Cincinnati

Along with other fire museums across the country, the Cincinnati Fire Museum showcases the history of fire fighting in the area from the early 1800s to the present. This fire museum, however, does more than display antique equipment, it provides hands-on, participatory exhibits for children. Starting with a video about fire safety, children move on into the museum to explore an old water pumper fire truck, slide down a fire pole, call 911, and use three interactive computer programs to learn more about fire safety. Antique equipment is on display, along with memorabilia from firefighters through the generations in Cincinnati.

Info in brief: Both hands-on and visual displays are offered.

Location: Downtown Cincinnati in a National Register firehouse at the corners of Court and Plum streets.

Hours: Tuesday–Friday, 10 A.M. to 4 P.M.; Saturday and Sunday, noon to 4 P.M.; closed Monday and holidays.

Admissions: Under 6, free; children, $5; adults, $7; seniors, $6.

Other sites of interest nearby: BB Riverboats, Inc., Behringer-Crawford Museum, Children's Museum of Cincinnati, Cincinnati Historical Society Museum, Cincinnati Museum of Natural History, Cincinnati Railway Museum, Paramount's Kings Island amusement park, and more.

For further information write to Cincinnati Fire Museum, 315 W. Court St., Cincinnati, Ohio 45202, or call (513) 621-5553. *www.cincinnatifiremuseum.com*

Cincinnati Museum Center at Union Terminal, Duke Energy Children's Museum
Cincinnati

Officially opened in 1994, the Children's Museum of Cincinnati became a part of Cincinnati Museum Center at Union Terminal in October of 1998, and was renamed the Duke Energy

Children's Museum in 2007. The museum features eight major exhibit areas and is regularly in the top ten most visited children's museums in the country. The eight exhibit areas include: "Energy Zone" (climbing and nature), "Water Works" (natural and physical uses of water), "Little Sprouts Farm" (infants and toddlers), "Kids' Town" (dramatic play), "Kids at Work" (building and construction), and "Children Just Like Me" (world cultures). The museum also features a small theater for live performances, programs for children, workshops for adults and families, and school programs, distance learning and outreach for schools.

The Duke Energy Children's Museum features 28,000 sq. ft. of exhibit space and is a part of Cincinnati Museum Center at Union Terminal, which also includes the Museum of Natural History and Science; Cincinnati History Museum; Cincinnati Historical Society Library, several changing exhibit halls, and the Robert D. Lindner Family OMNIMAX Theater. The museum also creates and tour several traveling exhibits.

Info in brief: A hands-on children's museum with over 200 experiences for children ages 10 and under and their families.

Location: Historic Union Terminal

Hours: Monday–Saturday, 10 A.M. to 5 P.M.; Sunday, 11 A.M. to 6 P.M. Additional hours vary for special exhibits and the Robert D. Lindner Family OMNIMAX Theater.

Admissions: Under 1, free; toddlers (1–3), $4.25; children (3–12), $5.25; adults, $7.25. Member ACM, ASTC.

Other sites of interest nearby: Paramount's Kings Island, Cincinnati Zoo, Cincinnati Art Museum, National Underground Railroad Freedom Center, and other Cincinnati tourist attractions.

For further information write to The Cincinnati Museum Center at Union Terminal, 1301 Western Ave., Cincinnati, OH 45203 or call (513) 287-7000 or 1-800-733-2077. *www.cincymuseum.org* E-mail: *information@cincymuseum.org*

Cleveland Children's Museum
Cleveland

This small museum features four interactive exhibit areas which encourage creative and dramatic play. Intended to serve children ages 2 to 10 years, these areas are: "Over and Under Bridges," "Water-Go-Round," "Little House Under Construction" (rotating exhibit), and at least one other traveling exhibit from the Youth Museum Exhibit Collaborative (YMEC) at all times. The intent is to keep the museum growing and changing.

Info in brief: Hands-on, exploratory museum for children and caregivers.

Location: Cleveland's University Circle at the intersection of Euclid Ave. and Martin Luther King Blvd.

Hours: Daily, 10 A.M.–5 P.M.

Admissions: Under 11 months free; ages 1–12, $7; all others, $6. Memberships available. Member ASTC.

Other sites of interest nearby: Cleveland Orchestra, Cleveland Museum of Art, Cleveland Museum of Natural History, African American Museum, the Cleveland Playhouse, Cleveland Clinic, Western Reserve Historical Society, the Health Museum.

For further information write to the Cleveland Children's Museum, 10730 Euclid Ave., Cleveland, Ohio 44106-2200, or call (216) 791-7114 or fax (216) 791-8838. *www.clevelandchildrensmuseum. org*

COSI, Center of Science & Industry
Columbus

COSI first opened its doors in 1964, on an Easter Sunday, with more than 5,000 people in attendance (paying 25 or 50 cents each). The museum was then housed in Memorial Hall, and stayed there with numerous improvements over the years. Thirty-five years later, having outgrown that space, COSI moved to its current location in downtown Columbus, with 320,000 sq. ft. of exhibit space. COSI, originally designed using the Chicago Museum of Science and Industry as its inspiration, is now one of the most respected science centers in the nation. The museum offers more than 300 interactive exhibits throughout its "discover-based and themed exhibition areas." Some of the exhibits include: Ocean, Space Gadgets, Life, little kid-space, Progress, WOSU@COSI, and Big Science Park. Hallways also hold fun, learning activities like Electrostatic Generator Show. Other offerings include the only High-Wire Unicycle in the country, a seven-story Extreme Screen theater, a Science 2Go! Retail store and the Atomi-cafe restaurant. Changing traveling exhibits from other museums are available throughout the year.

COSI has received numerous awards for its ground-breaking, education programs.

Info in brief: Premier hands-on, interactive science museum for children and their families.

Location: Downtown Columbus.

Hours: Regular hours: Wednesday–Saturday, 10 A.M. to 5 P.M.; Sunday, noon to 6 P.M. Mondays open: Martin Luther King Jr. day, President's Day, Memorial Day and Labor Day. Some days offer extended hours (be sure to contact the museum). Closed New Year's Day, Easter Sunday, July 3–4th, September 4–21, Thanksgiving, Christmas Eve and Christmas Day.

Admissions: COSI ticket only: under 2, free; youth (2–12), $7.50; senior (60+), $10.50; adult (13–59), $12.50. Value Passes available (add $6) for all movies. Extreme Screen Movie Ticket: under 2, free; all others, $7.50. Active military personnel, certified teachers, and Big Brothers/Sisters with Little admitted free to exhibits. Membership available. Member ASTC. Discounts to AAA and COESRA members.

For further information contact: COSI, Center of Science & Industry, 333 West Broad St., Columbus, Ohio 43215-3773, phone: (614) 228-2674. *www.cosi.org*

Duke Energy Children's Museum
Cincinnati

One of the museums in the Cincinnati Museum Center, Duke Energy Children's Museum opened in 1998 and has consistently ranked in the top 25 children's museums in the country since then. Children can climb, crawl, explore and learn about themselves and the world around them in the 8 educational and dramatic exhibit areas. Two areas are for preschool age and younger children.

Info in brief: A multidisciplinary museum for children. One of a complex of museums on this site.

Location: Cincinnati Museum Center at Cincinnati Union Terminal.

Hours: Monday thru Saturday, 10 A.M.–5 P.M.; Sunday, 11 A.M.–6 P.M.

Admissions: Single Attraction Price: toddlers, $4.25; children (3–12), $5.25; seniors (60+), $6.25; adults, $7.25. Combo tickets are also available. Contact the Museum Center for more information.

For further information write to The Cincinnati Museum Center at Union Terminal, 1301 Western Ave., Cincinnati, OH 45203 or call (513) 287-7000 or 1-800-733-2077. *www.cincymuseum.org* E-mail: *information@cincymuseum.org*

Inventure Place
Akron

Inventure Place has something to offer the entire family. Its unique architectural structure is one of the most interesting in Akron. The courtyard in front of the sail-like structure actually enters the building several levels above the bottom floor. From the top floors, which contain the National Inventors Hall of Fame, visitors can see all the way down to the bottom floor, which is where the hands-on, interactive exhibits for children (and their families) are housed. Interactive exhibits include a harp, with lasers where strings are normally placed, cameras that allow visitors to create stop-motion simulations, water play, magnets, electricity and others that encourage visitors to learn more about technology and its applications.

Info in brief: Multi-story facility with both visual and hands-on exhibits for both adults and children.

Location: Downtown Akron.

Hours: Tuesday thru Saturday, 9 A.M.–5 P.M.; Sunday, noon–5 P.M.

Admissions: 2 & under, free; seniors & kids (3–17), $6; adults, $7.50.

Other sites of interest nearby: Pro Football Hall of Fame, Dover Park, MetroParks, and the Cuyahoga Valley National Park.

For further information write to Inventure Place, 221 S. Broadway St., Akron, Oh 44308-1505 or call (330) 762-6565. *www.invent.org*

Museum of Natural History & Science
Cincinnati

Opened in 1990, The Museum of Natural History & Science is one attraction at the Cincinnati Museum Center. Visitors are treated to both visual and hands-on displays. Interactive exhibits include displays of the human body, a natural trading post, and migration and extinction demonstrations are offered. Visitors can also walk through a glacier and step back 19,000 years into the Ohio Valley during the Ice Age or explore a limestone cave with waterfalls, streams, fossils and a live bat colony.

Other museum/attractions in the complex are The Cincinnati History Museum, The Duke Energy Children's Museum, and an Omnimax Theater.

Info in brief: A natural history and science museum for families. One of a complex of museums on this site.

Location: Cincinnati Museum Center at Cincinnati Union Terminal.

Hours: Monday thru Saturday, 10 A.M.–5 P.M.; Sunday, 11 A.M.–6 P.M.

Admissions: Single Attraction Price: toddlers, $4.25; children (3–12), $5.25; seniors (60+), $6.25; adults, $7.25. Combo tickets are also available. Contact the Museum Center for more information.

For further information write to The Cincinnati Museum Center at Union Terminal, 1301 Western Ave., Cincinnati, OH 45203 or call (513) 287-7000 or 1-800-733-2077. *www.cincymuseum.org* E-mail: *information@cincymuseum.org*

Wm. McKinley Presidential Library & Museum
Canton

The Wm. McKinley Presidential Library & Museum is located on 26 acres adjacent to the McKinley National Memorial — burial site of William McKinley, 25th President of the United

Dinosaurs are a favorite of visitors of all ages at the William McKinley Presidential Library and Museum.

The streets of yesteryear at the William McKinley Presidential Library and Museum.

States, and his family. The Museum complex includes the McKinley Gallery, Street of Shops, Keller Gallery, Hoover-Price Planetarium, Ramsayer Research Library, and Discover World, all relating the story of life in Stark County and the legacy of William McKinley.

The Planetarium and Discover World are of special interest to children. Exhibits in Discover World are both visual and interactive. As visitors enter the area, they are greeted by the roar of a life-sized, robotic Allosaurus. Dioramas of pre-historic life fill this area. On display are a series of ponds displaying underwater wildlife, and a working beehive. "Space Station Earth" is of special interest, as many hands-on exhibits are in this area. A Museum Shoppe offers both educational and entertaining items for visitors to purchase.

Info in brief: Definitely a full-day experience with both hands-on and visual displays available.

Location: 800 McKinley Monument Drive N.W., Canton, Ohio (It is suggested that you visit their website for specific travel instructions.)

Hours: Monday–Saturday, 9 A.M. to 5 P.M.; Sunday, noon to 5 P.M.

Admissions: Adults, $7; children (3–18), $5; seniors (60 & over), $6. Member ASTC.

Other sites of interest nearby: Tourist attractions in Cleveland, Ohio, or Pittsburgh, Pennsylvania.

For further information write to the McKinley Museum, 800 McKinley Monument Dr. N.W., Canton, Ohio 44708-4800, or call (330) 455-7043. *www.mckinleymuseum.org*

OKLAHOMA

Hands-On!! Interactive Children's Museum
Tulsa

Hands-On offers more than 25 interactive exhibits that encourage self-discovery.

For further information write to Hands-On!! Interactive Children's Museum, 7704 E. 38th St., Tulsa, OK 74103 or call (918) 663-3333.

Jasmine Moran Children's Museum
Seminole

This 28,000 sq. ft. of children's museum offers indoor exhibits based on the theme of a child-sized town. All exhibits are interactive and hands-on. An outdoor play area, complete with the SuperSONIC Express train is also featured.

Hours: Tuesday thru Saturday, 10 A.M.–5 P.M.; Sunday 1–5 P.M.; Closed Mondays, major holidays and the first 2 weeks after Labor Day.

Admissions: 2 & under, free; 3 years & older, $7 + tax; over 60, $6 + tax.

For further information write to Jasmine Moran Children's Museum, 1714 Wrangler Blvd., or 1714 Hwy 9 West, Seminole, Oklahoma 74868 or call 1-800-259-KIDS. *www.jasminemoran.com*

Science Museum Oklahoma
Oklahoma City

The Science Museum Oklahoma contains three independent museums in one 10-acre facility. However, visitors pay only one admissions charge, which covers all three museum areas. Museums included are the Kirkpatrick Science and Air Space Museum, the International Photography Hall of Fame and Museum, and Red Earth Indian Center. Of special concern to this publication is the Kirkpatrick Science and Air Space Museum, which itself contains five main areas. These areas are the Hands-on Science Museum, the Air Space Museum, Kirkpatrick Galleries, Botanical Gardens and Greenhouse, and Kirkpatrick Planetarium.

The Hands-on Science Museum has been operating for nearly 40 years. Its primary aim is and has always been to promote science literacy in Oklahoma. Today, it is considered to be the premier interactive science center in Oklahoma, with over 300 hands-on exhibits and numerous educational programs. Some of the theme exhibit areas include: Perception, Light, Sound, Life Sciences, Energy Sources, Meteorology, KIDSPACE, Physics, Agriculture and Nutrition. In 1996, *Parents* magazine named the Hands-on Science Museum as one of the nation's best museums for children.

The Air Space Museum was founded in 1980 to "recognize and honor those in aviation and space who have contributed significantly to the advancement of aviation and space exploration." (Oklahoma has produced more astronauts than any other state.) One-week summer camp programs offer an extensive aerospace experience for children ages 3–16. Visitors can experience a NASA moon landing, fly an actual mission at the AWAC's control center, fly a real World War II link trainer, fly an F-16 Combat Flight Simulator, and man a unique Mercury capsule simulator that recreates the first space mission by a U.S. astronaut.

The other areas of the Kirkpatrick Science and Air Space Museum are also of interest to children and their families, but offer little in the way of hands-on experiences. Displays of miniatures, toys, and wildlife, however, are enough to hold their interest, so plan on allotting an entire day to this visit.

The Science Museum Oklahoma is a Smithsonian Affiliate.

Info in brief: A multifacility museum with plenty of hands-on activities and interactive displays for children of all ages and their caregivers. Also includes a planetarium, botanical gardens and more.

Location: Northeast Oklahoma City near the zoo and Remington Park racetrack.

Hours: Monday thru Friday, 9 A.M.–5 P.M.; Saturday, 9 A.M.–6 P.M.; Sunday, 11 A.M.–6 P.M. Closed Thanksgiving and Christmas Day. Planetarium show times vary, so be sure to contact museum for updated schedule.

Admissions: Under 3, free; seniors/children, $8.25; adults, $9.50; Dome Theater — senior/children, $6.75; adult, $8.25. Member ASTC. Member Oklahoma Museum Network. Free parking is available.

Unique feature: Seven museums under one roof.

Other sites of interest nearby: Oklahoma State Firefighters Museum, Amateur Softball Association, National Softball Hall of Fame and Museum, Lions Family Fun Park, The National Cowboy Hall of Fame and Western Heritage Center, Oklahoma City Zoo, Remington Park (horse racing), and Frontier City theme park.

For further information write to Omniplex, 2100 N.E. 52nd St., Oklahoma City, Oklahoma 73111-7107, or call 1-800-532-7652 or (405) 602-6664 or fax (405) 602-3768. *www.omniplex.org*

Stillwater Children's Museum
Stillwater

Stillwater Children's Museum is designed for young children and their caregivers. Opening date not yet set.

For further information write to the Stillwater Children's Museum, P.O. Box 1299, Stillwater, OK 74076 or call (405) 533-3333. *www.stillwaterchildrensmuseum.org* E-mail: *info@stillwaterchildrens museum.org*

Will Rogers Memorial & Birthplace
Claremore

The Will Rogers museum in Claremore is a twelve-gallery comprehensive museum with three theaters, two interactive television kiosks and the family tomb. The museum also features a 3,000 sq. ft. children's participation area (opened in 1995). Children enter a time tunnel that starts with the Oklahoma mound dwellers of 20,000 years ago. The tunnel takes them past exhibits of the exiled 19th-century Cherokee Indians' civilization, past exhibits of taxidermed indigenous wildlife, and past live fish, then ends in the hands-on area depicting Will Rogers' career. Many role-playing situations are available here.

Info in brief: There are actually two attractions situated about 12 miles apart, one of which (in Claremore) offers participatory activities for children.

Location: Claremore; the Living History Ranch is on the shore of Lake Oologah.

Hours: Daily, 8 A.M. to 5 P.M.

Admissions: Free; donations welcome. Contact the museum for current charges.

Unique feature: The only museum in the world dedicated to maintaining the memory and humor of Will Rogers.

For further information write to the Will Rogers Memorial & Birthplace, P.O. Box 157, Claremore, Oklahoma 74018-0157, or call 1-800-324-WILL or (918) 341-0719 or fax (918) 343-8119. *www.will rogers.com*

OREGON

A.C. Gilberts Discovery Village
Salem

Opened in 1989, the Gilbert House Children's Museum is a hands-on museum whose mission is "to provide innovative and stimulating experiences to spark children's natural creativity and curiosity ... with fun and challenging exhibits and activities in the Sciences, Arts and Humanities." Each room and each exhibit has written guides, educational explanations, and lesson concepts posted for a more thorough understanding of each activity.

The museum grounds incorporate two two-story buildings which house various exhibits, including: "Recycle City," "Wet & Wild," "Artist Studio," "Cave of Wonders," "Secret Sleuths," "Kidspace," "Gilbert Room" (memorabilia display), "Chain Reaction" (physics), "Bienvenidos a México!," "Karaoke for Kids," "Children's Theater," a family resource center, classroom space, and various rotating exhibits throughout the year. Use of the portable planetarium is available at various times, and visitors are also allowed access to the Children's Discovery Garden.

Info in brief: Mostly hands-on museum designed for children.

Location: Housed in two historic Victorian homes on Salem's downtown riverfront.

Hours: Monday–Saturday, 10 A.M. to 5 P.M.; Sunday, noon to 4 P.M.; Open 361 days a year.

Admissions: Under 1, free; toddlers (1 & 2), $2.50; seniors, (60+) $4; all others, $5.50. Groups rates available. Member of Association of Youth Museums. Member ASTC.

Other sites of interest nearby: Elsinore Center for the Arts, Enchanted Forest (in Turner, 7 miles south), Oaks Park amusement park (Portland).

For further information write to A.C. Gilbert's Discovery Village, 116 Marion Street NE, Salem, Oregon 97301-3437, or call 1-800-208-9514 or (503) 371-3631. E-mail: *info@acgilbert.org*

Children's Museum
Jacksonville

The Children's Museum in Jacksonville features exhibits related to American Indians and early settlers to the area. Among other exhibits are a 1920's kitchen, a pioneer cabin, a Native American lodge, a puppet theater, a general store, and a barber shop.

Location: Next to the Jacksonville Museum in the old town jail.

Hours: June thru September: Daily, 10 A.M.–5 P.M.; October thru May: Closed Mondays.

Admissions: 2 & under, free; child (3–12), $3; seniors (65+), $3; adults, $5.

Other sites of interest nearby: Beekman House & Bank, Museum of Southern Oregon History.

For further information call the museum at (541) 773-6536 or visit their website: *www.sohs.org* or the following website: *www.planetware.com/jacksonville/childrens-museum-us-or-jvcm.htm*

The Children's Museum of Southern Oregon Historical Society
Jacksonville

The Southern Oregon Historical Society operates several museums and historical sites that are open to the public. One of these museums is The Children's Museum in Jacksonville. Opened in 1979, the museum is located in the 1910 former Jackson County Jail. Exhibits target children aged from preschool through fourth grade. It is a history museum, which provides hands-on history for all ages. The two floors of exhibits include an actual 1890s General Store, a Chinese laundry, a bank, and several other stations that encourage interactive play. The newest exhibit is titled "Miner, Baker, Furniture Maker"—chronicling technology's role in the development of early Jacksonville and Southern Oregon.

Info in brief: The Children's Museum is a hands-on, interactive museum for young children and their caregivers. Other museums run by the society are of interest to the whole family.

Location: 206 N. 5th Street, Jacksonville.

Hours: Wednesday–Saturday, 1:00 P.M.–4 P.M.

Admissions To the Children's Museum & adjacent Jacksonville Museum: Under 3, free; children (3–12), $3; seniors (60+), $3; adults, $5.

Other sites of interest nearby: (Operated by the society) The Southern Oregon History Center, Jacksonville Museum of Southern Oregon History, the C.C. Beekman House, and more; Enchanted Forest amusement park in Turner; Oaks Park in Portland; The Gilbert House Children's Museum in Salem; and the Oregon Museum of Science and Industry in Portland.

For further information write to The Children's Museum, 206 N. 5th St., Jacksonville, Oregon 97530, or c/o Southern Oregon Historical Society, 106 N. Central Ave., Medford, Oregon 97501-5926, or call (541) 773-6536 or fax (541) 776-7994.

CM2 — Children's Museum 2nd Generation
Portland

The mission of CM2 is "to inspire imagination, creativity and the wonder of learning in children and adults by inviting moments of shared discovery."

Info in brief: A children's museum with an emphasis on the arts.

For further information write to CM2, 4015 SW Canyon Rd., Portland, OR 97221. *www.portland cm2.org*

The High Desert Museum
Bend

The cultural and natural heritage of the "Intermountain West" is brought to life at the High Desert Museum. Situated on a 150-acre tract of land surrounded by the Deschutes National Forest, the museum offers visitors unusual activities both outside and inside. Outside, the rugged land between the Rockies and the Cascades, a unique area of timberland, rivers, volcanic hot springs and high desert land, enables the museum to offer visitors opportunities to observe otters in a pond, witness hand-feeding of native porcupines, watch a birds of prey presentation, walk through a settler's cabin and hike the trails. Inside, visual displays, hands-on activities, and interactive displays enable visitors to rediscover the sights and sounds of the past.

Info in brief: An indoor-outdoor museum offering a number of hands-on activities along with visual and interactive displays for the whole family.

Location: Six miles south of Bend, Oregon.

Hours: Open every day, 9 A.M. to 5 P.M. Closed Thanksgiving, Christmas and New Year's Day. Be sure to contact the museum for exact times of various demonstrations throughout the day.

Admissions: (October–April) 4 & under, free; youth (5–12), $6; adult, $10; senior (65+), $9. (May–September) youth, $9; adult, $15 (2 days); senior, 12. Memberships available.

Other sites of interest nearby: Deschutes National Forest, numerous outdoor recreational facilities. Contact the Chamber of Commerce and Tourist Bureau in Bend, Oregon, for more specific details.

For further information write to The High Desert Museum, 59800 South Highway 97, Bend, Oregon 97702, or call (541) 382-4754. *www.highdesertmuseum.org*

Oregon Museum of Science and Industry
Portland

Founded in 1944, OMSI started, as many children's museums do, in a house. After an unprecedented fundraising campaign, the huge new facility opened in 1992 on Water Avenue. Six exhibit halls, including seven interactive laboratories and an Early Childhood Education Center, a 330-seat Omnimax Theater, a 220-seat Murdock Sky Theater Planetarium/Laser Light

At OMSI, science is amazing.

Kids take a look through submarine periscopes at the Oregon Museum of Science and Industry.

Venue, the USS *Blueback* (a 219 ft. diesel electric submarine), a Science Store, Cafe and a 25,000 sq. ft. exhibit shop are offered. A total of 219,000 sq. ft. are incorporated in the facility. The five permanent exhibit halls represent specific scientific themes: Earth Science, Life Science, Information Science, Physical Science and Space Science. All halls house laboratories and hands-on activity areas as well as live science presentations throughout the day.

Besides the in-house exhibits and programs, the museum offers 26 traveling exhibits to museums throughout North America, making it the largest science outreach program in the United States.

Info in brief: A hands-on, participatory science museum for children and their caregivers.

Location: S.E. Water Ave. at the East end of the Hawthorne Bridge on the Willamette River.

Hours & Admission Prices: Visit the Museum's website, select a date from the calendar to see museum and café hours, showtimes, sub tours information and Omnimax and Planetarium hours and prices.

Unique exhibits: The facility incorporates the Historic Portland General Electric Turbine Hall, which once generated power for downtown Portland.

For further information write to OMSI, 1945 SE Water Ave., Portland, Oregon 97214-3354, or call (503) 797-4000. Website: *http://www.omsi.edu*

Portland Children's Museum
Portland

Celebrating more than 45 years of service, the Children's Museum in Portland is now administered by the Portland Bureau of Parks and Recreation. Little visitors (especially those ages infant to 10 years) are encouraged to use their imaginations as they slip into a firefighter's gear, climb onto a ladder truck, rev up pint-sized vehicles and follow roadways through a tunnel and bridge, pretend to operate a repair shop, restaurant, doctor's office, grocery store and more. The basement houses a clay workshop where all visitors may play with the clay for free, or can purchase their completed creations for a small fee. A playground is also located just outside in Lair Hill Park.

In conjunction with the museum — and just a short distance away — is the Children's Cultural Center, where contemporary American Indian life is explored. A 1,200 sq. ft. exhibit called "Living Legends" opened early in 1997, along with other cultural exhibits.

Admission to the Children's Museum includes free admission to the Cultural Center, or each museum may be visited separately.

Info in brief: A hands-on museum for younger children with some exhibits of interest to slightly older children. The Cultural Center attracts visitors of all ages.

Locations: In older downtown Portland.

Hours: Fall/Winter: Tuesday–Sunday, 9 A.M.–5 P.M.; Select Mondays (contact museum).

Admissions: Under 1, free; $3.50 for others. Member AYM.

Unique exhibits: "H_2Oh" exhibit — pumps, drawbridges and a bubble wall impel visitors to experiment.

Other sites of interest nearby: Cascade Sternwheelers, Crooked River Railroad Company Dinner Train, End of the Oregon Trail Interpretive Center, The High Desert Museum, Metro Washington Park Zoo, Mount Hood Railroad, Oregon Museum of Science and Industry, and more.

For further information write to the Children's Museum, 4015 SW Canyon Rd., Portland, Oregon 97221, or call (503) 223-6500 or fax (503) 823-3667. *www.portlandcm.org*

Science Factory Children's Museum & Planetarium
Eugene

The Science Factory Children's Museum exhibit hall has more than 50 interactive hands-on exhibits, including a large multi-room color playhouse, Polarized Windows, TV Colors, and Color Storm (a bicycle-powered machine that forms a flurry of colored feathers), and a giant Kaleidoscope. LaBallotory is a highly interactive exhibit that allows visitors to explore the physics behind simple machines through exhibits that use balls. Other exhibits include Bernoulli's, a Bike Wheel Gyroscope, a computer room and more.

Originally opened in June of 2002, the Science Factory has doubled their space to 10,000 sq. feet including the planetarium, classroom computer laboratory, exhibit hall and meeting space. They are currently in the process of planning another expansion.

Info in brief: A hands-on, interactive science museum for children and their caregivers.

Location: Alton Baker Park in the Eugene/Springfield metro area. 2300 Leo Harris Parkway, next to Autzen Football Stadium.

Hours: Exhibit hall: Wednesday thru Sunday, 10 A.M.–4 P.M. Planetarium: Saturday & Sunday, 1 P.M. and 2 P.M. Closed Memorial Day, July 4th, Labor Day, Thanksgiving Day, Christmas Day, New Year's Day.

Other sites of interest nearby: See Oregon City Carnegie Center for Kids.

Admissions: Exhibits only, $4; Planetarium only, $4; Exhibits & Planetarium, $7; under 2, free; seniors, $3 or $6 memberships available. Member ASTC and the Northwest Association of Youth Museums.

For further information write to Science Factory, P.O. Box 1518, Eugene, OR 97440 or call (541) 682-7888 or fax (541) 484-9027. *www.sciencefactory.org* E-mail: *info@sciencefactory.org*

Science Works Hands-On Museum
Ashland

Located in the facility previously occupied by the Pacific Northwest Museum of Natural History, Science Works claims to be Southern Oregon's world class science museum, featuring innovative exhibits, science shows and exploration for all ages. They celebrated their 5th anniversary in 2008.

Location: 15 miles north of the California-Oregon border between the Siskiyou and Cascade Mountain ranges.

Hours: Open Wednesday–Saturday, 10 A.M. to 4 P.M.; Sunday, noon to 4 P.M.

Admissions: Under 2, free; children (2–12), $5; seniors (65+), $5; adults, $7.50. Member ASTC.

Other sites of interest nearby: Crater Lake National Park, the Oregon Shakespeare Festival, the Peter Britt Music Festival, Cascade Lakes Tour, and Oregon Caves National Monument.

For further information write to Science Works Hands-On Museum, 1500 East Main St., Ashland, Oregon 97520, or call (541) 482-67676. *www.scienceworksmuseum.org*

Southern Oregon Historical Society Children's Museum
Jacksonville

The Southern Oregon Children's Museum has two main themes or "timelines" showing historic events in Oregon history from the 1850s to the 1930s. One timeline shows domestic events while the other emphasizes occupational changes. All hands-on activities in these areas offer children a chance to handle reproductions of objects from the past.

The 23 exhibits include an 1890's General Store, a Takeima Indian Lodge, a schoolroom, an 1890's kitchen, a pioneer cabin, a pioneer bank and a laundry.

Special family-type activities are also offered seasonally: Spring—Public Heritage Fair; Summer—Ice Cream Social; Winter—Victorian Christmas; and Fall—Multicultural Heritage Day. It is recommended to contact the museum before planning a visit.

Info in brief: Hands-on activities along with interpretive displays make this museum of interest to the whole family, with specific items just for children.

Hours: Wednesday thru Saturday, 1–4 P.M.

Admissions: Under 3, free; child (3–12), $3; adult (13–64), $5; senior (65+), $3.

Unique exhibitions: All exhibits based on Oregon history.

Other sites of interest nearby: Oregon Shakespeare Festival in Ashland, South Oregon History Center in Medford, the Beekman House (Living History) in Jacksonville and the Natural History Museum in Ashland.

For further information write to the Southern Oregon Historical Society Children's Museum, 106 N. Central Ave., Medford, Oregon 97501-5926, or call (541) 773-6536 or fax (541) 776-7994. *www.sohs.org* or E-mail: *publicrelations@sohs.org*

A boy looks through a bubble at ScienceWorks.

Umpqua Discovery Center
Reedsport

Visitors have the chance to experience a journey through time in the "Tidewaters and Time" cultural history exhibit. Genuine artifacts, high-tech sounds and lights, videos and sim-

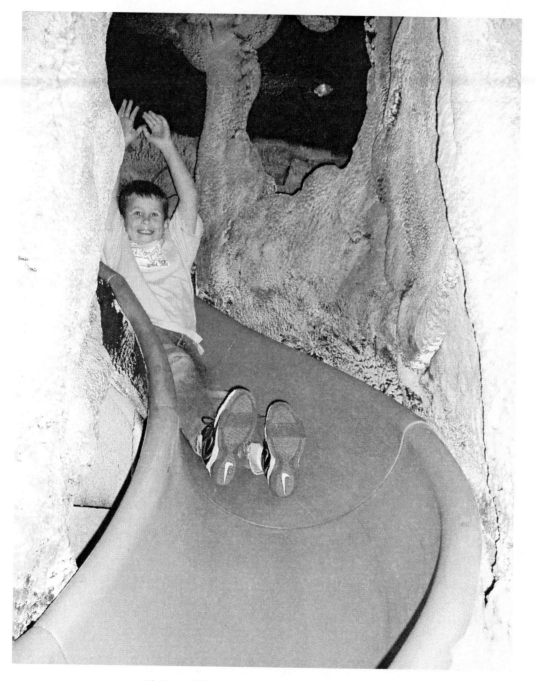

The bear slide at the Umpqua Discovery Center.

This totem greets visitors at the Umpqua Discovery Center.

ulated villages make the experience life-like. In the natural history exhibits "Pathways to Discovery," visitors are taken along on a simulated outdoor adventure, offering multiple environments: an estuary at sunrise in the fall, a deep forest in winter at mid-day (including a visit to a bear cave), a weather station visit, a high mountain meadow on a spring afternoon, a summer sunset in the dunes. These excursions end in the Subterranean Education Room where various videos are shown. A 35-foot periscope in the community room offers panoramic views of the beautiful Umpqua River.

Info in brief: A unique nature center with some hands-on activities for children.

Location: Scenic Umpqua Riverfront, accessible from either the street or a boardwalk along the Umpqua River waterfront.

Hours: (Summer — June 1–September 30) daily, 9 A.M. to 5 P.M. (Winter — October 1–May 31) daily, 10 A.M. to 4 P.M. Closed Thanksgiving, Christmas, and New Year's Day.

Admissions: Admissions charged (contact museum for current price).

Other sites of interest nearby: Many Reedsport–Winchester Bay area tourist attractions such as the Boardwalk, Jet Boats, Oldtown, Oregon Dunes National Recreation Headquarters, Umpqua River Lighthouse and Umpqua beaches.

For further information write to the Umpqua Discovery Center, 409 Riverfront Way, Reedsport, Oregon 97467, or call (541) 271-4816. *www.umpquadiscoverycenter.com*

Uppertown Firefighters Museum & Astoria Children's Museum
Astoria

Built in 1896, and revamped in 1928, The Uppertown Firefighters Museum houses an extensive collection of firefighting equipment dating from 1877 to 1963. Astoria's disastrous fires history is told with photographs and artifacts. The Astoria Childrens Museum is on the second floor and features interactive and educational exhibits for children and their families.

Other sites of interest nearby: Astoria Sunday Market, Columbia River Maritime Museum, Flavel House Museum, Fort Astoria, Heritage Museum, Maritime Memorial Park, Victorian Homes on Astoria's Hillsides, Youngs River Falls, and more.

For further information write to Uppertown Firefighters Museum & Astoria Children's Museum, 475 11th St., Astoria, OR 97103-4117 or call (503) 325-8669.

Working Wonders
Bend

Working Wonders is a children's museum with interactive displays that encourage imagination, learning, play and exploration. The 4,400 sq. ft. space houses exhibits that explore the arts, community, fitness, health, science, and world culture. Exhibits include: *KidVille, Passport, Busy Bodies, Pitter Patter, City Park, WonderMart, Pizza Parlor, Pet Hospital, Kidstruction, Mindstein's Lab, and Kaleidoscope Corner.*

Info in brief: An interactive children's museum.

Location: The Shops at the Old Mill District on level two.

Hours: Wednesday thru Saturday, 10 A.M.–5 P.M.; Sunday, 11 A.M.–5 P.M.

Admissions: Under 1 & over 99, free; seniors, $5; all others, $6. Family passes available. Member Northwest Association of Youth Museums.

For further information write to Working Wonders, 520 SW Powerhouse Dr., #624, Bend, OR 97702 or call (541) 389-4500. *www.workingwonders.org*

PENNSYLVANIA

Briar Bush Nature Center
Abington

This 12-acre woodland and wildlife sanctuary opened in 1962 as an educational facility, and celebrates its 100th year of "welcoming area residents to a world of wonders" in 2008, having been a refuge since 1908. A newly completed entrance, which embraces the natural landscaping, offers more parking and safe walking paths to and from the Center. The Center offers various activities; the former home of the original Quaker owners is now the Griscom Bird Observatory where visitors can enjoy the peace of bird-watching in a garden with a trickling stream and many feeders.

The center offers hands-on exhibits and games, natural history displays, live animals, a "Discovery Den," a crawl-through cave exhibit for guided groups, a library, gift shop, and kitchen facilities (for rentals). The outdoors area offers diverse habitats and woodchipped trails, a pond, a bird observatory, wildflower garden, and an active beehive. Numerous special programs and workshops are offered, along with ecological trips, day camps and more.

Info in brief: Hands-on nature experiences and experiments for children and their caregivers.

Hours: Trails open dawn to dusk. The Center, pond and observatory are open 9 A.M. to 5 P.M., Monday–Saturday; Sunday, 1 P.M. to 5 P.M.

A girl checks out the ball python at the Briar Bush Nature Center.

Admissions: Free. Some charges for some special programs. Memberships are available.

Unique exhibits: At BBNC, Children are actually encouraged to handle nature, not just look at it.

For further information write to Briar Bush Nature Center, 1212 Edge Hill Road, Abington, Pennsylvania 19001, or call (215) 887-6603 or fax (215) 887-9079. *www.briarbush.org*

Children's Discovery Workshop
Williamsport

Exhibits at the Children's Discovery Workshop include a 129-foot tunnel, a castle, shadow walk, a child-sized doctor's office and other hands-on activities.

Hours: September to May: Monday thru Friday, 10 A.M.—5 P.M.; Saturday, 11 A.M.—5 P.M.; Sunday, 1–5 P.M. June to August: Monday thru Saturday, 10 A.M.–4 P.M.

Admissions: $4 per person.

For further information write to Children's Discovery Workshop, 343 W. Fourth St., Williamsport, PA 17701-6401 or call (717) 322-5437.

Childventure Museum and Shop
Fort Washington

Childventure is a 2000 sq. ft. hands-on museum specifically for children 3 to 8 years of age. Interactive play spaces, cultural exhibits and imaginative play areas are offered along with state-of-the-art video programs. Changing exhibits are offered in the main exhibit area frequently, and occasionally in one of the smaller areas.

Info in brief: Hands-on participatory and some visual exhibits especially for children and their caregivers.

Location: Fort Washington Office Park.

Hours: Tuesday–Saturday, 10 A.M. to 4 P.M.; Sunday, 12 P.M. to 4 P.M. Closed Thanksgiving, Christmas, New Year's Day, and July 4th.

Admissions: $4. Member AAM.

Other sites of interest nearby: Morris Arboretum, Insectarium, Rodin Museum, Academy of Natural Sciences and several other museum. Only 32 minutes from Philadelphia.

For further information write to Childventure, 430 Virginia Dr., Fort Washington, Pennsylvania 19034, or call (215) 643-3233.

The Crayola FACTORY &
National Canal Museum
Easton

Visitors to the Crayola FACTORY are immersed in color and creativity. This unique hands-on discovery center for children and adults provides creative experiences through the arts. You can color, draw and create with the latest Crayola products. A number of creative stations invite visitors to "play and explore while learning and having lots and lots of fun." These stations are titled: *the Factory Floor, Crayola Meltdown, Easton Press and Bindery, Super Sculptures, The Light Zone, The Creative Studio, Cool Moves* and *Color Park*. Visitors can also see how Crayola crayons and markers are made.

Admissions to the FACTORY also includes a visit to The National Canal Museum and the Crayola STORE. The National Canal Museum gives visitors a chance to experience the early 1800s before railroads, highways and airplanes were in use. Interactive, hands-on exhibits help visitors understand how canals were and still are relevant today.

Location: Two Rivers Landing.

Hours: September to May: Tuesday thru Friday, 9:30 A.M.–3 P.M.; Saturday, 9:30–5 P.M.; Sunday, noon–5 P.M. Memorial Day to Labor Day: Monday thru Saturday, 9:30 A.M.–5 P.M.; Sundays, 11 A.M.–5 P.M.

Admissions: 2 and under, free; seniors (65+), $9; all others, $9.50. Military discounts and group discounts are available. Metered parking is available on the street, or parking for a fee is available at the municipal parking garage nearby.

For further information write to The Crayola FACTORY, 30 Centre Square, Easton, PA 18042 or call (610) 515-8000. *www.crayola.com/factory*

Da Vinci Science Center
Allentown

In 2003, the Discovery Center of Science and Technology and Leonardo Da Vinci's Horse, Inc., merged to form the Da Vinci Science Center. The original mission of the Leonardo Da Vinci's Horse, Inc., was to complete construction of a 24-ft bronze horse statue, which was completed in 1999. The Discovery Center was a hands-on science center. The facility today offers hands-on experiences with titles like *What's Alive? What on Earth? What's the Matter? Watts Up? What Works? View space, GyroSphere, Little Learners Lab, Wind Turbine* and *The Curiosity Shop.* In these exhibit areas, visitors can test their ability to pick out distractions and unsafe driving behaviors in the "Safety Car," interact with medical equipment in an ambulance and on a CPR mannequin.

For further information write to the Da Vinci Science Center, 3145 Hamilton Blvd Bypass, Allentown, PA 18103-3686 or call/fax (484) 664-1002. *www.davinci-center.org*

expERIEnce Children's Museum
Erie

More than 55 hands-on exhibits are featured in this museum that teaches children and adults about the natural sciences, social studies, the arts, and life experiences.

Hours: Winter (September to May): Wednesday thru Saturday, 10 A.M.–4 P.M.; Sunday, 1 P.M.–4 P.M. Summer (June to August): Tuesday thru Saturday, 10 A.M.–4 P.M.; Sunday, 1 P.M.–4 P.M.

Admissions: $5 per person; under 2, free.

Other sites of interest nearby: Erie Art Museum, Erie County Historical Society & Museum, Watson-Curtze Mansion, and the Planetarium.

For further information write to expERIEnce Children's Museum, 420 French St., Erie, PA 16507 or call (814) 453-3743 or fax (814) 459-9735. *www.eriechildrensmuseum.org* E-mail: *junep@eriechildrensmuseum.org*

The Franklin Institute Science Museum & The Tuttleman IMAX Theater
Philadelphia

The Franklin Institute was established in 1824 as the first professional organization of mechanical engineers and professional draftsmen in the U.S. Evolving over the years, the main goal of the institute has continued to be science and technology education. Current strategies include interactive exhibits, theater-based programming, educational programs and outreach programs. Included at this site are many interactive exhibits as well as the Fels Planetarium and the Tuttleman IMAX Theater. Permanent exhibits include: Sir Isaac's Loft: Where Art & Physics Collide, Electricity Hall, Franklin.... He's Electric, The Franklin Air Show, KidScience, Space Command, The Sports Challenge, The Train Factory, and The Giant Heart: A Healthy Interactive Experience.

Info in brief: A hands-on science museum, IMAX Theater and Planetarium.

Location: Center City Philadelphia, at the intersection of 20th Street and the Benjamin Franklin Parkway.

Hours: Daily, 9:30 A.M.–5 P.M. Closed New Year's Day, Thanksgiving, Christmas Eve & Day.

Admissions: Exhibits only: child (4–11)/military, $11.50; seniors (62+), $11.50; adult, $14.25; IMAX only: child/military, $9; senior, $9; adults, $9. Sci-Pass—Combo ticket: child/military, $16.50; senior, $18.25; adult, $19.25. The Sci-Pass includes admission to Museum, live science demonstrations, and one show in the Fels Planetarium. Admission to the Tuttleman IMAX theater is additional. There is a cost for parking.

For further information write to The Franklin Institute Science Museum, 222 N. 20th St., Philadelphia, PA 19103, or call (215) 448-1200. *www.fi.edu*

Hands-On House
Lancaster

Located in an historic Victorian farmhouse, Hands-On House features eight self-directed interactive exhibit areas geared for children ages 2 to 10 years. Discovery areas include "Space Voyage Checkpoint," "Once Upon a Forest," "Under Construction," "The Whatchama-Giggle Company," "Face to Face," "Corner Grocery," "Eye Spy," and "Switch on Art."

Besides the self-directed areas, the museum also offers special classes, workshops, special scout workshops, and group tours.

Info in brief: Hands-on, interactive exhibits for ages 2 to 10.

Location: Lancaster County, just north of Lancaster, close to Routes 30 and 272.

Hours: Memorial Day to Labor Day—Monday–Saturday, 10 A.M. to 5 P.M.; Sunday, 12 P.M. to 5 P.M. Labor Day to Memorial Day—See museum's website for these hours. Group visits by reservation at other times also.

Admissions: $6 (subject to change without notice). Memberships available.

Other sites of interest nearby: Lancaster County tourist attractions.

For further information write to Hands-On House, Children's Museum of Lancaster, 721 Landis Valley Rd., Lancaster, Pennsylvania 17601, or call (717) 569-KIDS (5437).

Peter J. McGovern Little League Museum
Williamsport

The Little League Museum is the only sports museum dedicated to a child's game, and consequently would be of interest to children. Although it is not a strictly hands-on museum, the eight theme rooms each offer some interactive participation for visitors. These themes are: the Lobby (with one of the largest photographic murals in the world), the Founders Room, the Play It Safe Room, the Play Ball Room (where visitors can bat and throw in safety cages), the Showcase Room, the Hall of Excellence, the Gallery of Achievement, and the Theater.

Now in its eleventh year of operation, the museum showcases the development of Little

League from its inception in 1939 as a three-team league to its current 2.5 million membership standing. The museum is full of displays, pictures, videos, and exhibits showcasing players, equipment, rules, history, the future and the fun of Little League.

Info in brief: A concept-based museum with interactive displays of specific interest to children and their families, especially those interested in sports; some hands-on activities, but mostly interactive, computer-controlled exhibits.

Location: U.S. Route 14, adjacent to the Little League Baseball World Series Stadium and the Little League International Headquarters.

Hours: (Memorial Day thru Labor Day) Monday–Saturday, 10 A.M. to 7 P.M.; Sunday, noon to 7 P.M. (Labor Day thru Memorial Day) Monday, Thursday, Friday, 10 A.M.–5 P.M.; Saturday, noon–5 P.M.; Sunday, noon–4 P.M. Closed Thanksgiving, Christmas and New Year's Day.

Admissions: Under 4, free; children (5–13), $1.50; seniors, $3; other adults, $5; family rate, $13. Member of AAM.

For further information write to the Peter J. McGovern Little League Museum, P.O. Box 3485, Williamsport, Pennsylvania 17701, or call (717) 326-3607. *www.littleleague.org*

Pittsburgh Children's Museum
Pittsburgh

The Pittsburgh Children's Museum is located in the historic Old Post Office Building, Allegheny Center, on Pittsburgh's North Side. Since its beginning in 1983, its mission has been "to enrich the lives of children" through the use of exhibits, artifacts, performances, interactive demonstrations, art activities and more. The goal is to foster creativity, discovery, learning and understanding.

The three-story building offers loads of hands-on fun through the use of permanent and revolving interactive exhibits, as well as visits by children's book authors and illustrators, Mister Rogers' Neighborhood puppets, Jim Henson puppets, Andy Warhol prints, "Stuffee" (a nine-foot-tall, blue-haired health exhibit), art activities in The Workshop, a recreation of a life-like street environment which teaches bicycle, school bus, car and pedestrian safety, and much more.

The museum also has a tremendous outreach program which includes assemblies, classroom programs, hands-on workshops, traveling trunks, festival arts packages and teacher classes for certification. Special classes and workshops are also offered throughout the year.

Info in brief: Three floors of hands-on exploratory exhibits—both permanent and revolving—for all ages.

Location: 10 Children's Way, Allegheny Center, Pittsburgh, Pennsylvania.

Hours: Monday–Saturday, 10 A.M. to 5 P.M.; Sunday, noon to 5 P.M.; open till 8 P.M. one Thursday per month (call 322-5058, press 6); Closed New Year's Day, Easter, Memorial Day, July 4th, Labor Day, Thanksgiving, and Christmas Day.

Admissions: Under 2, free; child (2–18), $8; adults, $9; senior, $8. Member ASTC.

Unique exhibits or exhibitions: "Stuffee" (the museum's trademark)—a nine-foot tall, blue-haired anatomy exhibit which unzips to reveal his internal organs (in pillow form) to illustrate how our bodies work. "Safety Street," a recreation of a life-like street environment to teach safety rules.

Other sites of interest nearby (phone numbers given): Carnegie Science Center (237-3400), Frick Art & Historical Center (371-0600), Carnegie Museums of Pittsburgh (622-3131), Duquesne Incline, The Andy Warhol Museum (237-8300), Tour-Ed Mine & Museum (224-4720), Riverboat Cruises (355-7980), and much more. Call the Visitor Information Hotline at 1-800-366-0093 for more information.

For further information write to The Pittsburgh Children's Museum, 10 Children's Way, Pittsburgh, Pennsylvania 15212-5250, or call (412) 322-5058 (recorded info.) or (412) 322-5059 (bus. office). *www.pittsburghkids.org* or E-mail: *stuffee@pittsburghkids.org*

Please Touch Museum
Philadelphia

The Please Touch Museum is probably the only museum in the country designed for children ages 7 or younger. For 30 years, all exhibits encourage children to touch, ride, climb, or otherwise interact with the materials provided. Exhibits include "Alice's Adventures in Wonderland," "Barnyard Babies," "Move It!," "Story Garden," "Sendark," "The SuperMarket," "Theater," "Kids Store," and "Collections."

Please Touch has earned several awards: 2002 Institute of Museum and Library Services' National Award for Museum Service; 2003 *Coming Up Taller Award* from the President's Committee on the Arts and Humanities, in partnership with the National Endowment for the Arts, the National Endowment for the Humanities, and the Institute of Museums and Library Services; and the 2004 *Promising Practice Award* from the Association of Children's Museums and the MetLife Foundation.

Location: Corner of 21st and Race Streets in the heart of Philadelphia's Parkway museum district.

Hours: Regular hours: 9 A.M. to 4:30 P.M.; Summer hours: July 1–Labor Day, Sunday–Thursday, 9 A.M.–4:30 P.M.; Friday–Saturday, 9 A.M.–5 P.M.

Admissions: Under 1, free; others, $10.95.

For further information write to The Please Touch Museum, 210 N. 21st St., Philadelphia, Pennsylvania 19103, or call (215) 963-0667. Member ASTC. *www.pleasetouchmuseum.org*

Quaint Corner Children's Museum
Altoona

Quaint Corner Children's Museum is a hands-on museum with 14 rooms for exploring and special events offered periodically.

Location: In the Alleghenies.

Hours: Thursday thru Saturday, 1 P.M.–5 P.M.

Admissions: Check with museum before visiting.

For further information write to Quaint Corner Children's Museum, 2000 Union Ave., Altoona, PA 16601 or call (814) 944-6830.

PUERTO RICO

Museo del Niño
San Juan

One little-known tourist attraction in San Juan is the Museo del Niño, a hands-on museum for children. Exhibits on display include "Pueblito" (playspace for kids 1–3 years old), "Gozando con Numeros" (math exhibit), "Diseno con Texturas" (creating designs with textures), "Dibuyo en Espajos" (drawing on mirrors), "La Barberia" (barber shop), "Vistitemos al Dentista," "Camerino" (imaginative play), "La Placita" (kids play in a traditional Puerto Rican town square), "Hazlo con Reciclaje" (art with recyclables), "Carpinteria" (using tools and wood), "Amigos de Aquí y Alla" (shortwave radio station — Saturdays only), "Nuestro Ambiente" (experience the ecosystems of Puerto Rican Rain Forests), "Burbujas" (soap bubbles and solar lighting), "Mi Mascota y Yo" (pet ownership), "Aedes Agypti" (microscopes and mosquitos), and "Observatorio" (using a powerful telescope to view solar spots).

Special activities and events are also offered at various times throughout the year. Contact the museum before visiting for a current schedule of events.

Info in brief: A small hands-on museum for children and their caregivers.

Location: Historic Old San Juan, Puerto Rico, next to the Convento Hotel on Cristo Street. Physical address: Calle Cristo 150, San Juan 00902-2467 Puerto Rico.

Hours: Tuesday–Thursday, 9 A.M. to 3:30 P.M.; Friday, 9 A.M. to 5 P.M.; Saturday and Sunday, 12:30 P.M. to 5 P.M.

Admissions: Ages 14 & under, $4; all others, $5.

Other sites of interest nearby: All of Old San Juan is a historical monument. Visitors can see Spanish architecture, El Morro Fortress, several museums, and the governor's mansion. Shopping and restaurants are also major tourist attractions.

For further information write to Museo del Niño, P.O. Box 9022467, San Juan, Puerto Rico 00902-2467 (no extra postage is required), or call (787) 722-3791 or (787) 725-7214 or fax (787) 723-2058. *www.museodelninopr.org*

RHODE ISLAND

Providence Children's Museum
Pawtucket

Providence Children's Museum is Rhode Island's only children's museum. It is a hands-on museum for kids ages 1–11 and their caregivers. Exhibits and program explore the arts, culture, history and science and are based on the developmental needs of children, embracing a range of learning styles and forms of expression. Visitors are encouraged to share with and learn from one another. Some of the exhibit areas include: Waterways, Pets & People, Teeth, and Hey Look!

Originally opened in 1977, after a move and several renovation projects were completed, the current location offers 17,000 square feet on two floors. An outdoor Children's Garden and a Gift Shop are also available.

Info in brief: A participatory learning center for children and their families.

Location: Providence's Jewelry District.

Hours: September to March: Tuesday thru Sunday, 9 A.M.–6 P.M. Open during school vacations, Monday holidays and until 8 P.M. the third Friday evening of each month. April to Labor Day: Daily, 9 A.M.–6 P.M. and until 8 P.M. every Friday evening in June, July and August.

Admissions: $6.50 per person; under 1 year, free. Parking is free. Memberships available.

For further information write to Providence Children's Museum, 100 South St., Providence, RI 02903 or call (401) 273-5437 or fax (401) 273-1004.

SOUTH CAROLINA

Children's Museum of South Carolina
Myrtle Beach

In 1994, the Children's Museum of South Carolina opened its doors with a 1,200 sq. ft. facility. In 1995 they acquired a 7,500 sq. ft. facility, renovated it and re-opened in 1996. In 1998, 1,200 more sq. ft. were added. The goal of the museum is to promote and stimulate self-discovery through interactive learning experiences for better understanding his/her global community.

Location: 2501 North Kings Highway in Myrtle Beach, across the street from the Sheraton Convention Center, on the ocean side of the Office Depot Building.

Hours: Tuesday thru Saturday, 10 A.M.–4 P.M.; Thursday, 10 A.M.–6 P.M. Closed New Year's Day, Memorial Day, July 4th, Labor Day, Thanksgiving, Christmas Eve and Christmas Day.

Admissions: 1 & under, free; all others, $7.

For further information write to Children's Museum of South Carolina, P.O. Box 1781, Myrtle Beach, SC 29578 or phone (843) 946-9469 or fax (843) 946-7011. *www.cmsckids.org*

Children's Museum of the Lowcountry
Charleston

Opening in 2003, CML is Charleston's first hands-on, interactive museum for children ages 3 months to 12 years and their families. The eight main exhibit areas offer experiences in the arts, humanities and sciences. The titles of these areas are: Creativity Castle, Castle Stories, Raceways, WaterWheel, Lowcountry Shrimping, Totally Toddler (and infants too), The Children's Garden, and Charleston Market.

The interactive, interdisciplinary environments help children develop creative thinking and problem-solving skills. Children are encouraged to play, explore, learn and create in all of the exhibit areas.

Info in brief: A hands-on, interdisciplinary museum for children ages 3 months to 12 years.

Location: Historic downtown Charleston, directly behind the Visitor and Information Center.

Hours: Closed Monday. Tuesday thru Saturday, 10 A.M.–5 P.M.; Sunday, 1–5 P.M. Closed New Year's Day, Easter, Fourth of July, Thanksgiving, Christmas Eve, Christmas Day.

Admissions: Under 1, free; all others, $7. Memberships available.

For further information write to the Children's Museum of the Lowcountry, 25 Ann St., Charleston, SC 29403. *www.explorecml.com* E-mail: *info@explorecml.org*

The Coastal Discovery Museum
Hilton Head Island

The Coastal Discovery Museum offers "hands-on exploring of the history, wildlife, and heritage of Coastal Carolina through both indoor and outdoor exhibits." The center of activity is in the Sea Island Classroom, the History Time-Line Exhibit and the Museum Store. Besides these indoor activities, the museum offers 11 different tours and cruises around the island that inform visitors about the island's unique history and ecology. The main exhibits are "Sea Island BioDiversity," which features presentations and displays on animals and interesting Carolina activities, and "Coastal Discovery Gardens," which features a butterfly garden, a perennial garden, and a marsh walk and deck. The Museum grounds are developed as outdoor exhibits focusing on the history and native flora and fauna of the area. Included are life-size models of Saxon vats used in the 1700s to produce indigo dye.

Info in brief: Although advertised as a "hands-on museum," most of the exhibits are actually visual.

Location: Situated on the north end of Hilton Head Island overlooking Jarvis Creek and the surrounding salt marsh. Physical address: 70 Honey Horn Dr., or 100 William Hilton Pkwy, on Hilton Head Island.

Hours & Admissions: Contact museum for current prices.

For further information write to The Coastal Discovery Museum, P.O. Box 23497, Hilton Head Island, SC 29925, or call (843) 689-6767. *www.coastaldiscovery.org*

EdVenture Children's Museum
Columbia

This 67,000 sq. ft. facility advertises as "The South's Largest Children's Museum." Eight galleries offer the following exhibits for children 12 years of age and younger: Eddie (the world's largest child), Body Works, World of Work, Mission Imagination, My Backyard, Over the Horizon, The Great Outdoors, and Critter Garden.

Info in brief: A large hands-on museum for children ages 12 and under.

Location: In front of the South Carolina State Museum.

Hours: Tuesday thru Saturday, 9 A.M.–5 P.M.; Sunday, noon–5 P.M.; Open some Mondays (check with the museum). Closed Thanksgiving, Christmas Eve & Day.

Admissions: Under 1, free; child, $6.95; adult, $8.95.

Other sites of interest nearby: The South Carolina State Museum.

For further information write to EdVenture Children's Museum, 211 Gervais St., Columbia, SC 29201, or call (803) 779-3100 or fax (803) 779-3144. E-mail: *info@edventure.org*

ScienceSouth, Inc.
Florence

ScienceSouth was established in 2000 and launched an outreach program in 2003. In 2007, construction was begun on a Phase One facility. The facility itself will be a lesson in science and technology, as it will consist of an aluminum frame, insulated cross section and an architectural membrane designed to withstand wind, fire, snow and other natural disasters. The building was planned to be a unique facility for unique activities. The building will also serve as the home base for ScienceSouth's growing outreach programming.

The new science pavilion offers families the opportunity to do real science in minds-on, hands-on workshops.

Info in brief: Hands-on science workshops for the entire family.

Location: 1511 Freedom Blvd., Florence, SC.

Hours & Admissions: Book family workshops in advance via the website.

For further information write to ScienceSouth, Inc., c/o Roche Carolina, 6173 E. Old Marion Hwy, Florence, SC 29506-9330, or call (843) 629-4040 or fax (843) 629-4341. *www.sciencesouth.org* E-mail: *info@sciencesouth.org*

SOUTH DAKOTA

Discovery Center & Aquarium
Pierre

The Discovery Center opened in 1989 and was the first Sci-Tech Center in South Dakota to be open year-round. The museum currently offers more than 60 hands-on exhibits for children. Most exhibits are geared around science explorations, especially in electricity and magnetism. Three aquariums with fish from the Missouri River are also on display, and planetarium shows are offered regularly. A permanent observatory and a Children's Science Theater are planned to open soon.

Info in brief: A hands-on, participatory science museum for children of all ages and their caregivers.

Hours: Winter (Labor Day — the day before Memorial Day): Sunday thru Friday, 1–5 P.M.; Saturday, 10 A.M.–5 P.M. Summer (Memorial Day — day before Labor Day): Monday thru Saturday, 10 A.M.–5 P.M.; Sunday, 1–5 P.M. Closed Thanksgiving, Christmas Eve & Day, New Year's Day, Good Friday and Easter.

Admissions: 2 & under, free; child (3–12), $3+ tax; all others, $4+ tax. AAA discounts, and group discounts. Member ASTC.

Other sites of interest nearby: Historic Fort Chouteau, Verendrye Museum, South Dakota National Guard Museum, the State Capitol, Fighting Stallions Memorial, Capitol Grounds Arboretum Trail, and the South Dakota Cultural Heritage Center.

For further information write to the South Dakota Discovery Center & Aquarium, 805 W. Sioux, Pierre, SD 57501, or call (605) 224-2865. Website: *sddcaklm@sd.cybernex.net*

Kirby Science Discovery Center
Sioux Falls

The Kirby Science Center offers visitors three floors of hands-on, interactive exhibits for children and their families. The main exhibit galleries have the following titles: Air and Space; The Stairway to Sound; Big Sioux River Banks: Light, Sound, Action! Nature Works; and Dynamic Earth. The Wells Fargo CineDome Theater is also on site. Also at the same location are the Discovery Store, Visual Arts Center, and the Husby Performing Arts Center.

Info in brief: Three stories of hands-on, interactive arts and sciences exhibits.

Location: Washington Pavilion of Arts and Science

Hours: *Kirby Science Discovery Center/Visual Arts Center*: Wednesday, Thursday, & Saturday, 10 A.M.–5 P.M.; Friday, 10 A.M.–8 P.M.; Sunday, noon–5 P.M. *CineDome Theater (shows at the top of each hour)*: Wednesday, Thursday & Sunday, 1 P.M.–4 P.M.; Friday & Saturday, 11 A.M.–8 P.M. Closed Thanksgiving and Christmas Day. Discovery Center closed on most Mondays and Tuesdays, Labor

Day through Easter. CineDome closed Tuesdays, Labor Day through Easter. CineDome hours are subject to change, so be sure to check with office before visiting.

Admissions: Kirby Science Discovery Center: child, $4.60; senior, $5.65; adult, $6.75. CineDome: child (3–12), $5.95; senior (62+), $6.75; adult, $7.55. Combo Tickets: child, $8.10; senior, $9.20; adult, $10.80. Children under 3 years are free. $5 First Friday—from 5–8 P.M. on the first Friday of each month. Member ASTC.

Other sites of interest nearby: Mount Rushmore (Hill City), Joe Foss Field Airport (Sioux Falls), State Historical Society (Brookings), Dacotah Prairie Museum (Aberdeen), Museum of Wildlife Science & Technology of NE South Dakota (Webster), Wild Life Museum (Wall), Clay County Historical Society (Vermillion), Great Plains Zoo/Dilbridge Museum (Sioux Falls).

For further information write to the Washington Pavilion of Arts & Science, 301 S. Main Ave., Sioux Falls, SD 57104, or call 1-877-WashPav (927-4728). Ticket Hotline: (605) 367-6000. *www.washing tonpavilion.org*

South Dakota Discovery Center & Aquarium
Pierre

The South Dakota Discovery Center & Aquarium features sixty hands-on, interactive experiments and exhibits on topics such as sounds, vision, light, electricity and motion.

Info in brief: A hands-on, interactive science center for children and their families.

Location: Old Pierre Municipal Power & Light Building.

Hours: Winter (Labor Day—the day before Memorial Day): Sunday thru Friday, 1–5 P.M.; Saturday, 10 A.M.–5 P.M. Summer (Memorial Day—day before Labor Day): Monday thru Saturday, 10 A.M.–5 P.M.; Sunday, 1–5 P.M. Closed Thanksgiving, Christmas Eve & Day, New Year's Day, Good Friday and Easter.

Admissions: 2 & under, free; child (3–12), $3 + tax; all others, $4 + tax. AAA discounts, and group discounts.

Other sites of interest nearby: Mount Rushmore (Hill City), Joe Foss Field Airport (Sioux Falls), State Historical Society (Brookings), Dacotah Prairie Museum (Aberdeen), Museum of Wildlife Science & Technology of NE South Dakota (Webster), Wild Life Museum (Wall), Clay County Historical Society (Vermillion), Great Plains Zoo/Dilbridge Museum (Sioux Falls).

For further information write to South Dakota Discovery Center & Aquarium, 805 W. Sioux, Pierre, SD 57501, or call (605) 224-8295.

TENNESSEE

Adventure Science Center
Nashville

Adventure Science Center is a hands-on, interactive museum for children and their caregivers. Permanent exhibits include Body Quest, Blue Max, Adventure Tower and Play Motion. Body Quest (a 9,000 sq. ft. area) presents a day in the life of your body. Adventure Tower (more than 75 feet tall) is packed with scientific explorations. Blue Max is a simulator ride where visitors can maneuver their own jet aircraft.

Hours: Monday thru Saturday, 10 A.M.–5 P.M.; Sunday, 12:30–5:30 P.M. closed Thanksgiving and Christmas Day.

Admissions: 2 & under, free: children (3–12), $7; seniors (60+), $7; adults, $9. Memberships available. Blue Max Simulator charge: $4, members; $5 nonmembers.

For further information write to Adventure Science Center (Cumberland Science Museum), 800 Fort Negley Blvd., Nashville, TN 37203-4899 or call (615) 862-5160 or fax (615) 862-5178. *www.adventuresci.com* E-mail: *info@adventuresci.com*

The Children's Museum of Memphis
Memphis

Opened in 1990, The Children's Museum of Memphis aims to provide interactive exhibits and programs in the arts, sciences, humanities and technology for children ages 12 or younger.

In 2002 an expansion added 16,000 sq. ft. of space, resulting in a cumulative 54,000 sq. ft. of floor space in three buildings which formerly housed the National Guard Armory. There are five exhibit galleries: Cityscape, Going Places, Art Smart, WaterWORKS! and Growing Healthy. The galleries collectively hold these exhibits: Tree House; City Friend; Playscape Park; Your House, My House/Windows to the World; Bank; Smiles, Inc.; Kid's Market; Garage; Skyscraper; Time Square/Sire Dance-A-Lot; Child Passenger Safety Van; Honeybee Hives; and Lighthouse. The Van Vleet Gallery also changes traveling exhibits every 3–4 months.

Info in brief: Hands-on museum for children ages 12 or younger.

Hours: Monday–Saturday, 9 A.M. to 5 P.M.; Sunday, noon to 5 P.M.; closed some major holidays.

Admissions: Under 1, free; children (1–12), $7; adults (13–64), $8; seniors (65+), $7. Member ASTC & ACM.

Other sites of interest nearby: Liberty Bowl Memorial Stadium, Mid-South Fairgrounds, Memphis Zoo, Pink Palace Museum, and other Memphis attractions.

For further information write to The Children's Museum of Memphis online at *www.cmom.com* or call (901) 458-2678 or fax (901) 320-3170.

Cookeville Children's Museum
Cookeville

The Cookeville Children's Museum's Grand Opening was held on December 1, 2007. Targeted audience is children ages 2–12 and their families. Visitors to the Museum can make music, play with science, solve a crime, explore art, be a diva, visit a farm, and play outside in a fenced-in yard.

Location: Cookeville's Westside.

Hours: Wednesday thru Friday, 10 A.M.–2 P.M.; Saturday, 10 A.M.–4 P.M.

Admissions: Under 2, free; 2 & older, $3; adults, $4. Memberships available. Member ACM.

For further information write to the Cookeville Children's Museum, P.O. Box 204, Cookeville, TN 38503. *www.cookevillechildrensmuseum.org* E-Mail: *info@cookevillechildrensmuseum.org*

Creative Discovery Museum
Chattanooga

Selected as the best museum in Chattanooga by *Family Fun* magazine and as one of the top 20 children's museum in the U.S. by *Child Magazine*, the Creative Discovery Museum is designed for kids from 2 months to 12 years old. Kids can climb up a crow's nest, dig for dinosaur bones, build robots, create a sculpture, see how bees make honey, spin whirligigs by spraying jets of water and more. Most exhibits encourage parents and children to experience the activity together. Exhibits include: *Rooftop Fun Factory, Riverplay, Little Yellow House, Artist's Studio, Excavation Station, Inventors' Clubhouse, Barsamian Sculpture,* and *Lookout Tower.*

An IMAX theatre and an aquarium are also on site.

Info in brief: A hands-on science/nature museum for children 12 and under and their caregivers.

Location: Downtown Chattanooga.

Hours: Labor Day thru February: Sundays, noon–5 P.M.; Monday thru Saturday, 10 A.M.–5 P.M. March to Labor Day: Sunday, noon–5 P.M.; Monday thru Saturday, 10 A.M.–5 P.M. Closed Wednesdays in the fall. (Be sure to contact the museum before visiting.) Closed Thanksgiving, and Christmas Eve & Day.

Admissions: Creative Discovery Museum: under 2, free; all others, $8.95. Triple Value Package (Museum, Aquarium and one IMAX movie): under 2, free; child (2–12), $21.95; others, $31.95. Military discounts are available. Discounts are also given with a visit to the aquarium. Membership available.

For further information write to Creative Discovery Museum, 321 Chestnut St., Chattanooga, TN 37402 or call (423) 756-2738. *www.cdmfun.org*

The Discovery Center at Murfree Spring
Murfreesboro

The Discovery Center is a hands-on, interactive museum and environmental center for children and adults of all ages. The aim of the center is that "each child, teen and adult who visits will grow in knowledge, competence and appreciation for themselves, their families, their community and their environment." The 18,000 sq. ft. center features 15 permanent, indoor exhibit areas, 20 acres of wetland habitat and several associated outdoor exhibits. Special programs are held regularly, celebrating special times and events.

Info in brief: A hands-on, interactive museum/environmental center for visitors of all ages.

Location: Downtown Murfreesboro.

Hours: Monday thru Saturday, 10 A.M.–5 P.M.; Sunday 1–5 P.M. Closed major holidays.

Admissions: Under 2, free; all others, $5. Memberships available.

For further information write to The Discovery Center at Murfree Spring, 502 S.E. Broad St., Murfreesboro, TN 37130, or call (615) 890-2300. *www.discoverycenteronline.org* E-mail: *info@ discoverycenteronline.org*

East Tennessee Discovery Center
Knoxville

The East Tennessee Discovery Center is actually two centers in one: the Science Discovery Center (which also features the AKIMA Planetarium) and the KAMA Health Discovery Center. (For the purposes of this book, information here is for the Science Discovery Center.)

Exhibits at the Discovery Center fit in one of three areas—Life Science, Physical Science and Earth Science. In the Life Science area, visitors can visit *Aquaria, Wentzscopes, Insects, Live Arthropods, Amphibians & Reptiles, and a Live Honey Bee colony.* In the Physical Science area are *Light & Vision, Sound, Simple Machines, and Energy.* The Earth Science area features *Fossils, Rocks & Minerals, Discovery Space Shuttle and a Computer Mini-Lab.* A special exhibit area which offers multiple hands-on experiences for young children is called *Kidspace.* Kidspace offers many math-oriented activities, including a large Lego Lab where imaginations can go wild.

Info in brief: A science discovery center for children and their families. Exhibits are mostly visual, but hands-on exhibit areas are featured.

Location: Chilhowee Park in Knoxville. Physical address: 516 N. Beaman St., Knoxville, TN 37914.

Hours: Monday thru Friday, 9 A.M.–5 P.M.; Saturday, 10 A.M.–5 P.M. Closed on major holidays and for certain events held at Chilhowee Park.

Admissions: 2 & under, free; children (3&4), $2; children (5+) & senior adults, $3; all others, $4. Memberships available.

Other sites of interest nearby: Chilhowee Park, Chilhowee Zoo, and many other Knoxville attractions.

For further information write to ETDC, P.O. Box 6204, Knoxville, TN 37914, or call (865) 594-1494. E-mail: *ETDC@comcast.net*

Hands On! Regional Museum
Johnson City

The mission of the Hands On! Regional Museum is to create a dynamic, educational, fun environment which stimulates discovery, thought and understanding through interactive exhibits, programs and events in the arts, sciences and humanities. Hands On! features 27,000 sq. ft. of exhibits developed to instill a love of lifelong learning and fun for visitors of all ages.

Kids can shop just like their parents at the Hands On Regional Museum in Johnson City.

Besides the permanent and touring exhibits, the museum offers daily programs, outreach programs, summer camps, birthday parties, and special events.

Info in brief: A hands-on, interactive museum for children and their caregivers.

Hours: Monday (June–August only), 9 A.M. to 5 P.M.; Tuesday–Friday, 9 A.M. to 5 P.M.; Saturday, 10 A.M. to 5 P.M.; Sunday, 1 P.M. to 5 P.M.

Admissions: Under 3, free; adults & children ages 3 & older, $8. Memberships available. Children under 16 must be accompanied by an adult. Member ASTC.

Other sites of interest nearby: Dollywood and Pigeon Forge (Pigeon Forge), Bristol Motor Speedway, and many historic museums located in the region.

For further information write to Hands On! Regional Museum, 315 E. Main St., Johnson City, Tennessee 37601, or call (423) 434-hand. *www.handsonmuseum.org*

Hands-On Science Center
Tullahoma

Officially opened in 1995, the Hands-On Science Center now offers more than 80 hands-on science exhibits for children of all ages. Besides the hands-on exhibits, the museum has a Real Flight R/C Flight Simulator, Animal Ally (with more than 15 live animals), Whisper Dishes, and many other exhibits which help to teach concepts about electricity, sound, light, aerodynamics, pressure and more.

Hours: Tuesday thru Saturday, 10 A.M.–5 P.M.; Sunday, 1–5 P.M.

Admissions: 2 & under, free; children & adults, $5; seniors (65+), $4. Member ASTC.

For further information contact: Hands-On Science Center, P.O. Box 1121, 101 Mitchell Blvd., Tullahoma, Tennessee 37388, phone: (931) 455-8387. *www.hosc.org*

TEXAS

Austin Children's Museum
Austin

The Austin Children's Museum is a private, nonprofit 12,500 sq. ft. hands-on museum which offers both permanent and changing exhibits. Permanent exhibits include "Austin Kiddie Limits" (stage area), "Dairy Cow," " Funstruction Zone," "Global City," "Kid Metro," "Rising Star Ranch" (for the under 2 age group), "Splish," and "Tinkerer's Workshop." Monthly calendars update visitors to the ever-changing special events and workshops sponsored by the museum. The museum also sponsors an International Children's Festival each year.

Info in brief: Hands-on participatory museum for children of all ages and their families.

Hours: Tuesday–Saturday, 10 A.M. to 5 P.M.; Sunday, noon to 5 P.M. Community Night, Wed., 5 P.M.–8 P.M. Closed most major holidays.

Admissions Under 1, free; toddlers (12–23 months), $3.50; children, 2 and up, $5.50; adults, $5.50. Member ASTC.

Other sites of interest nearby: Tourist attractions in Austin.

For further information write to the Austin Children's Museum, 201 Colorado Street, Austin, Texas 78703, or call (512) 472-2499. *www.austinkids.org*

The Bob Bullock Texas State History Museum
Austin

Three floors of interactive exhibits, special effects shows, artifacts, recreated environments, theater presentations and Austin's only IMAX Theatre tell the story of Texas. Visitors, especially children, will enjoy seeing the 35-foot-tall bronze Lone Star sculpture in front of the museum and the colorful terrazzo floor in the museum's rotunda that features a campfire scene and other scenes from Texas' past. An indoor/outdoor Café and a Museum Store make the visit a full-day experience.

Each floor of the museum is designed around a unique theme highlighting important chapters in the "Story of Texas." The first floor, "Encounters on the Land," tells the story of the land before it was called Texas. See how the Native Americans, Spanish, and French interacted on the land clear up through 1900.

The second floor, "Building the Lone Star Identity," explores the story of how Texas became an independent nation and how they celebrated their unique identity during the 1936 Centennial. Visitors interact with a giant time line of Texas history on a 60-foot video wall.

The third floor, "Creating Opportunity," shows how Texans persevered on the land and how they approached everything from ranching, to drilling oil to redefining world technology.

Although this is not a "hands-on" museum, the use of multi-media presentations makes the museum an attention-keeping experience for children 8 and older and their families.

Info in brief: A multi-media interactive museum (not hands-on).

Location: Downtown Austin. Physical address: 1800 N. Congress Avenue (intersection of Martin Luther King, Jr., Blvd).

Hours: Monday through Saturday 9 A.M.–6 P.M.

Admissions: SINGLE VENUE TICKETS: under 3, free to all events. Exhibit Areas—child (ages 3–4), free; youth (ages 5–18), $4; senior (65+)/military/college student, $6; adults, $7. IMAX Theatre—child & youth, $5; senior/military/college student, $6; adult, $7. Texas Spirit Theater—child & youth, $4; senior/military/college student, $4. COMBINATION TICKETS: (Exhibits & IMAX)—child, $5; youth, $7; senior/military/college student, $10; adult, $12. (Exhibits & TX Spirit Theater)—child, $4; youth, $6; senior/military/college student, $8; adult, $10. (Exhibits & both theaters)—child, $7; youth, $10; senior/military/college student, $12; adult, $15. Plans call for a "U2 3D" theater to open in June, 2008. Contact the museum before visiting. There is a cost for parking ($8 pre-pay, with $2 rebate w/ticket) in the Museum's underground parking garage.

Other sites of interest nearby: The many sites and attractions in Austin.

For further information write to the Bob Bullock Texas State History Museum, P.O. Box 12874, Austin, TX 78711 or call (512) 936-8746 or (512) 936-4649 (for ticket reservations). *www.thestory-oftexas.com* E-mail: *Contactus@TheStoryofTexas.com*

Children's Discovery Center, Rusk County History Museum, Depot Museum Complex
Henderson

The Depot Museum Complex houses the Rusk County History Museum and the Children's Discovery Center. Also situated on the 4-acre site are eight other restored buildings from the area's past. The complex includes an 1841 log cabin, an early 1900's printing shop, country doctor's office, reconstructed barn, broom shop, the famous Arnold Outhouse (see below), the Beall-Ross home, a red caboose and a syrup mill. Recent additions include new buildings, an oil derrick, country store, saw mill, and a cotton gin. A former 1901 Missouri–Pacific Depot houses the waiting rooms and station master's office and the cotton warehouse which has been converted into the children's learning center. All nine buildings combine to make an interesting village museum, of which one area is a children's exploratory museum.

Info in brief: Village museum with one small area dedicated to hands-on, exploratory experiences for children.

Hours: Monday–Friday, 9 A.M. to 5 P.M. (closed noon to 1 P.M.); Saturday, 9 A.M. to noon; Genealogy Center open 1 P.M. to 5 P.M. weekdays. Closed on all state and federal holidays.

Admissions: Children, $1; adults, $3, seniors, $2.

Unique exhibits: The Arnold Outhouse is the most publicized historical marker in Texas. It consists of a three-holer outhouse with louvered windows and a porch.

For further information write to the Depot Museum Complex, 514 N. High St., Henderson, Texas 75652, or call (903) 657-4303. *www.depotmuseum.com*

The Children's Museum of Houston
Houston

Designed by internationally acclaimed architect Robert Venturi, the Children's Museum of Houston offers a multitude of interactive exhibits that engage kids in the ultimate learning experience. Founded in 1980, the museum has grown to serve more than 750,000 people annually and is dedicated to its mission of transforming communities through innovative child-centered learning, focusing on bilingual (English/Spanish), learning programs for kids, ages birth to 12 years, along with workshops in reading, science, math, health, engineering, culture and social studies.

In 2005, the museum launched a capital campaign fund to double its exhibition space, increase outreach programs, and add an "Institute for Family Learning." In March 2009, the museum will open its doors to more than 39,000 sq. ft. of new exhibition space (83,000 sq. ft. total), including six new exhibits. Permanent exhibits to be added will be "Cyberchase—The Chase Is On!," "Invention Convention," "Power Play," "Flow/Works and "Kidtropolis, U.S.A." Current permanent exhibit areas include "Tot*Spot," "Think Tank," "How Does It Work?" "EcoStation," and the "Inventors' Workshop."

This museum was named "2005 Nation's #1 Children's Museum" by MSN.com City Guide and "Best Museum in Houston" by goCityKids.

Info in brief: An "action packed" hands-on museum for children and their caregivers.

Location: In Houston's museum district—1500 Binz at the Corner of Binz and LaBranch.

Hours: Tuesday–Saturday, 9 A.M. to 5 P.M.; Thursday, until 8 P.M.; Sunday, noon to 5 P.M.

Admissions: Under 2, free; seniors (65+); all others $5 until 3 P.M.; after 3 P.M., $3. Member ASTC.

Other sites of interest nearby: Several museums within walking distance, Southern Orient Express DRC Rail Tours, Texas Limited train excursion, AstroWorld amusement park, WaterWorld water park, and other Houston tourist attractions.

For further information write to The Children's Museum of Houston, 1500 Binz, Houston, Texas 77004-7112, or call (713) 535-7267 or (713) 240-4956 or fax (713) 522-5747. *www.cmhouston. org*

Children make jitterbug art at the Children's Museum of Houston.

The Legos area is a favorite of visitors to the Children's Museum of Houston.

The Children's Museum of the Brazos Valley
Bryan

The Brazos Valley Children's Museum is a hands-on museum for young children and their caregivers. The mission of the museum is to provide a child-centered hands-on, interactive environment for discovery and learning. Current exhibits include: PBS Area, Upside down Passage, Train Table, Village Arts (Dramatic Play Area, Face painting, Easels, Exploratory Art Table, and "The Bug"—a 1970 Super Beetle "canvas"), Valley Grocery, Small Town Play, Block Table, Sounds Around Town, Health and Fitness and Rocketship/Galaxy. Special events and programs are also offered periodically.

Hours: Monday thru Saturday, 10 A.M.–5 P.M. The museum is closed for major holidays.

Admissions: Under 1, free; seniors, $3; others, $4. Parking is free adjacent to the building.

For further information write to the Children's Museum of the Brazos Valley, 111 E. 27th St., Bryan, TX 77803 or call (979) 779-KIDS (5437).

Dinosaur World
Glen Rose

Dinosaur World in Texas was slated to open in the Spring of 2008, next to Dinosaur Valley State Park. For more information on exhibits, see Dinosaur World, Plant City, Florida.

For further information write to Dinosaur World, 1058 Park Rd. 59, Glen Rose, TX, 76043 or call (254) 898-1526 or fax (254) 898-1792.

Discovery Place
Texarkana

The Texarkana Museums System actually consists of three museums in downtown Texarkana. The Ace of Clubs House (ca. 1880–1940), the Texarkana Historical Museum, and the Discovery Place. The Discovery Place is the only building which would really qualify as a children's museum. Several hands-on exhibits help children learn about the past with such displays as the Caddo people's grass hut, an old school house, and a real early–Texas cooking kitchen. Children and their families can also learn about some basic scientific principles through exhibits that teach about speed and the power of momentum, and more.

Info in brief: A hands-on and historical museum for children and their caregivers; part of a triplex of museums which would interest the whole family.

Location: Downtown Texarkana at 3rd and Pine streets. Physical address: 215 Pine St.

Hours: Tuesday–Saturday, 10 A.M. to 4 P.M.

Admissions: Ages 5 & older, $4.50. Free 2-hour parking.

For further information write to the Discovery Place, c/o Texarkana Museums System, P.O. Box 2343, Texarkana, Texas 75504-2343, or call (903) 793-4831 or fax (903) 793-7108. *www.texarkana-museums.org*

Discovery Science Place
Tyler

The Discovery Science Place is a hands-on museum for kids of all ages. The three exhibit areas currently featured are *Discovery Landing, Hometown, USA* (a permanent exhibit) and *Weather Watcher.*

Location: 1½ blocks north of the Smith County Courthouse in Tyler.

Hours: Monday thru Saturday, 9 A.M.–5 P.M.; Sunday, 1–5 P.M.; Closed most major holidays.

Admissions: Under 2, free; all others, $5. After 3:30 P.M., special rate is offered. Memberships available. Member ASTC.

Other sites of interest nearby: Tyler Civic Ballet, Smith County Historical Museum, East Texas Symphony Orchestra, Booner-Whitaker McClendon House, and Fire Mountain Amusement Park.

For further information write to Discovery Science Place, 308 N. Broadway Ave., Tyler, TX 75702, or call 1-800-218-8073 or (903) 533-8011. *www.discoveryscienceplace.com* E-mail: *info@discovery-scienceplace.com*

Don Harrington Discovery Center
Amarillo

More than 60 permanent exhibits and 3 traveling exhibits a year are offered at the Don Harrington Discovery Center, where visitors are encouraged to "experiment, explore, create, tinker, play, solve and discover with their own hands." Some of the exhibits are named *Tiny Town, Weather, Aquaria, Optical Illusions, Puzzles, ExploraZone, Amazing Bodies* and *Science Café.*

The Center has also recently acquired a digital theater system, one of the five installations in the Digistar 3 group. This large screen theater immerses the audience in the learning experience.

Info in brief: A hands-on museum and Digistar 3 theater for kids of all ages and their families.

Location: In the Harrington Regional Medical Center.

Hours: (Museum) Tuesday thru Saturday, 9:30 A.M.–4:30 P.M.; Sunday, noon–4:30 P.M. Closed New Year's Day, Thanksgiving Day and Christmas Day. (Digistar 3) Tuesday thru Friday, 11 A.M., 1 P.M. & 3 P.M. Saturday, 11 A.M., 1 P.M., 2 P.M. &3 P.M. Sunday, 1 P.M., 2 P.M. & 3 P.M.

Admissions: Under 3, free; children (ages 3–12), $4.50; students (13–22), $5; seniors (60+), $5; adults, $5.50. Digistar 3 theater presentations are included in the museum admission price.

For further information write to the Don Harrington Discovery Center, 1200 Streit Dr., Amarillo, TX 79106 or call (806) 355-9547 or 1-800-784-9548 or fax (806) 355-5703. *www.dhdc.org*

Fort Worth Museum of Science and History
Fort Worth

This museum has quite a history. It was chartered in 1941 and opened in 1945 as the Fort Worth Children's Museum. In 1968, the name was changed to encourage all family members to attend. The Museum brags of many "firsts"—the very first children's museum in Texas, and one of the first children's museums in the nation; the OMNI Theater was the first IMAX in the Southwest; the Noble Planetarium was the first planetarium to be named after a female astronomer; and it was the very first children's museum in the world to have a planetarium. The museum now offers many large, world-class traveling exhibits, as well as many interactive, hands-on exhibits like DinoDig, ExploraZone, and Kidspace.

In May of 2006, the Museum announced plans for a new building which is expected to take 24 months to build. During that time, the OmniTheater will remain open (except for a few months when the sound system will be renovated), and a variety of hands-on exhibits from the museum will be housed on the lower level of the National Cowgirl Museum and Hall of Fame at 1720 Gendy Street in Fort Worth's Cultural District.

Although its name, location, size and scope have changed over the years, the purpose of the Museum remains the same—"to provide an extraordinary learning environment to the community."

Info in brief: A hands-on, interactive science museum for all ages.

Location: The new facility will be located at 1501 Montgomery Street.

Hours: Daily, Monday thru Saturday, 9 A.M.–5 P.M.; Sunday, noon–5 P.M.

Admissions: 2 & under, free; child (3–12) & senior, $7; all others $8. Memberships available. Be sure to check the museum's website before visiting, as tickets may be purchased for various facilities at various locations.

Other sites of interest nearby: Amon Carter Museum, Kimbell Art Museum, Modern Art Museum of Ft. Worth, Will Rogers Memorial Center, Casa Manana Theater and many other attractions in Fort Worth.

For further information write to the Fort Worth Museum of Science and History, 1501 Montgomery St., Ft. Worth, TX 76107 or call (817) 255-9300 or 888-255-9300 or fax (817) 732-7635. *www.fwmuseum.org*

Fredda Turner Durham Children's Museum at the Museum of the Southwest
Midland

The Museum of the Southwest was founded in 1965 by the Junior League of Midland to honor the ancestral heritage of those who forged the new life in the Great Southwest. An art museum was the first step in this plan to preserve the history, art and culture of the area. The museum complex has grown to include the Turner Mansion with art galleries (Thomas Gallery and the South Wing Exhibition Hall), the Marian Blakemore Planetarium (added in 1972), and the Fredda Turner Durham Children's Museum (begun in 1986).

The Children's Museum sits on property neighboring the Turner Mansion and offers a number of science and art exhibitions. Both permanent and rotating exhibits are available to the visitor. Some exhibits include The Lowe Learning Center (computer lab with software programs in Science, Strategy/Thinking Skills, Art/Music/Creativity, and Read-Along Books; Imagination Station (dress-up, role-playing area); Light and Color; and more. Six-day art courses are also offered for the young artist, along with special weekend workshops, summer concerts and more.

The Blakemore Planetarium offers a variety of programs throughout the year. Visitors should call ahead for updated schedules and to insure seating through the reservations clerk.

The museum was accredited by the American Association of Museums in June of 1992.

Info in brief: A complex of three museums, all of which are of interest to children, but one of which is specifically a hands-on museum for children.

Location: Midland, midway between El Paso and Dallas on I-20.

Hours: Tuesday–Saturday, 10 A.M. to 5 P.M.; Sunday, 2 P.M. to 5 P.M. Planetarium showtimes differ slightly. Contact the Planetarium before your visit.

Admissions: Under 2, free; others, $2 (to the Museum of the Southwest). Admission Fredda Turner Durham Children's Museum and the Art Museum is free. Sundays are free. Free admission during Septemberfest (contact museum for more info).

Other sites of interest nearby: The American Airpower Heritage Museum, and the Petroleum Museum.

For further information write to the Museum of the Southwest, 1705 W. Missouri Ave., Midland, Texas 79701-6516, or call (915) 683-2882 or (915) 570-7770 or fax (915) 570-7077. *www.museumsw. org/childrens/childhome/html*

Guinness World of Records Museum, Ripley's Haunted Adventure & Tomb Rider 3D
San Antonio

Although the Guinness World of Records Museum is not strictly a children's museum, the items on display are of definite interest to children (and their caregivers) around the world. With over 5,200 sq. ft. of exhibits, the museum brings "amazing feats" and "astonishing facts" to life in its three-dimensional displays. Visitors find exhibits, displays, rare videos, artifacts, computerized data banks, life-size replicas of famous people and much more.

Ripley's Haunted Adventure and Tomb Rider 3D adventures are at the same location, and combination admission tickets are available.

Info in brief: A visual museum with items of interest to most children, while the other adjacent "adventures" do offer some interactivity.

Location: Alamo Plaza Street, across from the Alamo.

Hours: (September–May) Sunday–Thursday, 10 A.M.–7 P.M.; Friday–Saturday, 10 A.M. to 10 P.M.; (June–August) Sunday–Thursday, 10 A.M. to 10 P.M.; Friday and Saturday, 10 A.M. to midnight.

Admissions: 1 Attraction: adult, $16.99; child (4–12), $9.99. 2 Attractions: adult, $19.99; child, $12.99. All three: adult, $26.99; child, $16.99.

Other sites of interest nearby: The Alamo, Riverwalk, and the many other sites of interest in San Antonio.

For further information write to the Guinness World of Records Museum, 329 Alamo Plaza, San Antonio, TX 78205 or call (210) 226-2828. *www.haunted-guinness-crockett.com*

Houston Fire Museum, Inc.
Houston

The Houston Fire Museum is located just south of Downtown Houston in historic Fire Station No. 7. Its mission is to educate the public about the importance of fire and life safety and to teach the history of fire service. Visitors can view exhibits showing the evolution of firefighting from the days of the "bucket brigades" to today's advanced firefighting and lifesaving services.

Several pieces of antique fire apparatus are housed there, including a 1938 Rex Reo truck (open for children to explore), an old steam engine and a 1912 water tower. Other displays include collections of smaller pieces of equipment, patches, gear, and more.

The building itself is listed on the National Register of Historic Places. When first opened in 1899, it housed horse-drawn equipment, a steam engine and a hose wagon. It was one of Houston's busiest fire houses for many years. After being closed for 12 years, it was renovated and reopened in 1982 as the museum and is now open both for individual visitors and group tours.

Info in brief: The exciting nature of the exhibits makes it of special interest to children. The only true hands-on exhibit is the 1938 Rex Reo firetruck with firefighting gear on board for children to wear as they fight imaginary fires with the equipment also on board. Group tours are not recommended for children under 5 years of age.

Location: 2403 Milan Street, Houston, Texas.

Hours: 10 A.M. to 4 P.M., Tuesday–Saturday. (Other times also available for special group tours.)

Admissions: "Nominal"—call for more information.

Unique exhibits or exhibitions: 1938 Rex Reo firetruck and firefighting equipment and gear.

Other sites of interest nearby: The many tourist attractions of Houston.

For further information write to the Houston Fire Museum, 2403 Milam Street, Houston, Texas 77006, or call (713) 524-2526, or fax (713) 520-7566. *www.houstonfiremuseum.org*

Laredo Children's Museum
Laredo

This small children's museum is located in an old military building on the campus of Laredo Community College. Hands-on exhibits include "Grocery Store," "Computer Room," "Construction Corner," "Pediatric Clinic," "Choo-Choo Train," "Stage & Theatre," and "Sound Pipes." Traveling exhibits are made available to visitors several times a year. Super Sunday Programs, summer camps, and weekend workshops and special festivals are also offered.

Info in brief: A small hands-on arts and humanities museum for young children and their caregivers. Near the Mexican border, this would make a nice side-trip after an exhausting Mexico-shopping trip.

Location: Campus of Laredo Community College, right on the Rio Grande.

Hours: Wednesday–Sunday, 1 P.M. to 5 P.M.; Saturday, 10 A.M. to 5 P.M.

Admissions: Children, $1; adults, $2.

Other sites of interest nearby: Mexican-American border.

For further information write to the Laredo Children's Museum, 5300 San Dario Ave., Ste. 109, Laredo, Texas 78041-3001, or call (956) 728-0404. *www.ci.laredo.tx.us/Museum*

Museum of Nature & Science, The Science Place (TSP)
Dallas

The Museum of Nature & Science consists of several buildings all located at Fair Park in Dallas. Formerly known as the Dallas Museum of Natural History and the Science Place, the two facilities merged in 2006, continuing to inspire minds through nature and science. The Dallas Museum of Natural History earned Smithsonian Institution Affiliate Museum status in 1999. The Science Place was founded in 1946 as "The Dallas Health Museum" and is one of the oldest science museums in the U.S. The two buildings that make up the Science Place are listed in the National Historic Registry. It has earned both ASTC and AAM accreditation.

The Science Place occupies a total of 150,000 sq. ft. and has more than 200 permanent hands-on exhibits on physics, astronomy, health, robotics, and nature. A special area for young children is also on site. Some of the exhibit names in the Science Place are: Ancient Microworlds, Lagoon Nature Walk, Paleontology Lab, Ice Age Dallas, Texas Dinosaurs, Wildlife Dioramas, Dental Gallery, Little Urban Farm, NetWorks, Astronomy & Space and Disaster Zone.

Also on the campus are an IMAX Theater and a new DigiStar 3 planetarium. There are a total of 8 museums on the Fair Park campus, including the Museum of Nature & Science. (See "Other sites of interest nearby" below.)

Info in brief: A merger of two of the oldest science museums in the U.S. with both visual and hands-on exhibits. Visitors can spend their time in one section of the museum, or both sections, for a full day of thoughtful and fun science discovery.

Location: Fair Park in Dallas. The Nature Bldg. is located at 3535 Grand Ave, the Science Bldg is located at 1318 South Second Ave., and the Planetarium Building is located at 1620 First Ave. just a few minutes east of downtown Dallas.

Hours: Monday thru Saturday, 10 A.M.–5 P.M.; Sunday, noon–5 P.M.

Admissions: Under 3, free to all bldgs.; Exhibits: child (ages 3–11), $5.50; youth (ages 12–18) & student (with ID) & senior (62+), $7.75; adult, $8.75; IMAX: adults, $7; all others, $6. Planetarium: $4 for all visitors. Fair Park One Price Ticket: visit all 8 museums for just one price — 40% off the regular retail price. (NOTE: State Fair ticketing is separate from museum ticketing.) Memberships available. Member ASTC and AAM accredited. Parking is always free.

Other sites of interest nearby: *Fair Park Museums*— Age of Steam Railroad Museum, Dallas Aquarium at Fair Park, Hall of State, Texas Discovery Gardens, The Women's Museum. Also, the State Fair of Texas, Kennedy Assassination Museum and sites, Six Flags over Texas (nearby), and more.

For further information write to The Science Place, P.O. Box 151469, Dallas, TX 75315 or call (214) 428-5555 or fax (214) 428-4356.

Museum of the Southwest *see* The "Fredda Turner Durham Children's Museum at the Museum of the Southwest"

The National Center for Children's Illustrated Literature
Abilene

The NCCIL is a non-profit organization that creates exhibitions of the finest original artwork in children's literature. Established in 1997 as a partnership between artist William Joyce and the Abilene Arts Council, the museum was originally housed in the historic downtown Grace Hotel. In 2000, the beautifully renovated Rhodes Building, circa 1920's, was opened to the public and became the NCCIL's permanent home.

The NCCIL collaborates with award-winning artists to produce exhibitions of his/her artwork that are distinctive and appealing to museum visitors of all ages. In addition, each exhibition eventually travels to museums, public libraries and galleries nationwide.

As a community-based organization, the NCCIL provides free weekly hands-on art activities for families and special art camps for children. Throughout the year, the museum also hosts school tours and provides many seminars and training sessions for teachers and educators. Admission is always free.

Info in brief: More of a visual display/performance-type of museum, but with items of interest specifically for children.

Location: Downtown Historic District, across from the restored Texas & Pacific depot.

Hours and Admissions: Not yet established at the time of this writing.

Unique exhibits: The entire concept of a museum with these characteristics as its main interest is a unique concept.

Other sites of interest nearby: Texas & Pacific depot (restored), Museums of Abilene (see listing), and other tourist attractions in Abilene.

For further information contact the National Center for Children's Illustrated Literature at *www.nccil.org*

The New Braunfels Children's Museum
New Braunfels

The New Braunfels Children's Museum in New Braunfels is a 5,000 sq. ft. hands-on, exploratory museum for children of all ages. Some of the exhibits offered include "Where in the World?," "Once Upon a Time," "CMN-TV," "Magic School Bus Science Corner," "Puppet Place," "Picnic in the Park," "Grandma's Attic," and "Make 'N' Take" (recyclable arts center). Workshops, classes, and special events are also offered.

Info in brief: A small hands-on museum especially for younger children and their caregivers.

Hours: Monday–Saturday, 9 A.M. to 5 P.M.; Sunday, noon to 5 P.M.

Admissions: Under 1, free; all others, $2.50. Memberships available. Be sure to check with the museum for current prices.

Other sites of interest nearby: Rio Raft Co. rafting tours, the New Braunfels Conservation Society living history museum buildings and the other shops in the New Braunfels Factory Stores mall.

For further information write to The Children's Museum in New Braunfels, 386 W. San Antonio St., New Braunfels, Texas 78130-7939, or call (830) 620-0939. *www.nbchildren.org*

The Science Place, Southwest Museum of Science & Technology *see* Museum of Nature and Science

The Science Place (TSP), Science Spectrum
Lubbock

The Science Spectrum is a hands-on science and technology center offering exciting demonstrations, interactive hands-on exhibits and exploratory areas. Some of the experiences available include Bubble Fun, "Flight and Space," computer experiences, Kidspace for preschoolers, Whisper Dish and more. Traveling exhibits are offered through the year. Science Saturdays programs are offered free of charge each Saturday. An OMNI Theater is also on site.

Info in brief: A hands-on children's science museum.

Hours: Monday–Friday, 10 A.M. to 5 P.M.; Saturday, 10 A.M. to 6 P.M.; Sunday, 1 P.M. to 5 P.M.

Admissions: (Museum only) under 3, free; children (3–16), $4.50; adults, $6; seniors (60+), $5. (Omnimax Theater only) under 3, free; children, $6.50; adults, $6; seniors, $6.50. (Combination — both facilities) under 3, free; children, $9; adults, $11; seniors, $9. Member ASTC.

Other sites of interest nearby: Lubbock Lake Landmark State Historical Park, Moody Planetarium of the Museum of Texas Tech, The Museum of Texas Tech University, Ranching Heritage Center, Buddy Holly Center, American Wind Power Center, Silent Wings Museum, American Museum of Agriculture, and The Louise H. Underwood Center for the Arts.

For further information write to Science Spectrum, 2579 S. Loop 289, Ste. 250, Lubbock, Texas 79423, or call (806) 745-2525. *www.sciencespectrum.org*

Sci-Tech Discovery Center
Plano

Sci-Tech previously hosted preview exhibits at the Shop at Willow Bend, but has now closed down in the process of actively pursuing the establishment of a permanent facility. While a website is up and running, it is suggested that you contact the museum by phone (see number below) for accurate information.

Admissions: Not yet set. Member ACM.

For further information write to Sci-Tech Discovery Center, P.O. Box 261544, Plano, TX 75023 or call (972) 546-3050. *www.mindstretchingfun.org*

The Witte Museum, H-E-B Science Treehouse
San Antonio

The Witte Museum has been existence for more than 80 years, with the goals of engaging the imaginations of young and old and providing "encounters with artifacts and information only available in a museum." The Witte offers a large number of permanent exhibits that include dinosaur skeletons, wildlife dioramas, cave drawings and much, much more. Several historic homes have been moved to the site and renovated, one of which is now the H-E-B Science Treehouse, which is the children's hands-on science museum. The Treehouse offers 4 levels of experimentations with simple machines, LASERS, sound, electricity, air and weather. The "Small World Science" area offers a chance for young children and their caregivers to explore science at their level.

Info in brief: A large visual multidisciplinary museum, with an emphasis on the sciences. Some hands-on, interactive experiences are available in some of the exhibits. One building on the campus is designed especially for children.

Location: Brackenridge Park on the bank of the San Antonio River.

Hours: Daily, year round, except for the 3rd Monday in October, Thanksgiving Day and Christmas Day. Monday & Wednesday thru Saturday, 10 A.M.–5 P.M.; Tuesday, 10 A.M.–8 P.M.; Sunday, noon–5 P.M.

Admissions: Ages 3 & under, free; children (ages 4–11), $5; seniors (65+), $6; adults (ages 12–64), $7. An additional surcharge may apply to special exhibits. Member ASTC. Admission is free on Tuesday from 3–8 P.M.

Other sites of interest nearby: The Alamo, RiverWalk, IMAX Theatre, and many, many more San Antonio attractions.

For further information write to the Witte Museum, 3801 Broadway, San Antonio, TX 78209 or call (210) 357-1900. *www.wittemuseum.org*

The Woodlands Children's Museum
The Woodlands

The Woodlands Children's Museum is newly located inside the Woodlands Mall. The museum now provides more hands-on, interactive learning experiences "designed to immerse children and adults in play that stimulates curiosity and provides opportunities" to learn in a nurturing environment. These experiences are provided in the areas of science, health, nature, the environment, history and the arts. The names of the exhibit areas are *Critter Room, Dinoventure, A House For Me, Spirit of the Sea, Build It Big, Bank It, All Aboard! International Market & Café de Fun, Creation Station, Geology, Operating Room, Got Germs? Open Wide, Read-a-lot Kingdom, Post Office* and *Art Car.* Many special programs and events are offered weekly.

Info in brief: A children's hands-on museum.

Location: Woodlands Mall — Upper Level at 1201 Lake Woodlands Drive and I-45, The Woodlands, TX 77393-0864.

Hours: Tuesday thru Saturday, 10 A.M.–6 P.M.; Sunday, noon–5 P.M. Closed New Year's Day, Easter, Thanksgiving, Christmas Eve & Day.

Admissions: $5 per person ages 2 & older. Member ACM.

For further information write to The Woodlands Children's Museum, P.O. Box 130864, The Woodlands, TX 77380 or call (281) 465-0955 or fax (281) 465-0956. *www.woodlandschildrensmuseum.org*
E-mail: *info@woodlandschildrensmuseum.org*

UTAH

Discovery Gateway
Salt Lake City

The Children's Museum of Utah (TCMU) was founded in 1978. Doors were opened on the museum, housed in the former Wasatch Warm Springs Plunge building, in 1983. But, the dream of offering a world-class, hands-on learning center continued, until 2006, when The Children's Museum, in partnership with Junior Achievement of Utah and Salt Lake County, opened a larger, updated children's museum, with four floors and over 60,000 sq. ft. of interactive, hands-on, fun activities for all ages. With this improvement came a new name — "Discovery Gateway." Some of the more than 140 permanent exhibits now include: "The Garden," "Kids's Eye View," "Story Factory," "Media Central," "The Studio," "The Terrace," and "Jr. Achievement City."

Info in brief: A hands-on museum for children and their caregivers.

Location: Downtown Salt Lake City.

Hours: Monday, 10 A.M.–9 P.M.; Tuesday–Thursday, 10 A.M. to 6 P.M.; Friday, 10 A.M. to 9 P.M.; Saturday, 10 A.M. to 6 P.M.; Sunday, noon to 6 P.M. Call ahead for holiday hours.

Admissions: Under 1, free; Utah residents, $8.50; all others, $9.50.

Unique exhibits: A 747 Flight Simulator.

Other sites of interest nearby: Golden Spike National Historic Site in Brigham City; Heber Valley Railroad in Heber City; Lagoon, Lagoon A Beach, and Pioneer Village in Farmington.

For further information write to The Children's Museum of Utah, 840 North 300 West, Salt Lake City, Utah 84103-1413, or call (801) 456-KIDS (5437). *www.discoverygateway.org*

Treehouse Museum
Ogden

Treehouse Museum features dozens of award-winning exhibits based on literacy, literature and the arts. Exhibits are categorized as "Play" or "Literacy." Imaginative play exhibits are titled *The Treehouse, The Baby Place, Grandma Sophie's Kitchen and Garden Market, Day of the Knights, Pick up a Stick and Play Music Room,* and *One World Village.* Hands-on Literacy Exhibits are titled *Great American Map, Oval Office, Dinosaur Discovery, the One Room School, Mapping Utah, Millennium Tales* and *Native Peoples Area.* The Art Garden and Castle Theater are also featured. Special programs for little ones are offered regularly.

Info in Brief: A hands-on children's museum focusing on the arts.

Location: About 35 miles north of Salt Lake City.

Hours: Monday, 10 A.M.–4 P.M.; Tuesday–Thursday & Saturday, 10 A.M.–6 P.M.; Friday, 10 A.M.–6:30 P.M. Closed Sundays, New Year's Day, July 4th, July 24th, Thanksgiving Day and Christmas Day.

Admissions: Under 1, free; children (ages 1–15), $5; adults (16 & up), $3. Angled parking is available on the street around the building. Memberships available.

For further information write to Treehouse Museum, 347 22nd St., Ogden, UT 84401 or call (801) 394-9663. *www.treehousemuseum.org*

Utah Science Center
Salt Lake City

The Utah Science Center is slated to open in early 2010 as part of The Leonardo, on Library Square in Salt Lake City. It will be the first science center/museum in Salt Lake City, and will feature interactive, hands-on exhibits. The Leonardo's program will then provide a multi-level facility offering activities in the arts, culture and sciences for all visitors.

Info in brief: Planned to open in 2010, the USC will be a large, hands-on, interactive multidisciplinary museum for visitors of all ages.

Location: Library Square in Salt Lake City.

Hours & Admissions: Not set at time of publication.

Other sites of interest nearby: Many attractions in Salt Lake City.

For further information check the website at *www.theleonardo.org*

VERMONT

Green Mountain Children's Museum
Burlington

In April 2007, a probable site for the Green Mountain Children's Museum was set — at the renovated Moran Plant on Burlington's waterfront. When the museum opens, it will provide young children with a place where they can be physically and mentally active in the hands-on, interactive facility.

Info in brief: A hands-on, interactive children's museum, still in the planning stages.

For further information visit their website at *www.childrensmuseum.org* or E-mail them at *info@ gmcm.org*

Montshire Museum of Science
Norwich

The name Montshire comes from the combination of Vermont and New Hampshire, which is the area that the museum serves. Opening in 1976 in Hanover, New Hampshire, the museum moved to its larger facility in Norwich, Vermont in 1989. Montshire received the 1996 National Award for Museum Service in 1995, enabling it to receive some grants and monetary awards which will further increase both the size and the quality of the services offered.

Montshire, although not strictly classified as a children's museum, is a hands-on museum with exhibits on natural and physical science, ecology and technology. Science Park is a two-acre outdoor exhibit area with displays on water flow and natural history. Outside, more than 110 acres of woodland offer more than 2½ miles of nature trails to explore. Inside, two floors are packed with dozens of hands-on exhibits targeted for visitors of all age ranges. "Explainers" are on hand to answer questions, or visitors are free to explore the facilities on their own. A few special events are held during the year, and school field trips are encouraged. Traveling outreach programs are also offered.

Some major exhibits offered include, "Air Flow," "Andy's Place" (for preschoolers), "Bike-vator" (energy), "Bubbles," "Electricity Bench" (circuits, resistors, etc.), "Flow Tunnel," "Honeybees," "Kinetic Energy Machine," "Microscopes," "Mathematics" and much more.

Info in brief: While not advertised strictly as a children's museum, there are plenty of hands-on activities (most exhibits are) in this small museum to keep children (and adults) of all age ranges busy and entertained.

Location: On the banks of the Connecticut River in Norwich, just across the river from Hanover. Exit 13 off I-91 to Montshire Road.

Hours: Daily, 10 A.M. to 5 P.M.

Admissions: Under 3, free; children (3–17), $7; adults, $9. Memberships available. Member of ASTC.

Unique feature: Montshire received a $1.2 million National Science Foundation grant to be the lead organization of TEAMS (Traveling Exhibits at Museums of Science), a collaboration of five small science centers, with original exhibits to be shared among the participants.

Other sites of interest nearby: Winter skiing, beaches, Conway Scenic Railroad (North Conway, New York), Hobo Railroad (Lincoln, New Hampshire), The Mt. Washington Cog Railway (Mt. Washington, New Hampshire), White Mountain Central Railroad (Lincoln, New Hampshire), White River Flyer (White River, Vermont), Lamoille Valley Railroad (Morrisville, Vermont), Shelburne Museum (37 historic buildings near Shelburne, Vermont), Alpine Slide at Mount Mansfield Resort (Vermont), Pico Alpine Slide (Rutland, Vermont), Santa's Land amusement park (Putney, Vermont), and five amusement parks in New Hampshire: Canobie Lake Park (Salem), Santa's Village (Jefferson), Six Gun City (Jefferson), Storyland (Glen), and Whale's Tale Water Park (Lincoln).

For further information write to Montshire Museum of Science, One Montshire Rd., Norwich, Vermont 05055, or call (802) 649-2200. *www.montshire.org*

VIRGINIA

Amazement Square,
The Rightmire Children's Museum
Lynchburg

Amazement Square is a hands-on learning museum where visitors are encouraged to explore the arts and humanities, culture, science, technology and their interdisciplinary relationships. Four floors of interactive exhibitions, workshops and educational programming are featured. Amazement Tower is one of the most popular exhibits—"a meandering tangle of pathways, tunnels, illuminating stairs and glass elevator, connects all the Museum's exhibitions, and is the tallest indoor, interactive climbing structure in the United States."

Some of the permanent exhibit areas are named *Once Upon a Building, Raceways and Voltageville, Imagination Studio, On the James, Indian Island, Your Amazing Body, Big Red Barn* and *Kaleidoscope.* A changing exhibit gallery is also on site for traveling and rotating exhibits.

Info in brief: A multi-story, multidisciplinary children's museum.

Location: Historic J.W. Wood Building on the riverfront in downtown Lynchburg.

Hours: Tuesday thru Saturday, 10 A.M.–5 P.M.; Sunday, 1–5 P.M. Memorial Day–Labor Day, open on Mondays from 1 to 5 P.M.

Admissions: Under 2, free; seniors (60+), $6; all others, $7. Memberships available. Family Fun Nights, 2nd & 4th Wednesdays of every month, 3–8 P.M., $2.

For further information write to Amazement Square, 27 Ninth St., Lynchburg, VA 24504 or call (434) 845-1888 or fax (434) 845-5221. *www.amazementsquare.org* or E-mail: *pr@amazementsquare.com*

Chesapeake Planetarium
Chesapeake

Although not strictly a children's museum, this site's main emphasis is on children's programming. Chesapeake Planetarium was the first planetarium to be built by a public school system in Virginia and is open daily for school programs and one night each week for public shows.

Info in brief: A planetarium with an emphasis on children's programming.

Location: Chesapeake Municipal Center off I-64. (Near the site of the "Battle of Great Bridge" and a short distance from the Intracoastal Waterway.)

Hours: Contact planetarium for current schedule of programs.

Admissions: Public shows are free; group rate is $45. (It is recommended that children below the first grade level not be admitted to the planetarium chamber.)

Other sites of interest nearby: Virginia Beach beaches and hotels, American Revolution historic sites and more.

For further information write to Chesapeake Planetarium, P.O. Box 16496, Chesapeake, Virginia 23320, or call (757) 547-0153, Ext. 208. *www.cpschools.com* (check their directory).

The Children's Health Museum
Charlottesville

The Children's Health Museum, established 11 years ago by the Junior League and the University of Virginia Medical Center, has as its main goal to serve children who are visiting the hospital for a variety of reasons. It is a small hands-on museum which encourages children ages 3 to 8 to learn about their bodies, health and the hospital experience in general.

One-on-one attention is the museum's main goal. After a child "checks in," a volunteer "adopts" him or her for the remainder of the visit and helps with the activities, which vary according to age. Activities include a ride in a child's wheelchair, a slide (dental health), a nutrition board, two anatomically correct dolls which help children learn about health and surgical procedures, hand and foot board, scales, "picket fence" (measure height), coordination board, X-ray box and distorted mirrors.

Many of the exhibits are portable and can be taken to classrooms for special workshops. School groups may also visit the museum itself, but small groups will be formed.

The museum is staffed by two full-time employees and more than 40 volunteers, including Junior League members, hospital personnel, and college students. The main goal for volunteers and staff alike is to help children learn that they do not have to be afraid of the hospital.

Info in brief: Hands-on, participatory exhibits with one-on-one attention a primary goal.

Location: Corner of the Primary Care Center of the University of Virginia's Health Sciences Center.

Hours: Monday–Friday, 9 A.M. to 4 P.M.

Admissions: Free.

For further information write to The Children's Health Museum, University of Virginia Health Sciences Center, Box 231-94, Charlottesville, Virginia 22908, or call (434) 924-1593. *www.health-system.virginia.edu/internet/health-museum*

Children's Museum of Richmond
Richmond

The Children's Museum of Richmond opened its doors in 1981, offering a special place for children and their families in Central Virginia. With the central theme: "Me, My Community, and My World." eleven main sub-theme areas include: Playworks, Children's Bank, Health & Safety Area, WRCM-TV Studio, SuperMarket!, Computer Station, The Cave, Art Studio, Stage-Play, In My Own Backyard, and KidShop, inviting visitors to explore their world and its cultures from a child's perspective.

Special holiday activities, camp-ins, a Peanut Butter 'n' Jam Family Concert Series and other special programs are also offered throughout the year. Visitors should contact the museum before visiting to get a current schedule of events.

Info in brief: A hands-on, exploratory museum for children and their caregivers.

Hours: (Labor Day–Memorial Day) Tuesday–Saturday, 9:30 A.M. to 5 P.M.; Sunday, noon to 5 P.M. Closed to the public on Mondays EXCEPT major school holidays; (Memorial Day–Labor Day) Monday–Saturday, 9:30 A.M. to 5 P.M.; Sunday, noon to 5 P.M. Closed Thanksgiving Day, Christmas Day, New Year's Day, and Easter Sunday. OPEN these Monday holidays Labor Day, Columbus, Martin Luther King, Jr. Day, President's Day and Memorial Day.

Admissions: Call 1-800-kids-443 (543-7443) for current admissions charges.

Other sites of interest nearby: Science Museum of Virginia, Old Dominion Railway Museum, Busch Gardens–Williamsburg (in Williamsburg), Paramount's Kings Dominion (Doswell).

For further information write to The Children's Museum of Richmond, Richmond, Virginia 23220, or call (804) 474-7085 or fax (804) 474-7099. *www.c-mor.org*

Children's Museum of Virginia
Portsmouth

The Children's Museum of Virginia displays interactive exhibits that encourage students to learn in a fun way about science, art, music, communication, technology and cultural diversity. The twelve main exhibit areas include "The City," "Science Circus," "Rock Climb," "Every Body," "Art Moves," "Blockbuster," "Bubbles," "Play Space," "New2Do Gallery," "You and Me," "Too Cool Gallery" and a Planetarium. Other special exhibits, activities, events and programs are also offered throughout the year.

Info in brief: Hands-on, interactive displays, grouped together by themes.

Location: Historic Olde Towne Portsmouth.

Hours: (Winter) Tuesday–Saturday, 9 A.M. to 5 P.M.; Sunday, 11 P.M. to 5 P.M. (Summer — Memorial Day to Labor Day) Monday–Saturday, 9 A.M. to 5 P.M.; Sunday, 11 A.M. to 5 P.M. Closed most Mondays; open some Monday holidays. Groups by reservation at other times.

Admissions: Under 2, free; all others $6. Memberships available. Under 14 must be accompanied by an adult.

Unique feature: The Children's Museum is within walking distance of four other museums that have banded together under the name of "Portsmouth Museums" (see below).

Other sites of interest nearby: Other Portsmouth museums — Naval Shipyard Museum (757) 393-8591, Lightship Museum (757) 393-8741, The Arts Center (757) 393-8543, and the Virginia Sports Hall of Fame (757) 393-8031. Many other Virginia tourist attractions are within a short driving distance.

For further information write to Children's Museum of Virginia, 221 High St., Portsmouth, Virginia 23704, or call (757) 393-8393 or 1-800-ports va. *www.childrensmuseumva.com*

Explore and Moore Children's Discovery Museum
Woodbridge

Explore and Moore is a hands-on, interactive children's museum where children can "explore, create, learn and exercise their imaginations!" Exhibits include *Puppet Theater, Dress Up Closet, Magnet Mania, Sand Box, Climbing Wall, Beauty Shop, Medical Center, Space Command Control Station, Grocery Store,* and *Toddle Town.*

As of early 2009, the museum announced that it was closed indefinitely.

Other sites of interest nearby: Veterans Memorial Park, Occoquan Bay Refuge, Commonwealth of Virginia Visitor Center. Washington, D.C. sites are nearby.

For further information write to Explore and Moore Children's Discovery Museum, 12904 Occoquan Rd., Woodbridge, VA 22192 or call (703) 492-2222. *www.exploreandmoore.com*

Harrisonburg Children's Museum
Harrisonburg

The Harrisonburg Children's Museum is a not-for-profit organization whose goal is to provide a hands-on, interactive museum for children ages 2–12 and their families. Emphasis is on culture, science and technology. HCM was voted "BEST Museum of the Valley 2007" by readers of the *Daily News-Record.* Interactive exhibit areas include *Creation Station Art Studio, Construction Zone, Science Area, Game Corner, Theater/Performing Arts, Down on the Farm, Country Kitchen and Market, Mountain Climb* and more.

Location: Downtown Harrisonburg on Court Square.

Hours: Tuesdays, 10 A.M.–7 P.M. Wednesdays–Saturdays, 10 A.M.–4 P.M. Free Fridays—1st Friday of each month, 5–8 P.M. Closed Christmas Eve & Day, New Year's Day, and all Harrisonburg Public School holidays.

Admissions: Under 2, free; all others, $4. Memberships available.

For further information write to Harrisonburg Children's Museum, 30 N. Main St., Harrisonburg, VA 22802 or call (540) 442-8900. *www.hcmuseum.org* E-mail: *explore@hcmuseum.org*

The Naturalist Center
Leesburg

This public facility offers more than 30,000 natural history and anthropological specimens, as well as books, microscopes, measuring tools, and other equipment for visitors. Although not a "hands-on" experimental type of museum, visitors are allowed to handle many of the artifacts.

Info in brief: A science museum for visitors 10 years old and older, offering some hands-on experiences.

Location: Leesburg Airpark Business Center, 45 minutes from the National Mall.

Hours: Tuesday thru Saturday, 10:30–4 P.M. Closed Sundays, Mondays and all federal holidays.

Admissions: Free

Other sites of interest nearby: 30–45 minutes from Washington, D.C.

For further information write to the Naturalist Center, 741 Miller Drive SE, Leesburg, VA 20175 or call (703) 779-9712 or 1-800-729-7725.

Science Museum of Western Virginia
Roanoke

Established in 1970, the Science Museum of Western Virginia offers interactive exhibits for people of all ages. Included are two newly renovated galleries— The Science Arcade (with more than 40 interactive exhibits) and Body Tech: Science Behind Medicine. Other permanent exhibits include a weather station, Chesapeake Bay Touch Tank, Computers Then and Now and a simulated rainforest. At least one traveling exhibit is always on display. The Hopkins Planetarium, a 120-seat theater, is also part of the facility. Although it is not advertised as a children's museum *per se*, the type of exhibits and the atmosphere of the museum make it a true family-fun experience at which children will not be bored or frustrated.

Info in brief: A hands-on, interactive and participatory museum for people of all ages.

Location: Center in the Square building at 1 Market Square in Roanoke.

Hours: Monday–Saturday, 9 A.M. to 5 P.M.; Sunday, 1 P.M. to 5 P.M. Closed Thanksgiving, Christmas, and New Year's Day.

Admissions: (Exhibits) Under 3, free; children (3–12), $6; seniors (60+), $7; adults, $8. Add MegaDome, $3; add Planetarium, $2. (MegaDome only) child, $4; adult, $5; senior, $4.50. (Planetarium only) $3. Sluice (when available), $4. Paid parking is available; free parking on Saturday and Sunday. Member ASTC.

Other sites of interest nearby: The Art Museum of Western Virginia (next door), Roanoke Valley History Museum (next door), Virginia's Transportation Museum, Mill Mountain Zoo, Virginia's Explore Park, Salem Museum, To the Rescue, and the Harrison Museum of African American Culture.

For further information write to the Science Museum of Western Virginia, One Market Square, Roanoke, Virginia 24011, or call (540) 342-5726. Planetarium E-mail address: *www.@SMWV.org*

Shenandoah Valley Discovery Museum
Winchester

At the Shenandoah Valley Discovery Museum visitors of all ages can touch, crawl, explore and have fun while discovering the natural world around us all. Current exhibit areas include: Raceways, A Stop Along the Moccasin Trail, Emergency Clinic & Ambulance, Paleo Lab, Simple Machines, Natural History, Ranger Station and more. Each area contains a number of fun, hands-on activities. Plans also call for new exhibits, activities and even a "Museum in the Park" to be added to the existing facility.

Info in brief: A hands-on natural history museum for children and their caregivers.

Location: Downtown Pedestrian Mall. Physical address: 54 S. Loudoun St., (22601).

Hours: Monday thru Saturday, 9 A.M.–5 P.M.; Sunday, 1–5 P.M.; 1st Friday, 5–7:30 P.M.

Admissions: Under 2, free; all others, $6. Parking, $.50 per hour. Member ASTC, ACM, VAM and the Southeast Museum Conference.

For further information write to Shenandoah Valley Discovery Museum, P.O. Box 239, Winchester, Virginia 22604 or call (540) 722-2020 or fax (540) 722-2189. *www.discoverymuseum.net* or E-mail: *mlawson@discoverymuseum.net*

Virginia Air & Space Center
Hampton

The Virginia Air & Space Center is the visitor center for NASA Langley Research Center and Langley Air Force Base. Visitors can launch a rocket, pilot a space shuttle, come face-to-face with the Apollo 12 Command Module, and a DC-9 passenger jet. A 3D IMAX theater is also on site. Dozens of hands-on air and space exhibits are on site along with an interactive aviation gallery that spans 100 years of flight. Both permanent and traveling exhibits are featured. A Hampton Carousel is also on site as well as an IMAX Theater.

Location: Downtown Hampton.

Hours: Winter (Labor Day–end of May): Monday thru Saturday, 10 A.M.–5 P.M.; Sunday, noon–5 P.M. Summer (end of May–Labor Day): Monday thru Wednesday, 10 A.M.–5 P.M.; Thursday thru Sunday, 10 A.M.–7 P.M. Also open evenings for special programs and IMAX films.

Admissions: Under 2, free. Exhibits Only: child (ages 3–18), $7; senior (65+), $8; adult, $9. IMAX only: child, $6.75; senior, $7; adult, $9. Exhibits & 1 IMAX Feature: child, $11; senior, $13; adult, $14. Exhibits & 2 IMAX Features: child, $15.25; senior, $17.25; adult, $18.25. Several other admissions plans are available. Be sure to contact the museum. A ride on the Hampton Carousel, $1.50. Free parking is available.

Other sites of interest nearby: Hampton History Museum.

For further information call The Virginia Air & Space Center at (757) 727-0900 or visit their website at *www.vasc.org*

Virginia Discovery Museum
Charlottesville

Opened in 1981, the Virginia Discovery Museum is located in the east end of the Downtown Mall (across from the post office).

Besides the regular exhibits, the museum offers various classes, special events and special activities throughout the year. An after-school science club for the whole family meets every Thursday with topics changing weekly.

In 2007 over 53,000 people visited the museum itself, with approximately 2,000 more people taking advantage of the special group tours and classes.

Permanent exhibits on display at the Virginia Discovery Museum include an 18th-century log house, "Virginia Faces" (a dress-up area), Playscape, a carousel, and a working beehive. Numerous rotating exhibits are changed around every four months.

Info in brief: Hands-on science, history and art exhibits.

Location: East end of the Downtown Mall in Charlottesville, Virginia.

Hours: Tuesday–Saturday, 10 A.M. to 5 P.M.; Sunday, 1 P.M. to 5 P.M.; Closed Mondays; group reservations required.

Admissions: Ages 1–13, $4 (must be accompanied by an adult); adults, $4; seniors, $4; AAA discount, $.50. Memberships are offered. Member ASTC and ACM.

Unique exhibits or exhibitions: A complete 18th-century log house.

Other sites of interest nearby: Charlottesville tourist attractions.

For further information write to the Virginia Discovery Museum, P.O. Box 1128, Charlottesville, Virginia 22902, or call (804) 977-1025. *www.vadm.org* E-mail: *vadm@vadm.org*

WASHINGTON

The Children's Activity Museum of Ellensburg
Ellensburg

Hours: Thursday–Saturday, 10 A.M. to 5 P.M.; Sunday, 1 P.M. to 5 P.M.

For further information write to The Children's Activity Museum of Ellensburg, 400 N. Main, Ellensburg, Washington 98926, or call (509) 925-6789.

The Children's Museum
Seattle

Opened in 1981 as a private nonprofit corporation, The Children's Museum (TCM) now has 23 full-time and 23 part-time employees who work with more than 130 volunteers to keep the museum running smoothly year-round. Through their efforts, the museum has won several national honors and awards.

The Children's Museum is located on the first level of Center House at Seattle Center. A recent expansion project stretched the museum space to 32,200 sq. ft., with 22,000 of that as exhibit space and 5,200 as program/activity space. TCM offers 12 permanent exhibit areas, two temporary exhibits, several year-round and seasonal programs and community outreach programming. Traditionally, the museum uses multicultural themes in the literary, visual and performing arts, including topics on illustrating, the environment, history and communication. Names of exhibits: *Construction Zone, Bijou Theatre, Grocery, LaCocina Del Cacto, Discovery Bay, Mountain Forest, Global Village, Mind Scape & KD22 Radio, Cog City, Imagination Studio* and more.

Info in brief: A hands-on museum (emphasizing the arts and humanities) which also offers numerous workshops and special programming throughout the year.

Location: Center House at Seattle Center, a municipally-owned park in Seattle.

Hours: Monday–Friday, 10 A.M. to 5 P.M.; Saturday and Sunday, 10 A.M. to 6 P.M. Summer hours are longer—contact the museum before visiting. Closed Thanksgiving, Christmas Day and New Year's Day.

Admissions: Under 1, free; adults & children, $7.50; grandparents, $6.50. Memberships are available.

For further information write to The Children's Museum, 305 Harrison St., Seattle, Washington 98109-4645, or call (206) 441-1768 or fax (206) 448-0910. *www.thechildrensmuseum.org*

Children's Museum of Skagit County
Mount Vernon

The Children's Museum of Skagit County has been a hands-on museum for children and their families. There were eight main exhibit areas: The Transportation area (a real Semi-Cab from Freightliner with a play Truck Stop Diner attached); Light, Shadow, Action; Science Exploration Zone; an art studio, a farm area, Toddler Play Station; Drama area; a Reading/Quiet area; and a Natural Habitat (Tree House, Mountaintop and Sand Play).

Info in Brief: A hands-on museum for young children, ages birth to 8 years.

Location: Cascade Mall.

Hours: Monday–Saturday, 10 A.M. to 6 P.M.; Sunday, noon to 6 P.M.; Toddler Tuesdays, 8:30 A.M. to 10 A.M.

Admissions: $5 per person, under 12 months free.

For further information write to the Children's Museum of Skagit County, 550 Cascade Mall Dr., Burlington, WA 98233 or call (360) 757-8888.

The Children's Museum of Tacoma
Tacoma

The Children's Museum of Tacoma offers a range of permanent play spaces and rotating exhibits that "foster the power of play." Exhibits: Soar into Story, Bank on It!, New Digs, Becka's Studio, and traveling exhibits.

Location: 936 Broadway Ave., Tacoma, WA 98402.

Hours: Monday–Saturday, 10 A.M. to 5 P.M.; Sunday, noon to 5 P.M.

Admissions: Under 1, free; all others, $6; Half-price weekdays, 3 P.M.–5 P.M.; First Fridays, free, 10 A.M. to 7 P.M.

For further information write to The Children's Museum of Tacoma, 925 Court C, Tacoma, Washington 98402, or call (253) 627-2436 or 627-6031. *www.childrensmuseumoftacoma.org*

Children's Museum of Walla Walla
Walla Walla

Exhibit designers planned hands-on, interactive exhibits that children and their caregivers can experience together. Exhibit names include *Native American Exhibit, Science Sector, Tod-*

dler Meadow, Italian Restaurant, We Walla Harvest Market, The Enchanted Theater, Creative Play Forest, Bug Patch Party Room, Our Powerful Valley, We Walla Walla Clinic, Civil Service Exhibit, Construction Junction, Toddler Meadow, Me and My Shadow, Sasayama Exhibit (Sasayama, Japan is the Walla Walla's Sister City), Earthquake Simulation Exhibit and Art Nook.

Info in Brief: A hands-on, interactive museum for young children and their caregivers.

Hours: Thursday thru Saturday, 10 A.M.–5 P.M.; Sunday, noon to 5 P.M.

Admissions: Under 1, free; all others, $4.

For further information write to Children's Museum of Walla Walla, 77 Wainwright, Walla Walla, WA 99362 or call (509) 526-PLAY. *www.cmwallawalla.org* E-mail: *cmww@charter.net*

Hands On Children's Museum
Olympia

The Hands On Children's Museum in Olympia is an award-winning Children's Museum featuring 5 exhibit galleries, special early learning programming, field trips and school break camps as well as special events throughout the year. The Good For You! Gallery allows visitors to plant vegetables, pick flowers, shop in the grocery store and bakery, put together a healthy lunch, cook a family meal in the Family Kitchen and play on the Play Structure to get some exercise! The Backyard Gallery features a stage, a climbing tree, puppet theatre, and an animal Rescue Center. The Build It! Gallery offers a magnetic ball wall, house building with builder boards, a Design Studio, a huge pin wall for creating life-size fun shapes and a dump truck. The Working Waterfront Gallery provides a water table where children can play with and change the flow of water. There is also a giant crane and cargo ship as well as a Kapla Block table. The Art Studio provides over 100 recycled products and visitors can make and take any of their art creations. The Tot Spot! is a special place for children 0–4 years of age.

The museum also offers many early learning programs throughout the year including monthly parenting classes, weekly parent and child classes, monthly parents' night outs, preschool, school break camps and many other educational opportunities.

Info in brief: An award winning hands-on museum with 5 major galleries.

Hours: Monday–Saturday, 10 A.M. to 5 P.M.; Sunday, noon to 5 P.M. 1st Friday of the month, 5P.M.–9 P.M. (free)

Admissions: Under 1, free; toddlers (12–23 months), $4.95; children (age 2+), $7.95; seniors (55+), $6.95; adults, $7.95; military households, ½ price.

Other sites of interest nearby: Olympia Farmers' Market (April–December), Wolf Haven International (wolf sanctuary with narrated tours), Percival Landing, Heritage Park Fountain, and the Washington State Capitol buildings and grounds.

For further information write to Hands On Children's Museum, 106 11th Ave. SW, Olympia, WA 98501, or call (305) 956-0818. *www.hocm.org*

Imagine Children's Museum
Everett

Imagine Children's Museum provides interactive hands-on exhibits to children ages 2 to 12 and their families. The goal is to let them experience their community's history, culture, science and fine arts through exhibits laid out like a mini town. Some of the exhibits include a ferry, bank, clinic, construction area, farm art studio and more.

Outreach programs are also offered.

Info in brief: Small hands-on museum especially for children.

Hours: Tuesday, Wednesday & Saturday, 10 A.M. to 4 P.M. Thursday & Friday, 10 A.M. to 5:30 P.M.; Sunday, noon to 4 P.M. Closed New Year's Day, Easter, Christmas, Thanksgiving, Christmas.

Admissions: Under 1, free; all others, $7. (Admission half-price on Thursdays between 3:30 and 5:30.)

For further information write to Imagine Children's Museum, 1502 Wall Street, Everett, Washington 98201, or call (425) 258-1006. *www.imaginecm.org*

Pacific Science Center
Seattle

Pacific Science Center is a hands-on, interactive science & technology museum for children of all ages. Titles of major exhibits are: Dinosaurs, A Journey Through Time, Tropical Butterfly House, Insect Village, Puget Sound Model and Saltwater Tide Pool, Kids Works, Animal Exhibits, Boy Works, Adventures in 3Dimensions, Science Playground, and more. Technology exhibits and outdoor exhibits are also offered. A planetarium, laser show and IMAX theater are also on site.

Info in brief: Hands-on, interactive science & technology museum for children of all ages.

Location: Under the arches near the Space Needle.

Hours: Winter hours: Monday thru Friday, 10 A.M.–5 P.M.; Saturday & Sunday, 10 A.M.–6 P.M. Contact museum for Summer hours.

Admissions: Under 3, free to all facilities. Exhibits only: kids (ages 3–5), $6; juniors (ages 6–12), $8; seniors (65+), $9.50; adults (ages 13–64), $11. IMAX only: kids, $6; juniors, $7; seniors, $7.50; adults, $8. Exhibits & IMAX: kids, $10; juniors, $12; seniors, $13.50; adults, $15. Evening Laser Shows: Thursdays, $5; Friday & Saturday, $8. Special Engagement IMAX films require a special fee.

Other sites of interest nearby: The Space Needle, Music Project/Science Fiction Museum and Hall of Fame and more.

For further information write to the Pacific Science Center, 200 Second Ave. N, Seattle, WA 98109 or call (206) 443-2001 or fax (206) 443-3631. E-mail: *vs@pacsci.org*

Palouse Discovery Science Center
Pullman

"The Palouse Discovery Science Center promotes science, math and technology literacy through educational programs, exhibits, teaching collections and activities emphasizing hands-on learning." The 11,000 sq. ft. facility houses approximately 20 exhibit areas arranged in themes of Earth Systems, Biology and Physical Sciences with exhibits for all ages. Current exhibits include: *Making Connections— Communication Technology Across the Spectrum; The Space Place; The Great Mammoth Excavation; Light, Color & Vision; Little Learners' Lab; Wildlife with a whole assortment of animals;* the planetarium, and literacy and reading corners. All exhibits feature multi-age appeal and interactive materials.

Info in brief: An interactive, hands-on science museum for children of all ages.

Hours: Tuesday–Saturday, 10 A.M.–3 P.M.

Admissions: Under 2, free; senior scientists, (55+), $5; junior scientists (ages 2–12), $4; adult scientists, $6.

For further information write to The Palouse Discovery Science Center, 950 NE Nelson Ct., Pullman, WA 99163 or call (509) 332-6869 or fax (509) 332-6869. *www.palousescience.org* E-mail: *admin@palousescience.org*

Pioneer Farm Museum
Eatonville

The Pioneer Farm Museum is dedicated to providing living history, environmental and cultural educational opportunities through guided tours offering hand-on activities and experiences.

The Pioneer Farm Museum is a recreation of an 1880's settlement where children (and their caregivers) can tour log cabins, jump in the hay, pet animals and try other homesteader activities such as blacksmithing, woodworking, egg gathering, butter churning, wheat berry grinding, clothes scrubbing, and others.

The Ohop Indian Village offers visitors an opportunity to commune with nature in the woodlands, practicing hunting and fishing skills there, and then to return to the village to try preparing food items and working on winter craft activities, just as the Ohop Indians might have done.

Info in brief: A living history museum with an emphasis on hands-on learning.

Location: Between Hwy 161 and Hwy 7, 3 miles north of Eatonville in the Scenic Ohop Valley.

Hours: Summer (Fathers Day–Labor Day weekend) Pioneer Farm Tours— daily, 11 A.M. to 4 P.M. Native American Seasons Tour — Friday–Sunday, 1 P.M. and 2:30 P.M. Spring (March–Fathers Day week) and Fall (Labor Day–weekend before Thanksgiving) Pioneer Farm Tours— Saturday and Sunday, 11 A.M. to 4 P.M. Winter (Thanksgiving–February) Closed.

Admissions: Children (3–18), & seniors, $6; adults (19–61), $7.

Unique exhibitions: Large number of hands-on pioneering experiences available; all tours are guided only.

Other sites of interest nearby: The many tourist attractions in Seattle.

For further information write to The Rainier Legacy, 7716 Ohop Valley Road, Eatonville, Washington 98328, or call (360) 832-6300.

Three Rivers Children's Museum & Heritage Arts Center
Pasco

The Three Rivers Children's Museum opened in 1991 as a hands-on educational museum for children ages 2 to 10. The 3,000 sq. ft. facility offers activities in science, the arts, cultural understanding and history. The goal is to inspire children's curiosity and creativity, and to encourage them to add these to their lifelong value system. Another goal is to provide parents with a safe and fun place where they can interact positively with their children.

Current exhibits include *Computer Lab, Castle Performance Stage, Creative Kitchen, Lowe's Workshop, Magical Tree House, Reading Loft, Post Office, Puppet Theaters, School Bus, Science Explorations Area, Toddler Play Area, Union Pacific Train,* and *U.S.S. Friend-Ship.* Many special activities are also offered. Be sure to contact the museum or visit their website to find out about these activities.

Note: Kennewick and Richland are the other two cities which, with Pasco, make up the Tri-Cities metropolitan area. Some information about Three Rivers Children's Museum may list one of these cities as a location.

Info in brief: A hands-on multi-disciplinary museum for children ages 2 to 10 and their families.

Location: Broadmoor Square Mall.

Hours: Wednesday thru Friday, 10 A.M.–5 P.M.; Saturday, noon–5 P.M.

Admissions: $3 for all visitors. Member ASTC. Free parking available at the Mall.

For further information write to the Three Rivers Children's Museum, 52740 Outlet Dr., Pasco Washington 99301 or call (509) 543-7866. *www.childrensmuseumtr.org*

Whatcom Children's Museum
Bellingham

The Whatcom Children's Museum is located in one of the four buildings which make up the Whatcom Museum of History and Art campus. The other three buildings offer exhibitions for all ages, including interactive components for children, but the one building is exclusively devoted to children and activities designed around their specific needs. The other buildings are the Syre Education Center, the Arco Exhibits Building and the main museum building. The main museum building is the Old City Hall, which is listed on the National Register of Historic Places.

The museums offer both permanent and changing exhibits throughout the year. They also offer education and enrichment programs. The staff includes 32 professional paid staff members along with over 800 active volunteers.

The Children's Museum opened in 1989 as the Children's Museum Northwest. It became a part of the Whatcom Museum of History and Art in 1992 and underwent a full-scale renovation in 1995. The Children's Museum now occupies a 4,500 sq. ft. building with more than 3,500 sq. ft. of exhibit space.

Info in brief: One of four separate museum buildings, this one is designated and designed specifically for young children, with hands-on exhibits emphasized.

Location: Downtown cultural district of Bellingham on Prospect Street between Champion Street and Central Avenue.

Hours: Sunday, Tuesday and Wednesday, noon to 5 P.M.; Thursday, Friday and Saturday, 10 A.M. to 5 P.M. (Contact museum for hours of other buildings.)

Admissions: $3.50 per person for Children's Museum. Children must be accompanied by an adult. (Other buildings by donation.)

Unique exhibits: Four building set-up which can give a full day of museum visiting, both visual and tactile experiences being offered — visitors can look and do.

For further information write to the Whatcom Children's Museum, 227 Prospect St., Bellingham, Washington 98225, or call (360) 778-8970. *www.whatcommuseum.org*

World Kite Museum & Hall of Fame
Long Beach

The mission of the World Kite Museum & Hall of Fame, opened in 1990 in honor of the kite's 2,500-year-old history, is to tell the story of the kite by "preserving its past, recording its present, and honoring the people involved." The museum uses displays, education and activities to further this end. Various kite collections are displayed on a rotating schedule. Two new exhibits are featured each year to highlight a single aspect of kite-related history or culture. Two permanent exhibits document the Washington State International Kite Festival and members of the Hall of Fame.

Although most of the exhibits themselves are not hands-on, the museum does plan to keep at least one changing exhibit running which will provide hands-on activities for children. All children visiting the museum are also allowed to wear traditional Japanese *hapi* coats while they go through the facilities. A variety of kite-making classes, hands-on flying demonstrations, elder hostel lectures and school field trips are also sponsored regularly. Plans are underway to increase the size of the current facility, at which time more interactive displays will be available.

Info in brief: A unique collections–type museum with at least one hands-on exhibit area for children. The content of the museum itself is also of special interest to children.

Location: Corner of 3rd St. North and Boulevard in Long Beach. Physical address: 303 Sid Snyder Dr., SW (98631).

Hours: (May–September) daily, 11 A.M. to 5 P.M. (October–April) Friday thru Monday, 11 A.M. to 5 P.M.

Admissions: Children, $3; adults, $5; seniors, $4.

Other sites of interest nearby: Ilwaco Heritage Museum, Lewis & Clark Interpretive Center, Pacific Coast Cranberry Museum, Pacific Coast Historical Museum, Firefighter's Museum, Cape Disappointment Lighthouse, North Head Lighthouse, and more.

For further information write to The World Kite Museum and Hall of Fame, P.O. Box 964, Long Beach, Washington 98631 or call or fax (360) 642-4020. *www.worldkitemuseum.com*; E-mail: *info@worldkitemuseum.com*

Yakima Valley Museum
Yakima

The mission of the Yakima Valley Museum is to promote an "understanding of Central Washington history as it affects the lives of contemporary citizens." Through the collection, preservation, and exhibition of historic artifacts and stories, as well as related public programming, the museum provides residents and visitors with historical perspectives that may influence decisions about the future of the Valley. The museum houses permanent displays on the region's tree fruit industry, Supreme Court Justice William O. Douglas, Pioneer life, a large horse-drawn vehicle collection, an ice-age animal display, neon signs and an extensive Native American collection. Special exhibits are held throughout the year. Visitors may also visit the research library, gift and book shop, and enjoy a treat in the 1930's Art Deco soda fountain.

In 1996, the museum opened the "Children's Underground." This 2,500 sq. ft. area is a special historical and educational hands-on area teaching children about the valley's past, present and future. Available in this area are a freshwater "river biome" aquarium, a turtle habitat, a dress-up area, a four-building "child-size" town based on Yakima City in the 1880s, a pony cart and train car to climb in, and opportunities to handle the historic objects and artifacts from the area.

Info in brief: A family-oriented museum with a children's hands-on area.

Location: Next to Franklin Park.

Hours: (Museum) Tuesday–Saturday, 10 A.M. to 5 P.M., Sunday 11 A.M. to 5 P.M.; (Children's Underground), Tuesday–Friday, 1 P.M. to 5 P.M.; Saturday & Sunday, 11 A.M. to 5 P.M. (Tours by appointment).

Admissions (Includes museum and Children's Underground): 5 and under, free; students and seniors, $3; adults, $5; family, $12.

Unique exhibits: Special exhibitions and traveling exhibits change frequently.

Other sites of interest nearby: The historic H.M. Gilbert Homeplace; Union Gap Washington's historic attractions; Rail and Steam Museum (Toppenish); Yakima Indian National Cultural Center (Toppenish) and more.

For further information write to the Yakima Valley Museum, 2105 Tieton Dr., Yakima, Washington 98902, or call (509) 248-0747. *www.yakimavalleymuseum.org*

WASHINGTON, D.C.

Capital Children's Museum

The Capital Children's Museum closed permanently in August, 2004. Plans are currently underway for the new Museum which will be called The National Children's Museum. This new museum is scheduled to open in 2012. It is suggested that the visitor keep checking the website for updated information: *www.ccm.org*

For further information write to the Administrative Office, 955 L'Enfant Plaza North, SW, Suite 5100, Washington DC 20024 or call (202) 675-4120.

Discovery Creek Children's Museum

The Discovery Creek Children's Museum is a conglomerate of four environmental education centers, one mobile unit, and a central office. The museum itself is located at the Stable at Glen Echo Park (see address below). It is open to the public two days a week to visitors. The other locations offer programs during the week by reservation only. Environmental education centers are:

Stable at Glen Echo Park, 7300 MacArthur Blvd, Glen Echo, MD 20812
Historic Schoolhouse, 4954 MacArthur Blvd, Washington, DC 20007
Meadowlark Botanical Gardens, 9750 Meadowlark Gardens Ct., Vienna, VA 22182
Kenilworth Aquatic Gardens, 1550 Anacostia Ave., NE, Washington, DC 20019
"Rolling Rainforest" is the mobile unit which travels throughout the country. Contact them at the Discovery Creek website below.

Hours: The museum is open to the public on Saturdays and Sundays from 10 A.M. to 3 P.M.

Admissions: Under 2, free; seniors (65+), $3; all others, $5. Memberships available.

For further information write to the Discovery Creek's Offices, P.O. Box 70437, Washington, D.C. 20024 or visit the website at *www.discoverycreek.org* or call (202) 488-0627.

WEST VIRGINIA

Children's Museum of the Ohio Valley
Wheeling

The Children's Museum of the Ohio Valley is a hands-on museum for young children. The museum aims to provide a facility that "promotes and stimulates the intellectual and creative potential of children, by bringing a catalyst for the process of learning through hands on play." Children and their parents are encouraged to interact with the exhibits and with each other. Exhibits include: *K.I.D. Construction, The Art Box, the Lego Bar, Puzzle Math, Soft Spot and Read-*

ing Nook, the Vet's Office, *Where in Our World?*, the Rice and Train Tables, the Puppet Theater, the Stage and Backstage.

Info in brief: A hands-on museum for children and their caregivers.

Hours: Wednesday thru Saturday, 10 A.M.–5 P.M.; Sunday thru Tuesday, singles and groups by appointment only.

Admissions: Child, $4; adult, $2. Member ACM.

Other sites of interest nearby: Several museums in the West Virginia Area.

For further information write to the Children's Museum of the Ohio Valley, 1000 Main Street, Wheeling, WV 26003 or call or fax (304) 214-5437. *www.cmov.kids.org*

WISCONSIN

Betty Brinn Children's Museum
Milwaukee

The Betty Brinn Children's Museum is an interactive, hands-on museum for children ages 1 to 10 and their families. Special areas are reserved for infants and toddlers. Exhibits focus on real life experiences, arts and music, science and technology and are designed to "promote healthy development during the formative years." An emphasis is placed on having fun and learning together. Special programs are also offered periodically.

Location: Downtown Milwaukee.

Hours: Tuesday thru Saturday, 9 A.M.–5 P.M.; Sunday, noon–5 P.M.; Open Mondays during the summer, 9 A.M. to 5 P.M.

Admissions: Under 1, free; ages 1 & older, $5; seniors (55+), $4. 3rd Thursday of each month is free from 5–8 P.M. Free memberships are also offered to families in need. Memberships available. Metered street parking is available.

For further information write to the Betty Brinn Children's Museum, 929 E. Wisconsin Ave., Milwaukee, WI 53202 or call (414) 390-5437. *www.bbcmkids.org*

The Building for Kids (Fox Cities Children's Museum)
Appleton

The mission of The Building for Kids is to "build children's imagination, creativity, and confidence." It is designed for children ages birth to 12. (Groups of older children will NOT be admitted.) Exhibits include "Simple Machines," "Wall of Sounds," "The Happy Baby Garden," and "Starship Discovery," which offers panoramic views of land formations and bodies of water.

Hours: Tuesday thru Friday, 9 A.M.–5 P.M.; Saturday, 10 A.M.–5 P.M.; Sunday, noon–5 P.M.

Admissions: Under 1, free; others, $6.50. Special afternoon admission, Tuesday thru Friday, 4–5 P.M., $4.50.

For further information write to The Building for Kids, 100 W. College Ave., Appleton, WI 54911 or call (920) 734-3226 or fax (920) 734-0677. *www.kidmuseum.org*

The Children's Museum of La Crosse, Gertrude Salzer Gordon Children's Museum

La Crosse

The Children's Museum of La Crosse is a hands-on learning museum for children ages 1 to 12 and their caregivers. Opened in 1999, the museum offers three floors of hands-on exhibits and a variety of programs and activities. Some of the exhibits offered at the museum are *Bridges, Mighty Mississippi, Nana's Attic, Wiggles & Giggles, Fire Engine, Airplane, Me & My Shadow, Kwik Trip,* and more.

Info in brief: A hands-on, interactive museum for children ages 1–12 and their caregivers.

Location: Historic downtown La Crosse.

Hours: Tuesdays thru Saturdays, 10 A.M.–5 P.M.; Sundays, noon to 5 P.M. Closed Mondays and major holidays.

Admissions: Under 1, free; all others $5. Some free parking is available on the street. Metered parking also nearby.

For further information write to the Gertrude Salzer Gordon Children's Museum, 207 Fifth Ave., South, La Crosse, WI or call (608) 784-2652 or fax (608) 784-6968. E-mail: *info@childrensmuse umlax.org*

Discovery World at Pier Wisconsin

Milwaukee

Discovery World is the only science, economics and technology museum in Wisconsin and is named for James A. Lovell, commander of the Apollo 13 space mission who was raised in Milwaukee.

The idea for the museum was conceived in 1978 and has undergone numerous changes. The current 40,000 sq. ft. facility held its grand opening in October 1996 in the Museum Center, which also houses the Milwaukee Public Museum and the jointly-owned IMAX Dome Theater. The building consists of four stories with a copper foyer, classrooms and a small cabaret-style theater on the main level; exhibits on the second and third floors; a 160-seat theater on the third floor, and offices and workshops on the fourth floor. Exhibit areas include "Milwaukee Muscle: Simple Machines," "The Observatory," "Digital Thinkers," "Test Pilot Training," "Entrepreneur's Village," "Discovery World 4Cast Center," "Electricity & Magnetism," "Gears & Linkages," "Internal Combustion" and more.

More than 50 volunteers assist the 28 full-time and 20 part-time staff members to guide visitors through the hands-on and interactive displays. The staff also assist in outreach programs, Saturday workshops, special events and festivals and more.

Info in brief: An interactive, hands-on museum for children and their caregivers.

Location: Off of Lincoln Memorial Drive on Milwaukee's Lake Front, next to The Art Museum.

Hours: Tuesday–Sunday, 9 A.M. to 5 P.M.

Admissions: Under 3, free; students (3–17), $12.95; adults (18–59), $16.95; seniors (60+), $14.95; college students (9.95). Memberships available. Member ASTC.

Other sites of interest nearby: Milwaukee tourist attractions—Milwaukee has become the summer city of festivals. Contact the bureau of tourism there.

For further information write to Discovery World, 500 N. Harbor Dr., Milwaukee, Wisconsin 53202, or call (414) 765-9966 or fax (414) 765-0311. *www.discoveryworld.org*

Great Explorations Children's Museum
Green Bay

Great Explorations is a hands-on children's museum emphasizing the natural, technical and artistic aspects of their world. Exhibits include the "Mini Mart," "Wee Bank," "Wacky Wheels," "Investigation Station," "Healthy U," "The Locker Room," "The Play Park," "Tech-Know Junction," "Windows to the World," "Press-Gazette, Jr.," "From Pulp to Paper," "Imagination Station," "Oneida Past & Present," and "Water Works."

Info in brief: Hands-on, participatory museum exclusively for children and their caregivers.

Location: Port Plaza Mall, 2nd level, in Green Bay.

Hours: Monday (by appointment only); Tuesday and Friday, 10 A.M. to 8 P.M.; Wednesday and Thursday, 10 A.M. to 5 P.M.; Saturday, 10 A.M. to 6 P.M.; Sunday, noon to 5 P.M.

Admissions: Under 2, free; others $3. No one under 17 admitted without an adult. Memberships available.

Other sites of interest nearby: Green Bay Packers attractions, Heritage Hill State Historical Park, Hazelwood Historic Home Museum, New Zoo, Oneida Nation Museum, National Railroad Museum, Discovery Zone, and more.

For further information write to the Great Explorations Children's Museum, 320 North Adams Street, Green Bay, Wisconsin 54301, or call (920) 432-4397. *www.greatexplorations.org*

Madison Children's Museum
Madison

The Madison Children's Museum is a private, nonprofit museum whose mission is to offer hands-on learning and fun for children and their families. The exhibits center around the themes of culture, science, technology and art.

Besides the permanent hands-on exhibits, the museum offers special events, activities and workshops throughout the year. Family fun is encouraged.

Originally opened in 1980 as a traveling museum, the new permanent museum site opened its doors in 1990. Now a two-story building, the museum offers more than seven permanent exhibits along with special exhibits on display during different times of the year. Permanent exhibits include "Leap into Lakes," "Lookagain Lane," "Shadow Room," "The Children of Chernobyl" (visual display), "Let's Grow," "Cows, Curds and Their Wheys," and "Brazil: Beyond the Rainforest."

The museum also has developed the "Museum in a Shoebox Exchange Program" with Porto Alegre schoolchildren. This offers children in both countries the opportunity to be personally involved in different cultures.

Info in brief: Mostly hands-on exhibits, but various visual displays enhance the background and are meant to encourage critical thinking.

Location: Downtown Madison at the end of State Street, adjacent to the State Capitol building. Open only to city buses and bicycles, State Street contains unique shops, restaurants, coffee shops and the Children's Museum.

Hours: Weekdays, 9 A.M.–4 P.M.; Saturdays, 9 A.M.–5 P.M.; Sundays, noon–5 P.M.

Admissions: Under 1, free; child & adult, $5; senior (55+), $4; $.25 subsidized admission is available for qualifying families (visit website to apply), FREE admission — first Sunday of each month.

Unique exhibits: Children of Chernobyl — displaying works of art created by children who live in the Chernobyl Zone. This exhibit may be closed in order to be replaced by more hands-on exhibits.

Other sites of interest nearby: State Street attractions, the State Capitol, five other museums within walking distance, and two lakes.

For further information write to Madison Children's Museum, 100 State Street, Madison, Wisconsin 53703 or call (608) 256-6445. *www.madisonchildrensmuseum.org* E-mail: *bbaker@madisonchildrensmuseum.org*

Milwaukee Public Museum
Milwaukee

The Milwaukee Public Museum is a natural and human history museum located in downtown Milwaukee. The Museum was chartered in 1882 and opened to the public in 1884. MPM has three floors of exhibits that encompass life-size dioramas, walk-through villages, world cultures, dinosaurs, a rain forest and a live butterfly garden, as well as the Humphrey IMAX Dome theatre and the Daniel M. Soref Planetarium. In addition to housing more than 4.5 million objects in its permanent collections, only a very small number of which are on display at any given time, the Milwaukee Public Museum has also played host to several of the world's largest traveling exhibitions.

Info in brief: A history museum (both cultural and natural), one of the oldest and largest in the country, with numerous collections. A Humphrey IMAX Dome Theater and a Daniel M. Soref Planetarium are also on site.

Hours: Daily, 9 A.M. to 5 P.M. Closed Thanksgiving and Christmas Day and July 4th. Hours may be extended to accommodate traveling exhibitions.

Admissions: Under 3, free; students (4–17 and with college ID), $7; adults, $11; seniors (60+), $9. Milwaukee County residents with ID every Monday, free. Member ASTC.

Unique exhibit: Puelicher Butterfly Vivarium (walk-through indoor garden featuring live butterflies and plants), Streets of Old Milwaukee, world's largest known dinosaur skull.

For further information write to the Milwaukee Public Museum, 800 W. Wells St., Milwaukee, Wisconsin 53233 or call (414) 278-2700 or 2702 (TDD 278-2709). *www.mpm.edu*

Northwoods Children's Museum
Eagle River

Northwoods Children's Museum is a hands-on discovery museum for young children and their families. Some exhibits include *Sky & Space, Badger State, Farm Animals, Geography, Dinosaur, Cranberries, Turtles* and *Santa's Workshop.*

Location: Physical address— 346 W. Division St., Eagle River, WI.

Hours: (Labor Day to Memorial Day) Tuesday thru Friday, 10 A.M.–3 P.M.; Saturday, 10 A.M.–5 P.M.; Sunday, noon–5 P.M. Closed most major holidays. (Memorial Day to Labor Day) Monday thru Friday, 10 A.M.–5 P.M.; Saturday, 10 A.M.–5 P.M.; Sunday, noon–5 P.M. Closed July 4th.

Admissions: $6 per person — ages 1 to 100. Memberships available. Member ACM.

For further information write to the Northwoods Children's Museum, P.O. Box 216, Eagle River, WI 54521, or call (715) 479-4623 or fax (715) 479-3289. *www.northwoodschildrensmuseum.com*

WYOMING

The Science Zone
Casper

The Science Zone is a new community-based museum with science, math and technology exhibits for visitors of all ages. Exhibits offered include *Bubble Zone, Demo Zone, Tech City,* and more.

Location: Sunrise Center.

Hours: Monday thru Saturday, 10 A.M.–5 P.M.

Admissions: Under 3, free; children, $3; adults, $4. Member ASTC.

For further information write to The Science Zone, 3960 S. Poplar St., Casper, WY 882601 or call (307) 473-ZONE or fax (307) 261-6131. *www.thesciencezone.org* E-mail: *Julie@thesciencezone.org*

Wyoming Children's Museum & Nature Center
Laramie

All exhibits at the Wyoming Children's Museum are hands-on and interactive on topics such as the Oregon Trail and Native Americans. Besides the Museum, this facility also has a nature center, a discovery center, and pottery and ceramic youth classes. Traveling exhibits are also offered.

Location: Physical address— 968 North 9th Street, Laramie.

Hours: Tuesday thru Saturday, 10 A.M.–2 P.M.

Admissions: Under 3, free; child, $3; adults, $2. Memberships available.

For further information write to the Wyoming Children's Museum & Nature Center, P.O. Box 51, Laramie, WY 82073 or call (307) 745-6332 or fax (307) 745-4549. *www.wcmnc.org* or E-mail: *staff@ WCMNC.org*

Wyoming Territorial Prison State Historic Site
Laramie

Formerly known as the Wyoming Territorial Park, the Wyoming Territorial Prison State Historic Site is a village museum which offers a variety of hands-on experiences especially for children. Most of these experiences occur in the Old West Frontier Town, and include panning for gold, joining a prison break posse, participating in a Pioneer Puppet Theatre, digging for dinosaur fossils, calf-roping, rope-making, taking a stagecoach ride, and visiting a petting corral.

Other "sights to see" in the town include the working blacksmith's shop, a medicine show, a fiddler, singers, livery stable, and more. The three other major areas of the park include guided tours of the Wyoming Territorial Prison, the National U.S. Marshals Museum, and a dinner theater. Many special events are held in the park area during the year, so visitors should contact the park well in advance. Norma Slack, Calamity Jane's great, great niece, plays Calamity during numerous performances throughout the season.

Even though the prison is not a hands-on experience, it holds a great attraction for most children and their family members. It has been restored to its original 1890's condition, placed on the National Register of Historic Buildings, and is an important part of the rich Western history of the United States. The building has housed such prisoners as Butch Cassidy, Clark "The Kid" Pelton, Kich McKinney and Minnie Snyder. The National U.S. Marshals Museum is also historically significant.

Info in brief: Hands-on activities in the Wyoming Frontier Town only, but a full day of experiences are available throughout the entire park.

Location: Off I-80, 125 miles northwest of Denver, Colorado, and 120 miles northeast of Rocky Mountain National Park.

Hours: Grounds open year round. Frontier Town open weekends only; prison and exhibit hall open May through September. Dates, times and events are subject to change without notice. Call the park for exact information.

Admissions: Under 11, free; teens (12–17), $2.50; adults, $5. Reservations are required for the dinner theater.

Unique exhibits: Wyoming Territorial Prison.

For further information write to the Wyoming Territorial Prison State Historic Site, 975 Snowy Range Road, Laramie, Wyoming 82070, or call (307) 745-6161 or fax (307) 745-8620 *www.wyoparks. state.wy.us/Sites/TerritorialPrison/index.asp*

Appendix

Many museums are members of an association or associations which offer free admissions to visitors at other participatory museums which belong to the association. The most common association for children's museums is the ACM (Association of Children's Museums), formed in 1962 as the American Association of Youth Museums AAYM (American Association of Youth Museums). Approximately 340 museums all over the world belong to this association, but not all offer special admissions privileges. For further information, write to:

Association of Youth Museums
1300 L St., NW
#975
Washington, DC 20005
acm@ChildrensMuseums.org

Another large association is the Association of Science-Technology Centers Incorporated (ASTC). This is an international association and includes more than just children's museums. The Reciprocal Free Admission Program (RFAP) entitles visitors to free general admission to any ASTC museum, but does not include admissions to planetariums, large-screen theater presentations or any special programs offered by an individual museum. To obtain a list of participating museums, you must contact an ASTC museum. Membership in one participating museum provides membership in the RFAP.

In the Pacific Northwest, a group of museums have banded together to offer special admissions prices for museums in Oregon and Washington. All member museums provide visitors with a punch card which allows holders one free visit at each museum.

There are many other associations available, including VAM (Virginia Association of Museums) and AAM (American Association of Museums). It is strongly suggested that you contact your local or nearby museum to find out about membership there, and ask about reciprocal programs with other museums.

As stated in this book's Introduction, many small museums have a very tight budget and choose not to pay any association fees. This does not mean, however, that families cannot have a great visit. Caregivers are encouraged to teach their children that there are things to be learned from any and all experiences, and that they do not have to go to EPCOT or Disney World to have a great time.

Index